The Seventh Battalion
A. I. F.

BATTLE HONOURS

Seventh Battalion
(The Mount Alexander Regiment)
"CEDE NULLIS"

THE GREAT WAR—

Somme, 1916, 1918,

Pozieres, Bullecourt, Ypres, 1917

Menin Road, Polygon Wood, Broodseinde, Poelcapelle, Passchendale, Lys, Hazebrouck, Amiens, Albert, 1918, (Chuignes)

Hindenburgh Line, Epihy, France and Flanders, 1916-18

Helles, Krithia, Anzac, Landing at Anzac, Defence of Anzac, Suvla, Sari Bair—Lone Pine, Gallipoli, 1915

Suez Canal, Egypt, 1915-16.

The Seventh Battalion
A. I. F.

Resume of Activities of the Seventh Battalion in the Great War—1914-1918.

By
Arthur Dean
Eric W. Gutteridge

The Naval & Military Press Ltd

Published by
The Naval & Military Press Ltd
5 Riverside, Brambleside, Bellbrook
Industrial Estate, Uckfield, East Sussex,
TN22 1QQ England
Tel: +44 (0) 1825 749494
Fax: +44 (0) 1825 765701
www.naval-military-press.com
www.military-genealogy.com
www.militarymaproom.com

In reprinting in facsimile from the original, any imperfections are inevitably reproduced and the quality may fall short of modern type and cartographic standards.

ILLUSTRATIONS.

Major-General H. E. Elliott	facing page	7
Brig.-General C. H. Jess	,, ,,	32
Lieut.-Colonel E. E. Herrod	,, ,,	77

MAPS.

	Page
Locality Map of the Peninsula	14
Cape Helles	22
Lone Pine	22
The Somme	40
Ypres	88
The Somme to St. Quentin, 1918	118

CONTENTS.

		Page
Chapter	1—The Formation of the Battalion	7
,,	2—The Voyage	9
,,	3—Training in the Desert	12
,,	4—The Landing at Gaba Tepe	15
,,	5—The Attack on Krithia	19
,,	6—The Return to Anzac	23
,,	7—Lone Pine	25
,,	8—15th August to the Evacuation	29
,,	9—Egypt to Pozieres	31
,,	10—Pozieres	39
,,	11—Ypres	55
,,	12—The Winter on the Somme—	
	Part 1—The Mud	61
	Part 2—The Hun Withdrawal	70
,,	13—The Summer of 1917	77
,,	14—Internal Organisation	80
,,	15—The Battles of Passchendaele	87
,,	16—The Winter in Belgium	94
,,	17—The German Attack, 1918	98
,,	18—The Returning Ascendancy	106
An Appreciation		114
Chapter	19—The Great Offensive	119
,,	20—In Belgium—Battalion Breaks Up	131
Winners of Decorations		135
Award Statistics		137
Principal Engagement Casualties		138
Nominal Roll		139

Dedication

This Book is Dedicated to the
Memory of
The Seventh Battalion, A.I.F.
1914—1918.

Major-Gen. H. E. ELLIOTT
C.B., C.M.G., D.S.O., D.C.M., V.D.

CHAPTER 1.

THE FORMATION OF THE BATTALION.

WITHIN a few days of the entrance of the British Empire into the War the Australian Commonwealth Government offered, for service abroad, a complete infantry division and a brigade of light horse. Lieut.-Colonel H. E. Elliott, 59th Battalion, A.M.F., was appointed to command the Seventh Battalion. Elliott had, as a corporal, in the South African War received the D.C.M. With another man, he, finding a large party of Boers asleep, untied and led away their horses. Outspoken, impulsive, straight as a ruled line, intensely headstrong, he worked his men during their training perhaps harder than any other commander. In the field he abandoned the role of martinet, was a dour fighter, brave to a fault, happy to be sniping the enemy or personally reconnoitring a dangerous position. He was loved by his men, who nicknamed him Pompey Elliott.

He chose for his second-in-command Major W. Ramsay McNicol, and Lieut. C. Finlayson, A.I. Staff, as his adjutant.

The inception of compulsory training in 1910 had provided not only a number of partially trained officers and men, a supply of guns, equipment, rifles, etc., but a machinery for raising troops. The Battalion was allotted on a territorial basis.

- A Company from 59th Battalion—Brunswick and Coburg.
- B Company from 60th Battalion—North Carlton and Parkville.
- C Company from 57th Battalion—North-Eastern and Goulburn Valley.
- D Company from 58th Battalion—Essendon and Moonee Ponds
- E Company from 65th Battalion—Footscray, Spotswood and Bacchus Marsh.
- F Company from 66th Battalion—Castlemaine and Kyneton.
- G Company from 68th Battalion—Bendigo.
- H Company—Murray Valley, Echuca, Inglewood and Charlton.

By the 17th August recruiting and medical examination were in full swing. The drill-halls were besieged by long queues of men eager to be in the great adventure. The men offering were of splendid quality, the standard was very high and many were rejected.

The training camp was now ready at Broadmeadows, and on the 19th August at 9.30 a.m. the recruits assembled on the parade-ground at Victoria Barracks, Melbourne, the officers and a sprinkling of the men in uniform, the great majority in civilian clothes of every cut and colour. Their effects were carried in anything from a suit-case to a swag, from a biscuit-tin to a handkerchief. One man in uniform of a Highland Piper, a few others in odds and ends of khaki. Clerks, farmers, mechanics, swagmen in a heterogeneous collection, that by dint of much tutelage was worked into rough fours and swung out into St. Kilda Road behind a Citizen Force band and escorted by crowds of small boys and admiring friends. Through the city and up the Sydney Road to near the Carlton Oval, where a halt was made for a meal. An hour's spell and off again. Many were the halts, and the hard road made many sore feet, but somehow they arrived at the camp—a green plain rather high and wind-swept, with rows of pine trees and an old homestead.

The training was intense. Early parade at 7 a.m., physical drill, squad drill, rifle exercises and lectures filled the day, and gradually the recruits began to show that they had the makings of soldiers in them. After some weeks uniforms were issued—on the instalment plan—and bit by bit equipment came to hand. The weather was unpropitious and the clayey soil became a quagmire between the lines.

The Governor-General (Sir Ronald Munro-Ferguson) inspected the 2nd Brigade on the 11th September, and was well pleased with the parade. A fortnight later the Brigade under the Brigadier, Colonel J. W. McCay, marched through Melbourne.

On the 27th September orders to embark were issued. At that time the German ships Emden, Gneisenau and Scharnhorst had not been heard of for some days, and it was not considered safe to let the troops sail without a stronger escort than the H.M.A.S. Sydney and Melbourne. So the troops remained at Broadmeadows for a further three weeks.

CHAPTER 2.

THE VOYAGE.

IN the early hours of Sunday, the 18th October, the Battalion marched out of camp and entrained at Broadmeadows Station for Port Melbourne. There it embarked with the 6th Battalion on H.M.A.T. A20 S.S. Hororata, of the New Zealand Steamship Company, a fine new vessel of some 15,000 tons, built for emigrant traffic, with a main deck extending from stem to stern and athwartships. The upper deck was much encumbered with 120 horses, galleys and other erections. On the next day A20 steamed down the bay and cleared Port Phillip Heads at 11.40 a.m. After an uneventful voyage and a calm Great Australian Bight the ship arrived at King George's Sound on the 25th October.

Day by day Troopships arrived till the wide sound was thick with vessels moored in pairs. A few fortunate people visited Albany at the head of the harbour. With the appearance of the grey New Zealand Troopers and the Escort on the 28th the fleet was ready. Owing to the serious overcrowding of the Hororata, A Company, of the 6th Battalion, was transferred to the R.M.S. Omrah (A5).

On Sunday, the 1st November, the first convoy moved off. In single file past Breaksea Island at the entrance of the sound and out into the Indian Ocean, the convoy was in three lines—one mile apart—and with 800 yards between vessels. The Hororata was between the Star of Victoria and the Omrah, near the rear of the starboard line. The New Zealanders were in two lines astern. H.M.A.S. Minotaur was in front, the Sydney to port, the Melbourne at first on the starboard side, but with the arrival of the Ibuchi, the Japanese cruiser, she dropped astern.

The Australian coast had by now disappeared into the dim horizon. To many it was to be their last farewell.

Day by day the fleet sailed on a perfectly calm sea. There was some physical drill, a little signalling and exercising of horses and much basking in the sun and sports and boxing matches. "Ike" Saunders fought Darcy, the

6th Battalion champion, six hard rounds. The doctor refereed the private fights in the forrard well-deck.

All ranks received anti-typhoid inoculations and were vaccinated.

On the 7th November an enemy cruiser was reported to be in the vicinity, and all ships were ordered to be darkened down at night. The two 4.7 naval guns aft had crews allotted to them, and ammunition was placed in readiness. At dawn next day H.M.S. Minotaur received orders to proceed toward Mauritius and left the convoy. The Melbourne took the lead and the Sydney came up to the port side. As the dawn broke on the 9th the convoy was about 50 miles from Cocos Island, and swung a few points to port to regain the direct route to Colombo. At 6.24 a.m. wireless was heard from Cocos, and soon a message, "S.O.S. Strange warship approaching," Captain L'E. Silver, of the Melbourne, started for Cocos, but, realising his duty lay with the convoy, signalled the Sydney to go in his stead. She soon disappeared to the west. At 9.40 a.m. the Melbourne moved well over to the port beam. Some men stated that they could hear a noise like the beating of a big drum. The Ibuchi cleared for action, hammocks piled against her upper works, her decks naked and smoke pouring from her funnels. With huge battle-flags of the rising sun she sped across the bows of the convoy to help the Sydney. But the captain of the Melbourne refused her permission. The news had come from the Sydney at 9.30 that she had sighted the enemy steaming northward toward the convoy. At 10.45, "Am briskly engaging enemy." At 11.10 came the signal, "Emden beached and done for." It was a day of excitement to the men of the troopships and of heartfelt relief to the escort. The Emden had passed within 50 miles of the convoy during the night. If Captain Von Muller had managed to get among the fleet during the hours of darkness it would have been a holocaust.

The Konigsberg was still somewhere in the blue, so for another night the ships were darkened. Next day she was reported on the coast of Africa. From that time all fear of enemy interference in the Indian Ocean ceased. On the 11th the Hampshire relieved the Melbourne, which went on to Colombo to coal.

The weather still continued fine and the ordinary ship's routine continued. The skipper of the Hororata, Captain Cameron, insisted on a spotless ship. The mess tables had to be snowy white, the tinware shone like silver.

Colombo was reached on the 15th November. The Hororata entered the breakwater to refill her water tanks. The Sydney, bearing the marks of her battle, was already there, and lying nearby the Russian Askold, five-funnelled, and promptly christened "The packet of fags."

The convoy proceeded by divisions to Aden, reached on the 25th. More watering and on past Perim Island up the Red Sea. It was hot and the main deck an inferno at night.

It was believed that the troops were going straight to England, but it was deemed better not to take them to an English winter with its rigours, especially as huttage was not available. On the 28th instructions were received that training was to be completed in Cairo, and that the Australian and New Zealand Army Corps was to be placed under General Sir W. R. Birdwood. On the 1st December the ship reached Suez and passed up the canal. British troops, Sikhs, Punjabis and Ghurkas in trenches on the east bank welcomed the men. Machine guns were placed on the upper deck as a protection against marauding Bedouins. Port Said was passed, and after some delay the ship tied up at a wharf at Alexandria. The ship's crew refused to work the winches because it was a Sunday. In ten minutes the Battalion took over, found experienced donkeymen and lumpers and got all the baggage and equipment out of the ship to schedule time. Two trains of prodigious length took the unit through the flat Delta country, with its intense and antiquated cultivation, the mud villages and Old Testament figures, to Abu-Ela station on the outskirts of Cairo.

CHAPTER 3.

TRAINING IN THE DESERT.

A camp was in process of being made on the fringe of the desert at Mena, beneath the ridge on which stand the Pyramids and the Sphinx. By electric tram the Battalion was conveyed over the Nile to Ghezireh and out on the long straight road from Giseh known as the Avenue of the Empress Eugenie. The Pyramids stood out blackly against the dark blue sky. Turning to the right at Mena House they marched past two hastily built reservoirs and along a newly made road, beside which they rolled themselves in their blankets and slept. Tents arrived in a day or so, and soon the remainder of the Division had come in. The horses were weak after the voyage and had to be acclimatised to Tibbin. An Army Service dump of good Australian chaff had to be guarded day and night against marauding transport men.

Training recommenced seriously. From the lines stretched a sea of sand. Up past the Boojum Rocks, the Circus and Honeymoon Lane the Battalion marched daily to the hard shaly ridges. Every man stepped in the footmark of his predecessor and over all was a cloud of dust. Early in January, in accordance with the wish of the War Office, the original eight-company organisation was merged into the sixteen platoon, four company plan. Day after day training progressed. Platoon and company drill, company in attack, company in defence, outposts, with the figure of Lt.-Col. Elliott and his big black charger dominating the scene, physically, dynamically and orally. The men were hard driven and became lean and hard. They drilled like regulars. A boxing stadium was erected by the 7th and opened with a "Stupendous Scene of Stoush," with Lt. W. Conder as referee. On the 20th December the 3rd and 7th Battalions represented the A.I.F. at the accession of His Highness the Sultan of Egypt, Prince Hussein Kamel.

Early in February Djemal Pasha, with the Eighth Turkish Army Corps, delivered his long-expected attack on the Canal. On the 3rd February the 7th and 8th Battalions were railed to Ismailia. Lt.-Col. D. S. Wanliss,

5th Battalion, kindly sent his band to play the 7th into Cairo. Ismailia was reached at 9 p.m. and the Battalion bivouacked on the sand. Captain C. J. C. Mason and two platoons relieved the New Zealanders between Tussum Gare and Serapeum. The Turkish attack had failed. It was intended by Major General A. Wilson, in charge of the Canal defences, to launch a sortie against the enemy at Tussum, but as information was received that a large body of Turks was at Habeita, a few miles from Serapeum, the attack was abandoned. Captain A. Jackson and 60 men took 200 Turkish prisoners to Cairo. After five days pleasant rest in Ismailia, with its palm trees and greenery nourished by the Sweet-water Canal, the 7th returned to Mena Camp.

Major McNicol was transferred to command the 6th Battalion and Major Blezard became second-in-command. Captain Mason and Lieut. Layh received promotion.

On the 4th April the unit said farewell to the desert sands and marched into Cairo, entrained for Alexandria, and embarked on the S.S. Galeka, a Union Castle liner. Four days later she steamed out and proceeded to Mudros Harbour on the island of Lemnos, arriving on the 11th. For several days the troops were exercised in embarking on ship's boats with full pack, ammunition and shovels and landing on the shore. More ships were arriving and tied up two or three together. The Galeka lay beside the Cheang-Bee.

Lt.-Col. Elliott inspected the Gallipoli coast on H.M.S. Queen.

On the 24th April orders were issued for the attack on Gallipoli Peninsula, north of Gaba Tepe. Three days rations and 200 rounds of ammunition were to be carried by each man. At 10.30 p.m. the Galeka left the harbour and went round to the Bay of Purnea on the northern shore of Lemnos Island.

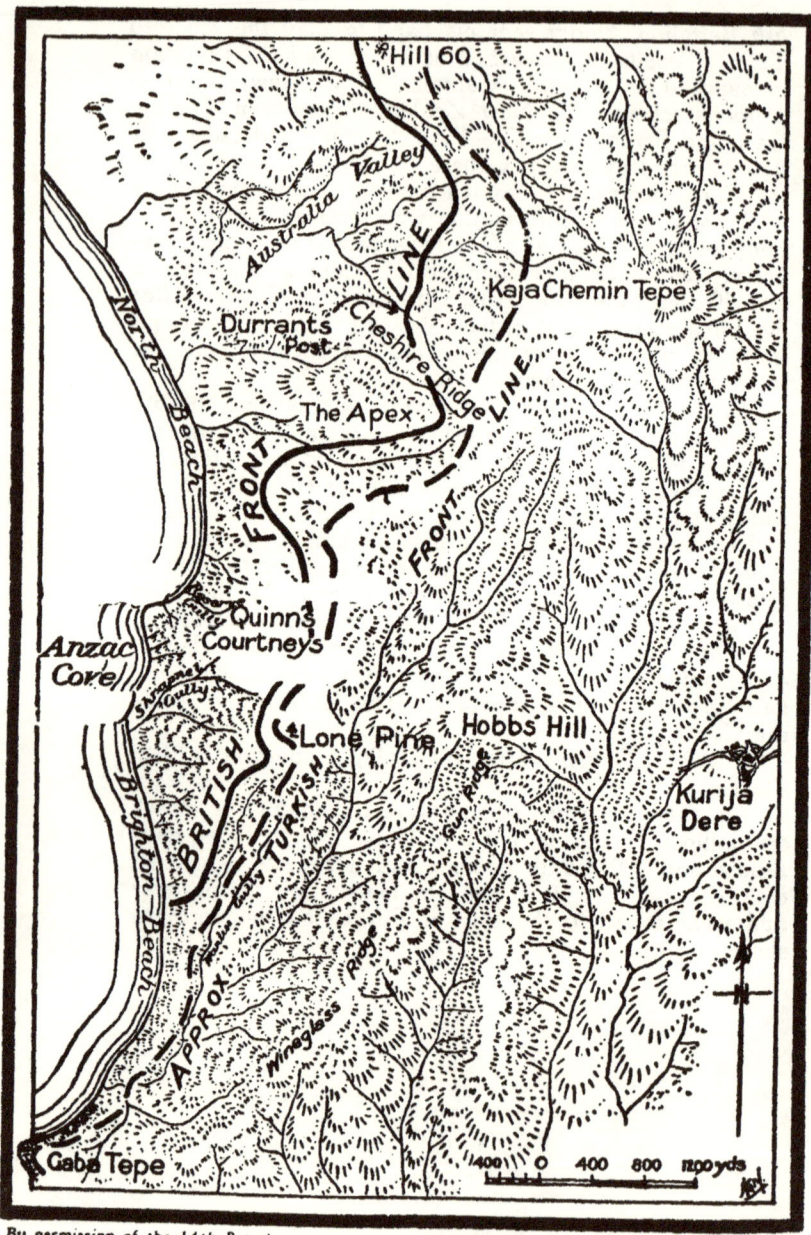

LOCALITY MAP OF THE PENINSULA

CHAPTER 4.

THE LANDING AT GABA TEPE.

THE plan of attack laid down by General Birdwood was for the 1st Australian Div. to make the landing. The New Zealand and Australian Div. was to follow. General Bridges detailed the Third Brigade to land as the covering force on the coast from Gaba Tepe to Ari Burnu. They were to push inland and seize the ridge from Gaba Tepe toward Battleship Hill and Chunuk Bair. This ridge, later known as Gun Ridge, was a mile from the shore. The 2nd Brigade was to be landed from its transports and was to secure the right or northerly flank from Battleship Hill to Hill 971. The 7th Battalion was to land just south of Ari Burnu, to proceed over Plugge's Plateau, along Russell's Top to Baby 700 and Battleship Hill, up the tangled slopes of Chunuk Bair, and to hold a line on the seaward slope looking northward. The 5th Battalion was to hold the crest of Chunuk Bair to the Koja Chemen Tepe (Hill 971), with the 8th on its right. Thus the 2nd Brigade made a triangle with the 5th at its apex on 971, the 7th on the left, the 8th on the right.

During the night of the 24/25th April the transports carrying the 1st and 2nd Brigades moved from the Bay of Purnea the 60 miles to the proposed landing place. The ships were in absolute darkness. In the black night after the moon set dark shapes of transports and warships could be dimly seen. Ahead breaking the starstrewn sky was a low mass of land. The excitement was intense. At 4.28 a.m. on the dark coast flared a bright yellow light, and a scattered fire commenced, growing in intensity. The landing party was ashore.

The Galeka, under Captain Bernard Burt, a Captain Kettle type, arrived punctually. There being no sign of the tows which should have been awaiting him after having landed the 3rd Brigade, Captain Burt took his ship 600 yards further in and anchored 1500 yards from the shore. The Gaba Tepe guns began to burst their shrapnel about the ship. Commander Somerville, the naval officer on board, decided that the 6th and 7th Battalions should land themselves by the ship's boats. Lieut.-Col. Elliott in accordance with the plan, ordered Major A. Jackson with Capt. H. T. C. Layh and three platoons of B Company to land about a mile north of the 3rd Brigade. As they neared the land they saw immediately north of Ari Burnu knoll the Red Cross flag of the 3rd Field Ambulance. The original orders being to guard the left flank from Fisherman's Hut up to 971, they rowed towards the Hut, under a severe rifle and machine gun fire. Casualties were severe. The boats were filled with dead and wounded. The survivors landed and occupied a trench on the knoll behind Fisherman's Hut. Of 140 officers and men only 38 reached the shore. Lieut. A. R. Heighway was wounded. Major Jackson went toward the 3rd Field Ambulance to arrange for evacuation of the wounded. A trawler came in and towed two of the boats away, but before all could be removed a Turkish attack developed between Walker's Ridge and the sea, and Layh was forced to withdraw his men along the beach. Many heroic attempts were made to rescue the remaining wounded. Bearers of the 2nd Battalion brought them in late on Monday afternoon (26th).

Lieut.-Col. Elliott, Lieut. Grills and the remainder of B Company were picked up by a steam pinnace and landed in the cove between the greater and lesser knolls of Ari Burnu—later simply known as the beach. It was recognised that the 3rd Brigade had landed a mile to the left of its objective, the beach from Hell Spit to Gaba Tepe—later known as Brighton Beach. Colonel E. G. Sinclair-MacLagan, Brigadier of 3rd Brigade, decided to divert the 2nd Brigade to take over the right flank. The 7th Battalion was to rendezvous in Shrapnel Gully. The later boats from the Galeka landed under heavy fire from the Turkish guns on Gaba Tepe. Major Mason's Company led in the advance up White's Valley, to the 400 plateau. Major I. Blezard was wounded. As the last companies of the 7th were disappearing over the crest, Elliott was told of the change in the plans, and that his Battalion was to fill a gap between the 9th and 10th Battalions on the Second Ridge. The projected advance on 971 from the 400 plateau was to be abandoned. Elliott climbed on to the plateau to see the position for himself. As he topped McCay's Hill a bullet hit him in the ankle and put him out of the fight. Henderson, Grills and Hunter advanced with the 9th Battalion toward Third Ridge to meet the Turkish counter attack. The 400 plateau was exposed "like the stage of a Greek drama," enfiladed by batteries from Chunuk Bair and Scrubby Knoll and subjected to a murderous rifle and machine gun fire from Third Ridge and from the ridges and spurs on each flank. The density of the fire and the thick scrub had torn to shreds all organisation. Isolated parties struggled through to the forward slopes of Lone Pine, the Cup, and down Owen's Gully. Grills occupied a Turkish trench on the inland side of the Pine. The units were inextricably mingled. Some of the 7th were with Flockart (5th Bn.) forward on Johnston's Jolly, with Wells' (6th Bn.) on 400 plateau south of Owen's Gully, a few strung out as a disconnected line on the Australian edge of the plateau. The counter-attack of the 27th Turkish Regiment at 10.30 a.m. pressed hard on the advanced parties, weakened by severe casualties. This attack came from Third (Gun) Ridge straight across the 400 plateau. By 1 p.m. some kind of a line had been established along the seaward slope of 400, running along Bolton's Ridge, with an advanced line on Sniper's Ridge and the Knife Edge. During the afternoon and evening the men lay in the open scrub harassed by shellfire and under a hail of bullets. At 4.30 p.m. came Mustafa Kemal's second attack with the 27th Regiment. They came across Gun Ridge towards Pine Ridge and Lone Pine, driving in isolated parties in front of these posts. A third attack was made more southerly on Bolton's Ridge later in the evening. With darkness it was possible to dig some form of protection. The parties out in front on Sniper's Ridge came in during the night.

On the 26th the remnant of the 6th and 7th Battalions under Lieut.-Col. McNicoll was to the south of 400 plateau. Soon after midday General Bridges ordered a small movement of the 4th Battalion to a new alignment on the Daisy Patch, to correspond with the 10th on the left and the 6th and the 7th on the right. Owing to a series of mistakes this minor movement developed into a general advance over 400 plateau, with a left form toward 971 bringing the attack between the Australian and Turkish lines. Casualties were heavy and the survivors had to retire to the Daisy Patch, where a line was being dug. This was subsequently known as the Pimple. The Battalion H.Q. were in the head of Brown's Dip, and next day a number of the Battalion who had been scattered along the line had rejoined. On the 29th the Battalion was relieved by the Deal Battalion of the 1st Naval

Brigade, and assembled on the beach at the foot of Victoria Gully. Lieut.-Col. R. Gartside, of the 8th Battalion, was appointed to command the 7th Battalion.

The casualties were:—

    Killed .... 2 officers   68 other ranks
    Wounded ... 15 ,,   229   ,,
    Missing. ....   —   ,,   227   ,,

Of the missing a proportion were afterward found to have been sent away without any record being kept.

Lieuts. Davey, McKenna, Blick, Allan Henderson and Chapman were killed or died of wounds. Major Blezard, Major Mason, Captain Jackson, Lieut. Heron, Captain Layh, Lieut. Scanlon, Lieuts. Heighway, Rogers, Connelly and Denehy were wounded.

CHAPTER 5.

THE ATTACK ON KRITHIA.

IT was decided by General Hamilton that two Brigades from Anzac should be sent to Cape Helles to take part in an attack on Krithia. On the evening of the 5th May the 2nd Brigade assembled on Brighton Beach, and early next morning the 7th Battalion embarked on the Folkestone, a deep sea trawler, whose crew made the men as comfortable as possible for the two-hour journey to "V" Beach. There under the shattered stone bastions and battered village of Sedd-el-Bahr the stranded River Clyde had been joined to the shore with moored lighters to form a pier. As the Battalion disembarked, it was greeted with shells from the Asiatic shore near the ruins of ancient Troy. For the next two days the Brigade was bivouacked in the damp green fields in front of Sedd-el-Bahr. The Brigade was part of the Composite Division under General Paris. It was intended to attack from the left flank and turn the Krithia position. By the 7th May this attack had not progressed, and on the morning of the 8th the 2nd Brigade was ordered to move up to a rear area in the Krithia Nullah. By 3.45 p.m. they were in old trenches behind the Indian Infantry Brigade in Reserve Line.

The toe of the peninsula was divided by three ravines —Gully Ravine on the left, Krithia Nullah in the centre, Kanli Dere to the right, forming four spurs—Ravine, Krithia, Central and Kereves. The Central Spur between Krithia Nullah and Kanli Dere led straight up to Krithia Village below the battlement-like eminence of Achi Baba. It was bisected by the Krithia Road and was a featureless, slightly swelling grassy moorland, exposed to fire from the trenches in front and from each flank.

General Hamilton had decided to make a frontal attack on the whole front at 5.30 p.m.—the New Zealand Brigade on Krithia Spur to the left, the 2nd Australian Brigade on Central Spur and the 2nd Naval Brigade and the French on Kereves Spur on the right. At 4.45 p.m. as the men were having a meal orders reached the Brigade. The order of advance was 7th on the right, 6th on the left, each on 500 yards frontage, the 5th and 8th Battalions in support. Gartside gave his officers two minutes to fall-in and detailed Captain R. H. Weddell to lead the two front companies. Major W. E. H. Cass, the Brigade-Major, was sent by McCay to hasten the 7th and led them to the right till they met the Krithia Road, when they wheeled to the front, crossing Reserve Trench held by the 14th Sikhs. Here they came out from some sheltering olive trees and were heavily shelled by a Turkish four-gun battery. They broke into artillery formation, and as rifle fire became intense, into line, had a short breather at the Tommies' Trench 300 yards in front and led by Cass went into the storm of bullets from front and flanks. A hundred-yard rush, with men falling fast, up again and struggling on by short stages, the severity of the fire and loss of officers and men brought the advance to a halt, approximately 500 yards in front of the Tommies' Trench and an equal distance from the Turkish trenches. Major Cass was wounded and Captain R. H. Henderson killed. Weddell was the only officer of the leading companies of the 7th. The supporting companies of the 7th reached the Tommies' Trench in the teeth of a furious fusillade. Lieut.-Col. R. Gartside was killed, Captain C. Finlayson, Adjutant, severely wounded as he reached the final line, Lieuts. Heron, S. M. DeRavin and J. M. West wounded as they were digging in. The right flank was completely in the air. Cass before he was again wounded swung round the 5th Battalion to guard this, and during the night the Naval Brigade came up and connected up with the French 2nd Division, which had succeeded in capturing Kemal Bay Tepe on the edge of the Straits.

The casualties of the Battalion were very heavy:—

Killed	3 officers	40	other ranks
Wounded	13 ,,	133	,,
Missing	— ,,	88	,,

Captain H. H. Hunter, a famous athlete was killed. Captain A. Fraser wounded. Lieuts. P. G. Wale, J. A. K. Johnston and T. McL. Carmichael and Capt. C. H. Permezel died of wounds. As darkness fell the battlefield for half a mile behind the foremost line was filled with the cries of the wounded. During the night stretcher-bearers brought many in to the R.A.P.'s at Tommies' Trench and along the Krithia Creek, and the Naval Brigade cleared the right flank. The Brigade was relieved by the Manchester Territorials on the night of the 11th May, moved back to the vicinity of "W" Beach, and returned to Anzac a week later by the Ionian, escorted by the Chelmer (Lt. Cdr. England). During this period the Battalion was commanded by Capt. Weddell, with Lieut. Grills the only other combatant officer.

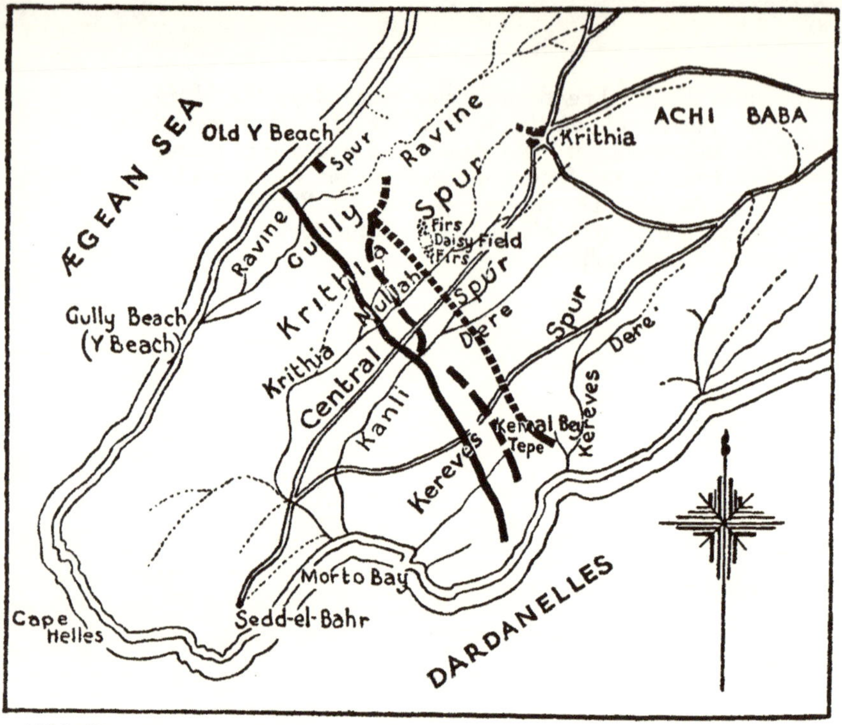

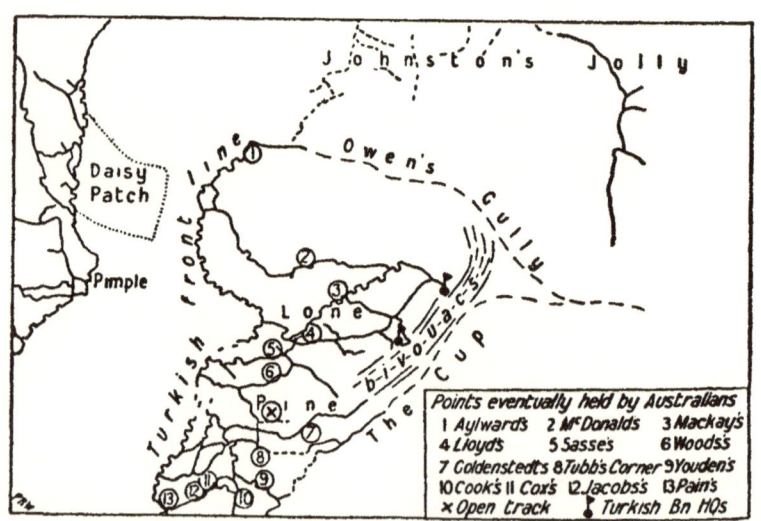

Official War History

CAPE HELLES, 6th, 7th, 8th MAY, 1915

Official War History

LONE PINE

CHAPTER 6.

THE RETURN TO ANZAC—17th MAY TO 5th AUGUST.

THE 7th Battalion, on arriving at Anzac, bivouacked on the Razorback, to the south of Shrapnel Gully. A steep slope gave protection in front, but there were two guns of the 5th Australian Battery emplaced to the right and two guns of the 21st Indian Mountain Battery immediately in the rear. General Birdwood visited the Battalion the day after its return from Cape Helles.

During the Turkish attack of the 19th May the 7th Battalion sent A Company to support the 3rd Battalion on the 400 plateau, facing Owen's Gully. Two men were killed and five wounded. The Battalion moved up next evening to support the 1st Brigade, but the Turks did not attack.

The 24th May was a day of armistice to bury the dead between the opposing lines.

On the 25th May H.M.S. Triumph was torpedoed at 12.26 and sank off Gaba Tepe. A destroyer, which remained pressed alongside the heeling ship until she was actually taking her final plunge, rescued almost the entire crew.

On the 31st May a shell burst on the Battalion drawn up on parade below the bivouac and wounded 15 men, one subsequently dying. Lieut.-Col. Elliott resumed command of the Battalion on the 4th June, and soon afterwards the unit moved to a site on the south of Monash Gully. The men were chiefly employed on fatigues, carrying water and ammunition. Some 50 assisted the Engineers in sapping under the Turkish trenches.

On the 11th June the 2nd Brigade took over the portion of the 1st Brigade front facing the German Officer's Trench, and on the 28th the 7th was holding Steel's Post. It was here on the 4th July that a tunnel—D21—running out beneath German Officer's Trench was blown up. Zeki Bey, the Commander of the 1/57th Turkish Regiment holding this trench, subsequently explored this tunnel on the 8th, pulling away the sandbag barricade at its entrance into the crater. Their entry being reported to Battalion H.Q., Elliott ordered Grills and Permezel to organise a party to drive the intruders out, and characteristically reconnoitred the position with two men. As he reached a point some 20 feet along the dark gallery a shot was fired from a Turkish sentry in the tunnel, wounding one of the men. They retired thinking Elliott, who was in front, was killed, and he held the tunnel sheltering behind a bend till Permezel's party came up and helped him build up a new sandbag barricade. Next afternoon a charge was placed in front of this and the Turkish barrier with the Turk sentry blown out, as the wad out of a gun. The roof fell in and Lieut. K. I. Walker and a party scrambled into the crater thus formed. This was subsequently known as Dyer's, and a Turkish raid was made on it next morning, but was easily repulsed. The crater was then evacuated. At 8.15 a.m. on the 11th, Lieut. N. J. Greig with 11 men entered the crater, killing three Turks, but was bombed from German Officer's Trench, into which the crater was widely open. Three were killed and all the rest wounded, and Lieut. Greig, having sent back all his men along the broken-down tunnel, himself covered their retreat till he was killed.

The Turks retaliated by heavy fire upon Steele's Post with 75's and a 6-inch Howitzer, and caused many casualties and a great strain upon the garrison.

CHAPTER 7.

LONE PINE.

EARLY in August, as a result of tunnelling and extensive mining operations, it was generally held that a big offensive was imminent. This in spite of the bad health of the Australian troops from dysentery and gastro-intestinal diseases from the monotony of the diet, lack of fresh vegetables and the swarms of disease-carrying flies.

The plan was as follows. The 6th Battalion was to take German Officer's Trench as a diversion while the 1st Brigade charged the Lone Pine position.

The 7th Battalion, drawn up opposite Johnston's Jolly, was, if the 6th was successful, to charge across the 120 yards between the A.I.F. position and the Turks and to be led by a special bombing platoon under Captain Hubert Jacobs.

It was hoped by these attacks to divert the attention of the Turkish command from the main landing of the British Divisions at Suvla Bay and the night advance of the British and New Zealanders on Sari Bair.

At 5.30 p.m. on the 6th August the 1st Australian Brigade attacked the Turkish trenches at Lone Pine. The 2nd Brigade concentrated a heavy machine gun and rifle fire upon the Turkish trenches on Johnston's Jolly. With the capture of Lone Pine, by dint of extremely heavy fighting, Infantry working parties under the 2nd Field Company connected up tunnels from Brown's Dip and the Pimple to the Pine trenches, a matter of about a hundred yards.

The 6th Battalion attacked from sapheads in an underground trench in front of German Officer's Trench. These sapheads were broken open at the time of the attack, but the steps leading up to them were so narrow that only one man could emerge at a time. This slow exit gave the Turks time to man their firesteps and the attackers were swept away as they appeared. The 6th lost 80 killed and 66 wounded in their valiant attempt. The attack by the 7th Battalion on Johnston's Jolly was therefore cancelled.

During the night the Turkish reserves, the 13th Regiment and the 9th Division began to arrive and counter-attacked heavily all next day. The 7th Battalion was ordered by Colonel N. Smyth, V.C., to support the 1st Battalion, and during the afternoon of the 8th August all, with the exception of one platoon, entered the captured position. The platoon of bombers under Capt. H. Jacobs were left covering the trenches of Johnston's Jolly and the Mule Gully, but later it too was sent to support the 1st Battalion under Col. McNaughton, and finally rejoined the 7th at dawn on the 19th, and was placed in the sector commanded by Lieut. F. H. Tubb.

The Official History states that the 7th Battalion bombers went into Lone Pine at 6 p.m. on the 7th August, and in the heavy fighting of that night the next day almost all had been killed or wounded.

By 3 p.m. on the 8th Colonel Elliott (7th Battalion) had relieved the 1st and the 2nd Battalions on the right. Lieut. W. J. Symons was in charge of the posts from Goldenstedt's to Wood's. On the extreme right, as Jacob's Trench appeared to be dangerously isolated, he increased the number of posts. Lieuts. W. Fisher and G. J. C. Dyett were in Jacob's Trench. Turkish attacks were heavy during the afternoon against the post at Jacob's barricade. At 7 p.m. another severe attack was launched against this position, extending to Goldenstedt's Post, now held by a portion of Lieut. Symons' company. The Turks again and again succeeded in forcing their way over the low barricade into the main position, but Symons bombed them out as often. Meanwhile in Jacob's Trench, Lieut. Dyett having been severely wounded, Lieut. West was placed in command; and since the fighting at Tubb's Corner also urgently required superintendence, Lieut. Tubb with half his reserve company from the Pimple was brought in to support and finally took over the New Flank Trench. By 2 a.m. on the night of the 8th August the fighting had died down.

On the fourth and last day of acute struggle at the Pine the Australian position was held in the north by the 4th Battalion, in the centre by the 3rd, and in the southern and largest sector by the 7th, whose front had been subdivided into three commands—Symon's, Tubb's and West's. At 4 a.m. from the enemy positions around the Pine, and also from Johnston's Jolly, there burst an intense machine gun and rifle fire, and a most violent general attack was directed against the whole line. Lieut. B. N. W. Edwards was killed and Lieut. A. N. Hamilton wounded in Wood's Trench. Symons himself took charge in the even heavier fighting which had again broken out at Goldenstedt's Post. Here by throwing the big gun-cotton bombs he temporarily subdued the enemy, but was called away by Col. Elliott for even more pressing work. Lieut. Tubb was then in command. Tubb had eight men on the parapet, while two corporals, H. Webb and F. Wright, were told to remain on the floor of the trench in order to catch and throw back the enemy's bombs or smother them with Turkish overcoats. Tubb was on the parapet, exposing himself recklessly. Soon Wright was killed, Webb had both his hands blown off, and Tubb, bleeding from bomb wounds in the arm and scalp, continued to fight, supported in the end only by Corporal W. Dunstan and a personal friend, Corporal A. S. Burton, of Euroa. An explosion blew down the barricade. Tubb drove the Turks off and Dunstan and Burton were helping to rebuild the barrier when a bomb fell between them, killing Burton. Tubb obtained further men from the next post, but the enemy's attack weakened and died away.

Meanwhile the struggle in Jacob's Trench had been as fierce. It was enfiladed by enemy machine gun fire, and all the garrison was killed except Lieut. West wounded and Pte. Shadbolt, who held the post till Lieut. H. H. Young brought up a few men. Further reinforcements under Lieut. T. J. Woodhouse, Lieut. H. E. Bastin came in, but were all killed or wounded and the post was lost. Lieut. Symons was ordered to retake it. He succeeded, drove out the enemy and rebuilt the barricade. Then, as the Turks were attacking the post from three sides, he asked Elliott's leave to abandon it. He then withdrew to some overhead cover at the western end of the trench, leaving fifteen yards of open trench to the enemy.

At 6.30 p.m. the enemy attack had definitely failed. An attempt was made to organise a counter-attack on the now thoroughly demoralised enemy and the 1st Battalion was brought in, but it was abandoned.

At midday on the 10th the remnant of the Battalion was relieved by the 5th Battalion.

Lieut. Tubb, Lieut. Symons, Cpl. Dunstan and Cpl. Burton were awarded the Victoria Cross, and Sgt. Ball and Cpt. Webb received the D.C.M.

The casualties were appalling. The Battalion went in with 14 officers and 680 O.R., and lost 12 officers and 342 O.R. The total losses of the 1st Australian Division were over 2000 men, the greater number incurred in sheer hand-to-hand fighting and bombing. The enemy's loss was heavier. The 16th Turkish Division is said to have lost 6930 men in five days.

The attack drew upon itself the whole of the immediate Turkish reserves, and for three days monopolised Essad Pasha's attention.

On the 11th of August, after 48 hours' rest, the Battalion returned to the Pine. There was no further counter-attack. The trenches were cleared of the dead and put into a state of repair. The re-entrant angle of the front line at Symons' Post was straightened out.

CHAPTER 8.

15th AUGUST TO THE EVACUATION.

WITH the failure of the Suvla Bay attack trench warfare recommenced. The 7th and 1st Battalions garrisoned Lone Pine, taking two days in the Pine and two days rest. The trenches were strongly fortified. Lieut.-Col. Elliott was evacuated sick on the 27th of August, and Major A. Jackson assumed command of the Battalion. On the 12th September the unit was finally relieved at Lone Pine by the 12th Battalion and next day left the Peninsula, arriving at Sarpi Camp, Mudros. There they remained for a month, resting and recuperating—food was plentiful and a bottle of stout per man was issued daily. The Battalion was inspected by General Munro, the new Commander-in-Chief, on the 27th October, and by Field-Marshal Lord Kitchener on the 11th November. Rough weather delayed the return to Anzac till the 25th November. The first bivouac was in Shrapnel Gully, but a snowstorm caused a move to Victoria Gully. Waterproof capes and rubber boots were issued to the troops. Elliott rejoined the Battalion on the 7th December. The Battalion relieved the 5th and 6th Battalions at Silt Spur on the 11th.

General Munro and Lord Kitchener having advised the necessity of withdrawing the troops from the Peninsula, preparations were being made. Major Layh, in charge of 7 officers and 199 other ranks, left the front line as the first party on the 18th December. Lieut.-Col. Elliott strained his ankle and had to be evacuated. Next day Major Hart with 5 officers and 224 other ranks left at dusk, stealing in small parties down the communication trenches with sandbags round their feet. At 8 p.m. Battalion Headquarters was moved to the firing line, and at 9.35 p.m. Major McCrae with 3 officers and 90 other ranks moved off. The Turks were apparently quite oblivious of any evacuation being carried out. At 2 o'clock next morning, the 20th December, C party, the last of the unit, left the trenches noiselessly and were embarked at 3.15 a.m.

Lance Corporal W. C. Surry devised a scheme for firing rifles after the last man had left. A weight attached to the trigger was suspended in such a way that it would be released through the overbalancing of a certain tin. Above that was placed another tin containing water but pierced with a small hole. When sufficient water had trickled into the lower tin the rifle was fired.

The Battalion was again at Sarpi Camp, Lemnos, from the 21st December till the 4th January, when it embarked on H.M.T.S. Empress of Britain for Alexandria, and thence by rail to Tel-el-Kebir, 70 miles from Cairo and 20 miles from Ismailia, the centre of the Canal defence system. Here, on the field where Lord Wolseley had defeated Arabi Pasha in 1882 and where the old trenches and breastwork could still be seen, the long lost Battalion Transport awaited the unit. The Transport, after some days off the Gallipoli coast, had been brought back to Alexandria and stationed at Max Camp, near Ramleh, and had remained there during the campaign.

CHAPTER 9.

EGYPT TO POZIERES.

WITH the departure on the 24th February, 1916, of Major Denehy with 12 officers and 466 other ranks to form the nucleus of the 59th Battalion, 15th Brigade (of which Lieut. Col., now Brig. General, H. E. Elliott was Brigadier), and the arrival the same day of 4 officers and 479 other ranks from reinforcements, the Battalion entered upon the second stage of its existence. Major C. H. Jess, who had been Brigade Major, was appointed to command with the rank of Lieut. Colonel, Major A. Jackson being second in command. Then began the work of welding the veterans and the recruits together into an efficient fighting unit.

We were engaged on outpost duty for some time, experiencing the hardships of desert warfare without the consolation of having an enemy near to share it, as no attack came. The early part of March was devoted to training, principally in musketry, when we were not required to supply guards and picquets, which duties were frequent and absorbed a great number of men.

The great compensation was that our camp at Serapeum, on the Asiatic side of the Canal, was quite close to the Canal, and every evening the Battalion bathed *en masse*, and washed away the dust and sweat of the day. It must have been an interesting sight to the passengers on the vessels passing along the Canal at this time to come on several hundreds of men bathing in the water alongside their ships.

The first intimation of our departure reached Brigade on the 2nd March, when it was learnt that we were to leave for France in about a fortnight. The news soon spread, and we were all filled with joyful anticipation of the good things to be expected there, among a civilised population, with quarters in respectable billets occasionally, and also with mixed feelings at the prospect of being at last pitted against the Germans.

Before we left we made our first acquaintance with H.R.H. the Prince of Wales, who rode through the camp and was heartily cheered. He appeared nervous upon this occasion, and quite boyish compared to the grizzled veterans of Anzac.

On the 25th March we left Serapeum under the command of Major Jackson, Lieut. Col. Jess being retained in Egypt as judge advocate at a general court-martial.

After a somewhat rough trip in open trucks across the desert by night through Ismalia and Tel-el-Kebir, we reached Alexandria at about 6 a.m. on the 26th, and immediately embarked on the "Megantic," together with the 8th Battalion. The ship was a very large one and the accommodation exceptionally good, every man having a cabin berth. As Captain Bastin, the newly appointed Adjutant, wrote in the War Diary, "All the men are berthed in cabins which is alright for them, but to the orderly officer it is a pest. He is just like a farmer digging up potatoes out of a field when he wants anyone for fatigue." The simile is hardly apt, for a potato can only be dug up once, while we were "dug up" almost as rapidly as we could get ourselves buried. There were numerous duties to be supplied, and many guards, the chief being "submarine guard," when the unlucky sentry leaned over a rail and scanned the sea for anything looking like his idea of a periscope. Fortunately nothing suspicious was seen, and in all respects the trip was a pleasant one, the only unpleasantness being caused by an enthusiasm displayed by the medical officers for inoculation. Everyone was duly punctured, but none rightly understood what disease he was now proof against.

We entered Marseilles on the 31st March. The previous night had been rough, and the breakfast parade that morning was poorly attended, but the day was glorious, and we shall not soon forget our first glimpse of the magnificent harbour—green hills rising from the sea to great heights, white houses with red roofs gleaming among the trees, dazzling sunlight dancing on the calm waters of the bay, all combined to make a joyous picture. On the wharves we saw indications of warfare, war material, anti-aircraft guns, and German prisoners at work. We were given no opportunity for exploration, disembarking at 7.30 p.m. We were marched a short distance to a train composed of trucks. Each truck bore a grim legend, happily as yet unintelligible to most of us, but one which

Brig.-Gen. C. H. JESS
C.M.G., C.B.E., D.S.O.

we were destined to know only too well in the days to come. "Hommes 40, chevaux (en long), 8." We soon learned to envy the "chevaux." In consideration of the long voyage before us, we were allowed the "luxury" of having only 35 men in each truck. Even then we found it impossible to lie at full length, and were much cramped. Officers travelled with their platoons. The train left at 9 p.m. At midnight there was a stop at Orange for hot tea. Then we "slept" again.

Everyone was awake again at the first sign of dawn, the sides of the truck were let down as far as possible, and we drank in the landscape with incredulous eyes. Every soldier who made that trip has written home describing it. It made the profoundest impression on every one of us. Coming, as we had, from the barren, dreary sands of Egypt, the green fields of France were like a glimpse into a new world to us. Eyes which had been long accustomed to the drab shores of Gallipoli, to the parched wastes of the desert, and to uncultivated wildernesses gazed enthralled at the new scenes which unfolded before us as our train crawled north. Vistas of green fields and orchards, trim farmhouses, clean white roads, wooded hills, and pretty villages surrounded by shapely trees, were opened around us. The villagers cheered us as we passed through, and neat looking girls threw kisses, and sometimes when we stopped at a station adventurous spirits secured a few real ones, in exchange for badges or buttons. "Pour souvenir, Monsieur." All the folk seemed to be in mourning and we saw no men, except aged and crippled. The war and what it was costing France was thus early borne in upon us.

We wound along up the Rhone Valley amid scenes of great beauty, stopped for a little while at busy Lyons, where the children in the street below scrambled for "souvenirs" in the shape of Egyptian coins, and had frequently to compete against their elders for possession of their trophies; then away across flatter and at times marshy country, by way of Dijon, towards Paris. We skirted the outer suburbs, through Juvisy and Saint Germains, on a glorious Sunday afternoon, and saw some charming suburbs buried among wooded hills; great numbers of people were walking in the woods, giving a holiday appearance to the scenes we saw; tea at Epûches, then on towards the coast. Next morning we caught glimpses of the English Channel from near Calais, then turning inland again, we arrived at about 2.30 p.m. on the 3rd April, after a journey of 66 hours, at our destination, Godes-waesvelde, on the Belgian frontier.

Detraining, we began a long tiring march, arriving about 6 p.m. almost exhausted at La Crêche, outside Bailieul. Here the troops were billeted very comfortably in barns, with clean straw for mattresses, and we soon began to explore. We were here for twelve days, and made our first acquaintance with the French people, the French language and French beverages. The large and ill-fated township of Baillieul was within easy walking distance, and as yet beyond the reach of enemy shell fire. Here we spent our pay, paying high prices for what we wanted. We met men from English and Canadian regiments, who gave us no very glowing account of warfare on this front.

We were soon busy training. Gas-masks were issued, the P.H. helmet type being then the one in use, a sort of large flannel bag, steeped in chemicals, which was put over the head, seized and held tightly at the throat, while the breath was expelled through a mouthpiece. A scout platoon was formed under Lieut. W. H. James; this platoon was the origin of a valuable arm. Cameras were collected and returned to England. On the 15th April we left La Crêche and marched in driving rain and sleet to l'Hallobeau, a few miles nearer the line. Here we were billeted in huts and resumed training. Lieut. Col. Jess rejoined us and resumed command.

Some officers and N.C.O.'s were sent forward to inspect the trenches, which were found to be entirely different from those at Anzac. Working parties, wearing the new steel helmets, were sent to the forward area on barb wire work behind the lines.

On the 29th April we moved still further forward to Fleur Baix, a village about a mile and a half from the front line.

"D" Company occupied a forward post at a farmhouse at Croix Marechal. The Battalion was in support to the 5th Battalion, and was occupied in work on the support trenches.

On the 3rd May we relieved the 5th Battalion in the front line, which consisted of ramparts raised above the ground, and not, as was usual, of trenches dug down into it. As we look back on the comfortable trenches and comparative safety of this tour of duty, we smile to think how deadly serious it was to us then. In reality it was a period of restful calm; a few night patrols or wiring parties, a continual improvement of the trenches (the Bantams had been in and in many places the parapet was too low), and some intermittent shell fire. Every shell fired was counted and faithfully reported in the day's intelligence summary. The weather was fine and warm. We sustained a few casualties, and soon learned the advantage of keeping our heads down.

Relieved by the 5th Battalion on the 28th May, we came back to Fleur Baix. From here we journeyed daily, either at night or by day, to the support area, and were employed on trench improvement. It was early summer and the country around us was bright with grass and meadow flowers, birds sang in the green-leafed trees, and it was difficult to imagine amidst such pleasant surroundings that man was bringing desolation upon a beautiful land.

The village of Fleur Baix consisted of a considerable number of houses, many of which had been damaged; but on the whole the town had been spared by the enemy and still held a few civilians.

Up near the support line, less than half a mile from the front line, was an estaminet occupied by an old couple and a boy. The Hun had never dropped a shell near this place. It was a curious sight to see the boy driving a small cart, drawn by a large dog, down the road (on which no soldier could appear) to the village for the daily provisions. On one occasion two French soldiers came along to Battalion Headquarters, enquiring the way to this estaminet where they said they had lived. As they appeared to be ignorant of its locality they were sent to Brigade under escort, and likewise under suspicion, and their ultimate fate is unknown.

When we came into the sector all the gun-pits of the artillery were covered over with moss and flowers. The guns had been in the same position for many months with little firing. The result was that as soon as our artillery renewed war-like operations they were promptly blown out of their pits, the location of which must have been long known to the enemy. They then inaugurated the practice of coming out into the fields by night and "pooping off," returning to shelter by day, leaving us to take the shelling of the enemy searching for them. These mobile batteries were the germ of the idea from which later on there sprang the well-known mobile brigades of artillery.

On the 9th June we were relieved and came back to Divisional Reserve, near Sailly, in comfortable barns. Sailly was a pleasant spot, surrounded by green, fresh country, intersected by the River Lys, and broad white roads. The town was large and filled with civilians, and our familiarity with the language grew. A certain amount of training and some fatigue duties were required, but on the whole the time passed very pleasantly. Our evenings were largely occupied by football matches, which usually began at about 7 or 7.30 p.m. and finished about 9.30 p.m. Daylight lasted till 10 p.m., and frequently "lights out" would be blown before the game was finished.

Early one morning a number of men smelt gas and woke up coughing; some gas from an attack by the enemy near Ploegsteert had drifted down the Lys Valley from the north. We sustained no casualties however, but the incident is interesting as showing the extent to which gas would penetrate behind the lines under favourable conditions, in this case upwards of ten miles.

On the 19th June we left, marching to Neuve Eglise, across the Belgian border and bivouacking for three days on a hillside at Aldershot Camp. On the 23rd we were in the line at Ploegsteert, of evil reputation, where we relieved the 3rd Battalion of the Rifle Brigade, facing Messines Hill. The line companies had in the main a quiet time until the 29th, when our trenches were shelled and B Company sustained heavy casualties.

A post, which it was necessary to place across the Messines Road was subjected to particular attention nightly by trench mortar from the direction of Messines village, which looked down on and completely commanded the position. A raid was carried out by the Buffs on the trenches opposite us, but it failed to reach the enemy lines. Gas, which was installed in our trenches, was at last discharged one night, and was last seen blowing over the enemy lines. This had caused considerable "wind up" for fear a shell should strike it. Subsequent reports indicated that severe casualties were sustained by the Hun.

We were relieved on the night of the 4th July by the 18th King's Royal Rifles and the 11th Royal West Kents.

Our casualties, practically all sustained on the left of our position on the Messines Road, were one officer killed (Lieut. Hoban), one officer wounded (Lieut. F. J. Smedley), 11 men killed and 27 wounded. Total 40.

On relief we came back to Neuve Eglise in heavy rain and again bivouacked on the hillside at Aldershot. Next day our first Battalion sports meeting in France was held.

On the 9th July we marched to Bailleul, and at 1 a.m. on the 11th we entrained for the Somme, where the great British offensive had been launched some ten days before. At 5 a.m. we reached Doullens, a large, quaint, picturesque town, and breakfasted in the main street. At 8.30 a.m. we began to march, and at 7 p.m. were still marching. It was well on towards 9 p.m. before we were all settled in billets at Bertaucourt after a gruelling day. That march, over 17 miles on paved and metalled roads, probably lives in our minds still as the biggest and most exhausting we ever accomplished, being soft from the trenches, but not a single man fell out of the ranks on the way. It was here that the inhabitants refused to let the billeting officers do their work, thinking "black" troops were coming. We set out at 11.30 a.m. next day, and began by climbing a steep hill. The road then lay through fields of corn flecked with poppies and cornflowers, and the country was most picturesque. After further marches and halts at Talmas and Rainneville, where we had our only practice of Battalion in attack, utilising an old quarry for the purpose, we reached Varennes on the 16th July. Here we dumped our blankets and packs, and, arrayed for the first time in the light equipment known as "fighting order," we set out for Albert on the 20th. At Albert we bivouacked just outside the town, and made final preparations for battle.

Maps of Pozieres were inspected and explained, and the scheme of the attack unfolded, half the officers being left in reserve at wagon lines. Moving forward in single file at 6.30 p.m. through Albert, much damaged by shellfire, beneath the famous statue of the Madonna and Child hanging in mid air from the top of the church steeple, out along the dusty, chalky roads, and by narrow winding paths, we arrived at the captured German trenches in Sausage Valley, La Boiselle, surrounded on all sides by guns.

The strength of the Battalion on the eve of Pozieres was 34 officers and 968 other ranks. It was considered by all of the "original" officers that the Battalion was now as efficient a fighting force as when it left Egypt for Gallipoli.

The week's marching forward from Doullens had hardened us wonderfully. It is worthy of note that throughout those long marches not a single man had failed to reach his billets, even four "diggers" under open arrest pending court-martial being just as keen as the others.

CHAPTER 10.

"POZIERES."

TO follow the part played by the Battalion in connection with the fighting at Pozieres, it is necessary to outline shortly the way the battle developed and the stage at which we came into it. The great offensive launched on the 1st July, 1916, had made substantial progress, but was held up at Pozieres, a commanding knoll dominating the country in every direction. Up to the 16th three separate assaults upon the village had failed. The 1st Division was to be thrown in to endeavour, if possible, to effect its capture. Until it was captured further progress on either flank was impossible, as the use of the ridge beyond Pozieres gave the enemy a wide view over our lines and denied us any observation over his. It was thus a key position, a fact which the Germans fully realised, as is witnessed by their stubborn defence.

The plan ultimately prepared was for a converging attack by the 1st and 3rd Brigades, with our Brigade, the 2nd, in reserve. The actual assault was launched at 12.30 a.m. on the 23rd July, as part of a major operation in which other troops were participating further to the right. The attack failed elsewhere, but our Division met with substantial success at Pozieres. Following upon a complete artillery preparation, a sudden attack met with comparatively little opposition at the beginning, and a line was formed along the south-east side of the Bapaume Road, running through the village, which was not captured till later. The village had been reduced to a large rubble heap by continuous shelling, and gradually it was cleaned up by scouting parties after tough fighting. During the night of the 23rd, the 6th and 8th Battalions attacked through the village and established posts beyond it. By the 24th, it could be said that the capture was complete, but holding was another problem, as enemy shelling never ceased, day or night.

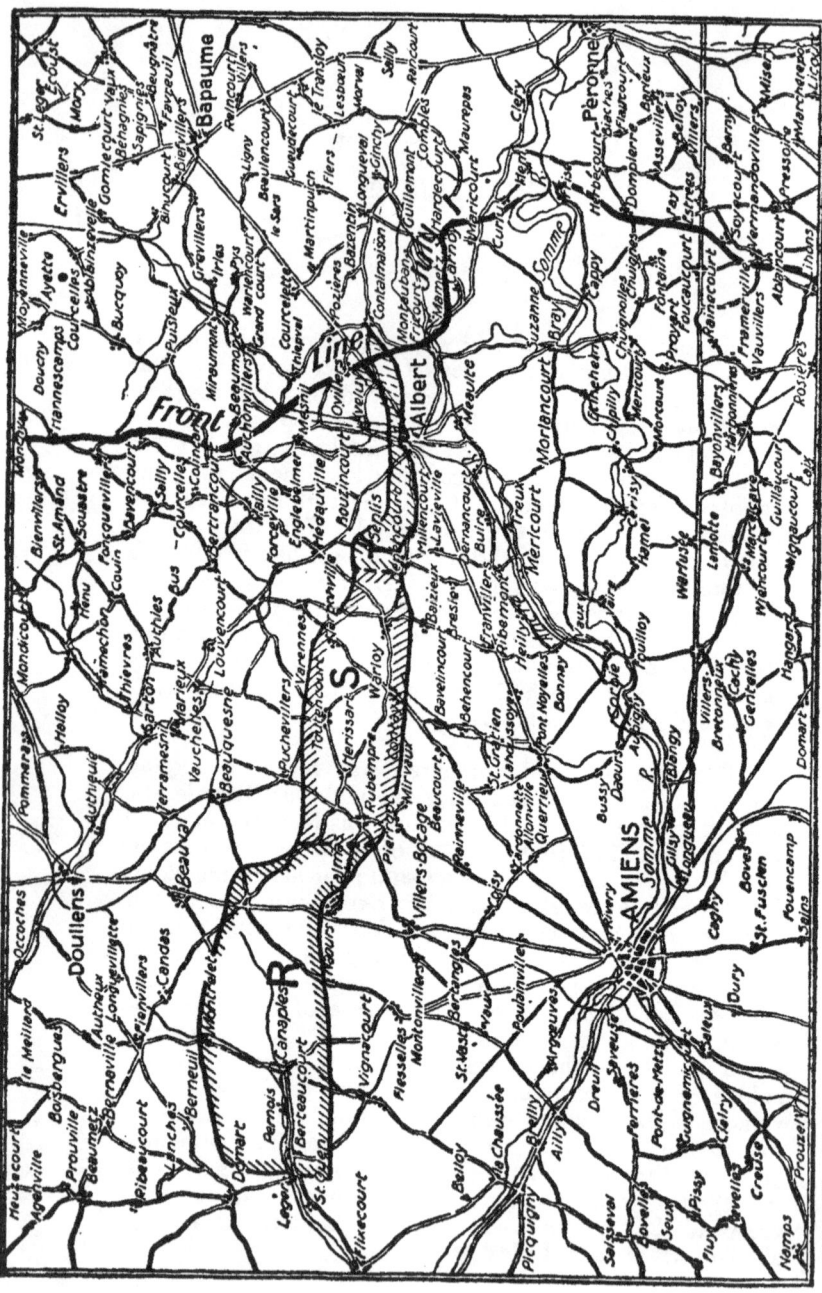

THE SOMME

To return now to our own operations. During the night of the 22nd/23rd July, we were at Sausage Valley, a mile and a half in rear, surrounded by artillery, which at the appointed hour opened fire with tremendous energy and was soon answered by the enemy. We waited anxiously for news of the battle in expectation of our own turn. By 3.45 a.m. we heard that the attack had succeeded. At 5 a.m., A and B Companies were called upon to go forward to Black Watch Alley, a communication trench near Contalmaison, to serve as reserve to the 3rd Brigade. At 5.45 a.m., C and D Companies followed. As we went forward in the grey light of the early morning, through a smoke laden atmosphere, we passed many dead enemy from the previous fighting and a great many prisoners who were being sent to the rear, and numbers of our own wounded coming from the battle. Passing through a barrage of heavy artillery fire we reached our destination in Black Watch Alley, and spent a far from quiet day there amongst the enemy gas and shrapnel shelling, A and B Companies being engaged in carrying rations and ammunition for the 3rd Brigade. On the 24th we received instructions for an operation early on the following morning. The operation was under the control of the 3rd Brigade, which was to have the use of the 5th Battalion and our two companies for the purpose. We were to deliver an attack on two lines of German trenches north-east of Pozieres known as "O.G.1" and "O.G.2," which terms meant "Old German Trench No. 1" and "Old German Trench No. 2." These lines were the scene of much heavy fighting.

The plan was for the 5th Battalion to attack on the right, and the two companies of the 7th on the left. The 5th were to employ two companies in front and two in rear and advance in six successive waves. The portion of the 7th on the left, between the Bapaume Road and an old light railway line, were to have one company in front and one in rear. The attack on O.G.1 was to be made at 2 a.m., and at 2.20 would go forward from O.G.1 to O.G.2 following the barrage. In our Battalion A Company was to take O.G.1 and B Company to go through them and capture O.G.2. C and D Companies were back again under the command of the C.O. and not concerned in the operation.

The ground was of course unfamiliar to us, under constant heavy shell fire, and we had no opportunity of reconnaissance. A tape was to be laid by the 5th Battalion to mark the starting position. Our companies were to leave Pozieres trench at 11 p.m., file northward in the dark across the shell holes to the Bapaume Road, then turn right so as to be facing O.G.1. The 5th Battalion was to follow. Owing to casualties the tape was not completely laid, and the plans for the attack went astray from the first. Instead of waiting for us to pass, the 5th Battalion began moving into position ahead of time, and we were obliged to wait until they were clear. B Company was misdirected by other troops, and in the darkness followed the remnants of a trench leading towards Pozieres. It was not until 2.10 a.m.—ten minutes after the attack was due to commence—that we were established and organised for attack; there was no time to carry out the preliminary movement planned; an enemy barrage in reply had descended on our troops, and in the darkness all was confusion. A Company negotiated the broken country as best they could in the attempt to get forward, but could not locate the enemy trenches. One platoon got to within 30 yards of them, but lacking support could advance no further. Of the whole attack only a small portion succeeded. At 6.45 a.m. the C.O. 5th Battalion, who had succeeded in getting into part of O.G.1, ordered two platoons of D Company into the line. No. 13 Platoon, led by 2nd/Lieut. Appleton, entered the front line trench, followed by No. 14. Appleton was immediately shot in the head by a sniper and killed, the whole of the two platoons having to step over his body as they passed along the trench. Led by Captain Oates, these two platoons bombed their way down O.G.1 towards the railway, and having gone as far as possible set about erecting a barricade. A heavy bomb fight and attacks ensued throughout 24 hours. Behind them the slaughter occasioned by artillery and machine gun or rifle bullets was terrific, and dead and wounded blocked the narow trenches. Stretchers and stretcher-bearers were not to be obtained. Enemy snipers accounted for a great many victims, the battered trenches giving inadequate protection. Relays of men, hastily organised by Oates, in a moment's respite, passed up bombs and sandbags. Oates and his small handful of men held the enemy at bay until 10 a.m. next day, when they were relieved. They had erected a substantial barrier in the trench, consolidating the position won. Subsequently Oates was awarded the D.S.O., D.C.M.'s being awarded to C.S.M. McDonald,

L/Corporal "Gorrie" Tucker (afterwards Lieut., who died of wounds in 1918) and Private Tracey, who lost a leg. Meantime C. Company had been engaged in carrying ammunition for the 5th Battalion, leaving only two platoons of D Company still under the command of the C.O., 7th Battalion. At 9 a.m. C Company of the 6th Battalion was placed under his command to assist in repelling a threatened counter-attack, and were disposed to fill a vital gap in the line just in time. This was delivered at 9.30 a.m., but was successfully repulsed.

By 1 p.m., except that as stated above, D Company, with Lieut. Bowtell-Harris, was still engaged on the left of the 5th, the Battalion was again placed under the C.O. The C.O. promptly set about the task of reorganising the Battalion, though still in the forward area and under continuous shell-fire; but it was many hours before all men were able to rejoin their own companies. At 2.30 p.m. we were instructed to withdraw the Battalion and complete reorganisation, where was not stated, and therefore the C.O. selected Bailiff Wood. The C.O. was called to 3rd Brigade for further instructions, and was told that we were to relieve two battalions of the 1st Brigade in Pozieres. We then withdrew through a heavy barrage about a mile to Bailiff Wood and were reorganised. Bombs were issued and at 9 p.m. we moved forward again through the intense barrage to Pozieres, relieving portion of the 1st Brigade in supports, and in the front area shell holes along the Pozieres Road. We remained here until the morning of the 27th under constant heavy fire from guns of large calibre, and subjected to shelling with gas shells. During the 26th conditions were such that the C.O. considered it to be his duty to inform Brigade that the men were occupying crater holes owing to the impossibility of making trenches in the crumbly soil; that they were continually being buried and dug out; that Pozieres was being subjected to constant bombardment by heavies, and that, despite the cheerful and resolute spirit of the men their dazed condition rendered them physically incapable of digging in or of strenuous resistance should fighting become necessary. He asked for support from the heavy artillery. The 6th and 8th Battalion concurred in his statement of the position. Brigade replied that the men must hang on. The C.O. answered that no suggestion of a retirement had been made, but rather that an enemy attack would be welcomed as a relief from the incessant heavy shell-fire. The enemy was seen moving his men forward, but artillery observers were finding it almost impossible to maintain communications as telephone lines could not remain intact during the barrage and gallant repairers were being killed in the attempt; none of our field guns were effectively shelling this enemy movement.

Fortunately at this juncture an observation officer of the Heavy Artillery scrambled through the shell-fire into Battalion Headquarters in a deep dugout, and by a stroke of luck brought an unbroken telephone line with him. He got on to Heavy Artillery Headquarters and just before his line was cut brought their fire on to the enemy infantry. The result was to dissipate the impending attack, which in the dazed and shattered condition of the men might well have been successful. If it had, the effect on subsequent operations involving the possible re-capture of Pozieres after the expenditure of so much effort can be imagined. Pozieres itself by this time had been razed to the ground, with not a particle of wall intact. The concentrated and continuous shell-fire of Pozieres was probably the severest ordeal we had yet encountered, and it lives to-day in the memory of many a man as a dreadful nightmare.

See Extract from " Dr. Bean's Official History" at end of chapter.

Towards evening our artillery became more active. This at once increased the enemy shelling, which, however, soon slackened to considerably less than that displayed during the day. At 2 a.m. on the 27th, A and B Companies were relieved by the 22nd Battalion, and at 4 a.m. C and D were withdrawn, followed by Battalion Headquarters. The Battalion returned to the comparative calm of Sausage Valley, where, for the first time for many days, we slept. Thus ended for us the battle known as "First Pozieres."

Officially we were never in the fight at all. Our Brigade Headquarters did not have the carrying out of any operation except the holding of Pozieres. We were attached in parts to other battalions, which in turn were attached to another brigade, for the earlier portion of the period. Consequently nothing was reported in our name during the fighting, as is evidenced by the fact that on the 25th July, the Divisional War Diary is able to refer to us as being "lightly engaged and comparatively fresh," after two days and nights as described above.

Our casualties were:—

	Killed.	Wounded.	Missing.	Total.
Officers	2	10	—	12
Men	52	265	1	317
Total	54	275	1	329

The officers killed were 2nd/Lieuts. W. Appleton and H. J. T. Brown.

Tired, grimy, and aware of the vacancies in our ranks, we left for Albert the same evening, where we washed, ate, and had a real good sleep. Then marching by way of Vadencourt and La Vicogne, we reached Canaples on the 30th, recovering in energy and spirit each day. Here we bivouacked pleasantly in the open, and spent a delightful week in bright warm weather. Several drafts of reinforcements arrived to replace casualties, and after steady training the unit soon recovered itself. A week later we were moving forward again. A hot trying march on the 8th August brought us to Vadencourt Wood, where we were camped in huts, very comfortably, situated in the woods. Here training was resumed. A Company left for Puchevillers to unload shells at a railway siding. On the 10th, we lined the roads to cheer the King as he passed, and also saw the battle strain on units of the 2nd Division coming from Pozieres. On the 14th, we were at Albert again, and on the following night we relieved the 46th Battalion, about half-a-mile south of Pozieres, near the O.G. 1 and 2, which we had tried to capture on the night of the 24th July. Our strength was then 36 officers, 755 other ranks, including the absent A Company. The position on the front had not changed very much since we left there, except that a semblance of continuous trenches had been made. The line had advanced north beyond Pozieres on the Australian front in a deep salient as far as Mouquet Farm, but on the flanks had been held back despite desperate assaults. It was proposed that our Division should make two assaults—the 1st Brigade in a north-westerly direction towards Mouquet Farm, and the 2nd Brigade in a north-easterly direction south of the Bapaume Road, in the vicinity of the famous windmill.

There was a strong feeling that after our severe losses of two weeks before, a longer period of rest might have been allowed, during which our reinforcements might have become accustomed to their new surroundings and instructed in what lay ahead.

On the 16th August a party of 1 officer and 80 men was sent out to continue the digging of a "jumping off trench" (usually referred to as J.O.T.), in front of our lines in full daylight. As the enemy was on the reverse slope of the ridge, little trouble was experienced at his hands. At 10 p.m. a further party of 4 officers and 310 men, being the whole strength of the Battalion not employed on other duties, were ordered by Brigade to be sent out to carry on the digging in No Man's Land where the work had been commenced by a previous unit. The work was supervised by Engineers, who were responsible for the direction. The trench was being dug in two sections, which were to meet. The enemy by shell and machine-gun fire had nightly endeavoured to prevent the work being accomplished. We persevered, however, despite casualties, and a trench some 200 yards long and 4 feet 6 inches wide was dug during the night. This trench was intended to be in prolongation of another trench being dug by another unit further to the left, and only about 50 yards distant from it, but junction could not be made before the 18th, when at 7 a.m. we relieved the 5th Battalion in the line. The trenches, the O.G. 1 and O.G. 2 of our first Pozieres experience, could not be occupied in strength owing to constant shelling, and two platoons of B Company were established in the newly dug J.O.T., the remainder of the Battalion along a sunken road in rear. Late in the day it was found that the ends of the J.O.T., had not met owing to bad direction, probably caused by the machine gun fire of the previous night, and this was the cause of most of our subsequent trouble.

The C.O. received instructions that the Battalion, with the 8th Battalion, was to attack on a night to be ordered later, and plans were made as follows:—B and C Companies were in front, B on the right, C on the left; our left was to rest on and include the Bapaume Road, where we joined the 6th Battalion. Our right was 80 yards north of the tramline, where we linked up with the 8th Battalion. D Company was to follow the leading Company and help as required, by occupying the J.O.T., and unless called on, dig communication trenches forward to the newly-captured line. A Company had not yet returned from Puchevillers. Stoke mortar and artillery co-operation were arranged for, shelling on the enemy strong points on the right and left of the objective being particularly asked for. C Company, prior to the assault, was to move forward from their J.O.T. so as to get in line with B Company, and arrangements were made for tapes to be put out to mark the line on which they were to form up. The Battalion bombers were to go with the left of the Battalion to assist in taking and holding a strongpost at the junction of the two roads.

These were the plans. Unfortunately, though verbally communicated to Company commanders the written orders arrived too late to be promulgated among those who were to carry them out. The first mishap was the non-arrival of the messenger with the order for the attack to be carried out that night, and the zero-hour as fixed by higher authority, and it was not until 5 p.m. that the hour—9 p.m.—was learnt by the C.O. from the 8th Battalion. The jumping-off trenches had not been joined, the central section being still undug. C Company in consequence were obliged to occupy the old firing-line which, beginning about 75 yards behind the left flank of B Company, ran diagonally forward and across the front towards the Bapaume Road, gradually becoming shallower until it petered out about 30 yards short of the road. In consequence it would be necessary for C Company to execute a half-left wheel to come up into alignment. Prior to the attack two platoons of C Company were withdrawn to make room for fatigue parties to pass through; these platoons were to return as soon as the trench was clear. At 8.40 p.m. the company commanders received word that the attack would be at 9 p.m. The trench was still blocked with the fatigue party, and C could not re-occupy it. At 8.55 p.m. an enemy barrage descended upon our crowded positions, causing great confusion and loss. Captain Campbell (C Company), and others to whom the laying of the tapes and the direction of the attack had been entrusted, became casualties, and Lieut. Anthony took over the Company, and at 9.10 he received the orders for the attack, which should have begun ten minutes earlier. At this stage he was buried by a shell, and after extricating himself had to search for and dig out the orders, and examine them by the light of a small electric torch. The Company was then moved forward, but it was too late to get in touch with B Company on the right, which had moved from the assembly position. C Company therefore went blindly forward against a hail of bullets, but, having nothing to guide them, lost direction. Anthony, wounded in the arm at the outset, pressed forward, and finally collapsed from loss of blood. On regaining consciousness he found himself alone in a shell-hole. He endeavoured to make his way back, but stumbled into the enemy trenches, and was captured. He had evidently crossed the first enemy posts in his advances. This supports the theory, held by some at the time, that the Germans, instead of occupying a continuous trench, were really scattered in isolated positions in front of their trench. It would account also for the inability of our troops to locate them. One platoon of C Company, with the bombers, succeeded in getting into the strong post on the Bapaume Road, but were driven back on to the 6th Battalion and D Company, who had followed the advance. They combined in a fresh attack in the darkness, but met with no success. They then dug in across the road in front of the strongpost and maintained themselves there. They established a strong-post only fifty yards short of their objective, and, although several times blown out, persistently re-occupied it, maintaining touch with the 6th Battalion. Extending to the right also D Company kept touch with the remnants of C Company.

Meanwhile B Company on the right had assembled and advanced on the objective, with the 8th Battalion on their right, but were opposed by heavy machine gun and artillery fire, from which they suffered severely. Advancing to the crest of the ridge they became visible on the sky-line, and came under a raking fire from the enemy in the trenches beyond. The centre of the company reached the enemy, where Captain Hoad was wounded on the German parapet, and taken prisoner. The few men who reached the enemy line were insufficient to capture it; the 8th Battalion on the right, despite gallant and determined attempts to overcome the opposition, were unable to gain a footing. B Company were now without officers, and the survivors were obliged to withdraw. In co-operation with the 8th Battalion the attack was renewed later, but the benefit of the barrage was by this time lost, intense darkness had set in, and the attack failed. Again a fresh onslaught was essayed; again the weary broken ranks were beaten back by strong opposition.

On the right the line then rested on the J.O.T., where Lieut. Hillard, who had been sent forward to take command of B Company, reorganised the ranks, which had been thrown into indescribable confusion by the heavy shelling and fruitless assaults.

This was a most difficult task, and on its completion a third attempt was made in conjunction with the 8th Battalion. The defence was again too strong, but some advance was made, and with thirty men of A Company and a Company of the 5th Battalion, the positions reached were consolidated. Heavy artillery fire, including some of our own 9.2 Howitzers, was raking the whole of the area occupied by the troops. Notwithstanding their constant labours of the past three days, the heavy shelling, and the high casualties, the men were resolutely determined to hold on to their positions; the response to a command to stand to, to resist an expected enemy attack, left no doubt as to their spirit.

The Battalion remained in these positions until the next day, the 19th, when B and C Companies were withdrawn, and A Company, fresh from Puchevillers, shared the front with D Company, and sapped forward towards the enemy line. That night, the 19th, because of an incorrect air report that our men were holding on in the enemy trenches, a further attack was ordered by Div. H.Q., two Companies of the 5th Battalion being made available to the C.O.; but owing to the determined action of the C.O., who resisted the order for needless slaughter, and only 23 bombers being available, the assault was abandoned, with the approval of Division.

It was subsequently ascertained that, at that period, the German trenches were packed with fresh relieving troops, and the fate of the attack, without artillery, can be well imagined.

Our trenches were subjected to constant bombardment, but, fortunately, the damage and casualties were slight, owing to our small numbers and the defensive posts being scattered. The Battalion was relieved on the night of the 21st, by the 19th Battalion, and by 1 p.m. on the 22nd was at Warloy. We marched to Rubempre next day, to Amptier the next, and entrained at Authieule for Belgium on the night of the 25th-26th August, glad to leave the Somme behind, and hoping for a period of rest.

The failure of the assault was due to many causes:— Insufficient and inaccurate information from outgoing units as regards the jumping-off-line, which could not be visited in daylight; the loss at critical times of officers, who alone had been able to obtain information as to the position, and to whom alone arrangements had been entrusted; the strength and preparedness of the enemy, who had watched our jumping-off trench being dug for some days previously, and knew exactly where to lay his artillery; the impossibility of previously reconnoitring and observing the enemy positions by reason of the intervening crest; his heavy artillery concentration at the moment of our attack; insufficient artillery preparation to destroy or damage the enemy posts, as particularly asked for in the plan; and the fact that our jumping-off-trench intended to connect with another trench on the left did not do so, so that instead of having a trench straight across the front, the line of assembly was something like this:—

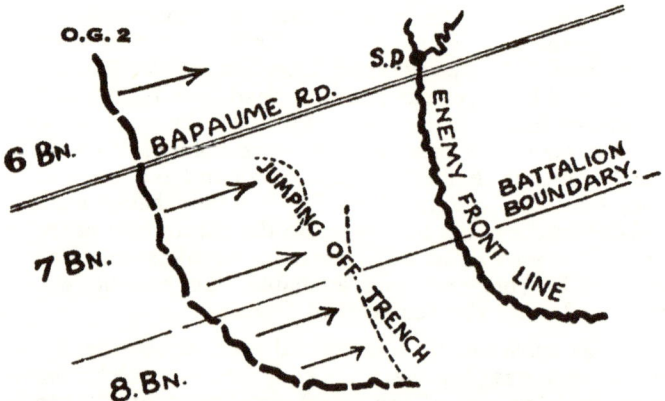

It was in no way the fault of the Battalion or of the 8th Battalion, on the right, that greater success had not rewarded our labours and sacrifices.

Looking back on the Pozieres battles in the light of subsequent experience, we can see more clearly than was possible then, the results of our work. At the time it seemed sheer folly. But we know now that Pozieres was the key to the situation on that front; that until the enemy was deprived of that position he had observation down the valley towards Thiepval on the right, Albert on his front, and on the left towards Contalmaison. While he held Pozieres and the ridge beyond, further advance of the Army was impossible. Previous assaults on the position had failed, and in capturing it the Australian troops gained great glory. Our part in the achievement, small though it was, and slight as our progress appeared to be, was of vast importance, and cleared the way for further advance, not here alone, but also on the flanks. The enemy was stronger than ourselves in men and guns; he was fully prepared for us; and we had to live in and attack over country which had been torn and broken by constant fighting. The attack on this front had begun on the 1st July; the element of surprise was therefore entirely missing. The wonder is not that we achieved so little, but that we achieved so much. Probably never during the whole war had we to meet such continuous and concentrated bombardment; certainly never had such heavy casualties been so meagrely rewarded by the amount of territory captured. But the new 7th had found itself, and had made good the Lone Pine reputation for sticking it out, and had laid the foundation of many future victories.

Our casualties were:—

	Killed.	Wounded.	Prisoners.	Total.
Officers	2	8	2	12
Men	76	151	2	229
Total	78	159	4	241

The officers killed were 2nd/Lieuts. Kozminsky and Jenkins.

Our total losses for the two engagements were:— Killed, 132; wounded, 444; taken prisoner, 4; total, 570; or 57 per cent. of our total strength, including those not engaged in actual fighting, such as the Transport and Quartermaster's and Headquarters Staffs.

Extract from "Official History of Australia in the War of 1914-1918," by C. E. Bean, Vol. III., pages 588-592 :—

The village, constantly hidden in rolling clouds of dust and smoke, was again the spectacle of the battlefield. At one time the bursts of German heavy shell—5.9-inch or larger—in its south-western corner averaged from fifteen to twenty every minute. Part of the upper chamber of Gibraltar—now the headquarters of the 7th and 8th Battalions—was smashed in, two signallers being killed. The roof of the log hut south of the road (the headquarters of Colonel Bennett, 6th Battalion) was struck six times but was saved for a time by the débris that had fallen upon it.[102] Runners whose way to these two headquarters lay up the sunken end of the Chalk Pit road, and the working and carrying-parties which had to pass up the same dreadful avenue to reach the north and west of the village, suffered heavily. The runners arrived exhausted and dazed. The line along the Bapaume Road, which had proved such a death-trap on the two previous days, was still being held by part of the 7th Battalion, the troops being now in shell-craters. Casualties were continuous. One by one the officers were wounded—the diary of the battalion commander (Lieut.-Col. Jess) shows:—

9.30. Lieut. Wright brought in—shell-shock.
1.50. Lieut. Hamilton wounded.
2.45. Lieut. Sutherland wounded.
3.30. Lieut. Hoban wounded (lost leg since).

The bombardment slackened at 11.30 but descended again at noon for half an hour. It then slackened till 1 p.m., when it recommenced, and, continuing hour after hour, was still in progress at sunset. In that half of the battlefield, except at Pozieres, very little was stirring. From the right sector of the III Corps the report was, "A very quiet day"; from the left (where the 23rd Division this day relieved the 1st British), "very little shell-fire," except where the flank touched that of the Anzac in the O.G. Lines, which were reported as being

shelled heavily all day and from time to time with great intensity.

Soon after the bombardment started General Walker (1st Australian Division) ordered one battery of the I Anzac Heavy Artillery to be detailed for counter-battery work all day.[105] At 1 o'clock the commander of the Reserve Army's artillery was appealed to and replied that the batteries of that army were already doing everything possible to suppress the German bombardment. At 4.5 p.m. Colonel Bennett, of the 6th Battalion, the young commander who had taken control of the Australian line at the Second Battle of Krithia, and whose headquarters in the log hut

---

[102] It was finally broken in shortly after Bennett and his staff left it.
[105] When the Corps heavy-artillery commander (who had been placed under Walker's orders) objected that his ammunition supply was not adequate for this and other tasks, Walker overruled the objection, insisting that the troops in Pozieres must thus be protected.

were kept in touch with the front line by his intelligence officer, Captain Rogers, reported:

> My men are being unmercifully shelled. They cannot hold on if attack is launched. The firing line and my headquarters are being plastered with heavy guns and the town is being swept with shrapnel. I myself am O.K., but the front line is being buried.

About 5 o'clock so tremendous was the bombardment that all the battalion commanders of the 2nd Brigade as well as the artillery officer at Gibraltar, who this day was to have begun directing fire from that point on the wire in front of the O.G. Lines, became convinced that an attack was portended. It happened that at 6.45 p.m. one telephone-line at Gibraltar was for the moment in working order, Lieutenant McCutchan, of the 1st Divisional Signal Company, though hit through the arm, having personally completed its repair. Through this line Colonel Jess, of the 7th, sent a message to the headquarters of the 2nd Brigade, describing the day's experience, and adding:

> It has been impossible to construct adequate trenches owing to the pulped nature of the ground. Those that were constructed N.E. of Pozieres are wiped out, and men are so dazed that they are incapable of working or fighting. Consider relief imperative as we could not resist attack if this is the preparation of it. 6th and 8th Battalions endorse this.

Then, taking the telephone, Jess personally told brigade headquarters that, as the smoke and brickdust round Gibraltar entirely prevented the artillery observers from seeing, the only safe course, if the attack was imminent, was to turn all guns upon the enemy's firing-line and render it impossible for the Germans to get through.

This message had the intended effect.[108] By 7.5 the whole artillery of the 1st Australian Division was firing heavily on the Germany front line. At 8.30 the enemy's fire paused for half an hour, but it fell again with great intensity at 9 o'clock. On learning this, Corps Headquarters at 9.55 appealed to Reserve Army for assistance from the artillery of the II and III Corps. Half an hour later the army staff answered that it had put every available heavy battery upon "counter-battery" work. As the heavy guns opened, a sudden change occurred in the

---

[108] On receiving Jess's alarming message at about 7 p.m. General Forsyth answered: "Men must and will fight if necessary. All artillery now turned on to stop bombardment." Jess at 10.16 explained: "No movement by officers or men in shelled area to retire has been made. Men have stuck to crater holes and no one will move in a rearward direction. Messages were sent to enable headquarters to realise the seriousness of the position."

enemy's action. Rockets and flares went up from his line, and, probably imagining that he was about to be attacked, his artillery changed to shrapnel and gas shell. His fire soon afterwards eased, subsequently breaking out once, but dying down at 11.30 until it was almost silent. At that hour the two battalions of the 6th Brigade (2nd Australian Division) which were to relieve the remaining infantry of the 1st Australian Division in the western and northern half of Pozieres began their movement into the village.[109]

No attack followed this tremendous bombardment. It is now known that the enemy had adopted a plan seldom if ever afterwards applied in the experience of Australian troops—that of laying down a day-long barrage, not in preparation for any intended offensive, but simply with the object of inflicting damage and loss. The bombardments of the 24th and 25th July were intended to make the village "sturmreif" ("ready for assault"); but, after the utter failure of the attempted assault on the afternoon of the 25th July, it was decided not to attack again, but to bombard Pozieres and its approaches throughout the 26th, the special feature of the operation, however, being a sudden synchronised "crash" by the artillery of three divisions[110] *after an interval of silence. This appears to have occurred shortly after 5 p.m., the concentration of fire lasting for half-an-hour.*[111]

The strain of this almost incessant fire from 7 in the morning until 11 at night was probably the heaviest yet placed on Australian troops; but the supreme test—that of being called upon to face an attack after such a bombardment—had not yet come, and the probable conduct of the troops in the contingency was still unascertained.

---

[109] The four battalion commanders of the 6th Brigade had visited Gibraltar from 3 to 3.50 p.m. to reconnoitre the position. Jess had recommended that no more than two battalions should be sent to replace the four in the village.

[110] 18th Reserve, 117th, and 26th Reserve Divisions. The enemy was also under the impression that he was being attacked by the Australians north-east of Pozieres about 5 p.m.

[111] In this concentration the following howitzers appear to have been employed:—
    Firing to the N.E. of Thiepval-Pozieres road: ten of 21-cm., twelve of 15-cm., eight of 10-cm.
    Firing to the S.W. of Thiepval-Pozieres road: eight of 21-cm., twelve of 15-cm., four of 10-cm.
    Firing on Pozieres Trench (Lattorf Graben): twelve of 15-cm.

CHAPTER 11.

"YPRES."

LEAVING the Somme behind we detrained at Godeswaesvelde on the 26th August, and marched to Vittoria Camp, Hesken. On the 29th, we moved to the large town of Poperinghe, still occupied by civilians, though damaged by shell-fire, and still occasionally shelled.

On the night of the 30th/31st August, we moved from Poperinghe by train; detrained at Ypres Asylum, and marched to the front line to relieve the 2nd Battalion. Duke of Wellington's Regiment (of the 4th British Division), for our first tour of duty in the Ypres salient. The sector of trench taken over extended from what was known as the Bluff on the south of the salient, a high bank of spoil along the Ypres-Commines Canal to the east. D Company was on the right, occupying a series of huge mine craters at the forward end of the bank, then C, B and A in adjoining trenches in the line and two in support. Our right rested on the canal, the opposite bank of which was held by Canadians. Here we got our first experience of mud. The trenches were half trench, half breast-work, and were in shocking repair, and knee-deep in sticky mud which rendered movement very difficult, and considerably delayed the relief. The sector was quiet enough, and casualties were few; but the discomfort of muddy trenches with no proper shelter compensated for enemy inactivity. It is almost superfluous to add that no time was lost in remedying this condition of affairs, and when we went out we left behind fairly dry trenches and comfortable shelters. The craters occupied by D Company were especially unpleasant for the troops. To get from the right platoon to the left it was necessary to crawl about 20 yards along a muddy tunnel, about three feet high, beneath a heap of mullock thrown up by the explosion of the mine which formed the crater. When two men going in opposite directions chanced to meet in the tunnel, one man had to retreat and begin again.

A spell of fine weather helped to improve conditions, though rain soon followed. The enemy's activity was virtually confined to mild shelling and to sniping at any targets presented, and some casualties were sustained in this way.

Listening posts and patrols were sent out into No Man's Land nightly, without encountering any enemy. Parties were also sent out to strengthen our barbed-wire defences. A feature of this tour of duty was the constant mining process. Beneath our line, tunnels were being dug forward under the enemy positions by mining units; mining material was sent forward every night, and bags of dirt were trucked out to the mouth of the tunnels. The enemy was similarly engaged, and the respective parties to this underground warfare frequently heard each other at work. We never knew when the ground beneath us might open and pitch us skywards. Crater-snatching parties were organised to be ready to rush forward and take possession of a crater should a mine be blown. However, we were spared the experience. The positions occupied by D Company were in a series of craters, each about 90 ft. deep by 100 ft. across, the crest of which commanded good observation over the enemy positions. The ground was very soft and after rain formed disagreeable mud, the bottom of each crater being always a quagmire. The soft ground also rendered trench repair and shelter construction exceedingly difficult.

On the night of the 12th/13th September, we were relieved by the 6th Battalion, and came back to Brigade Reserve, A Company in strong posts, B Company in the spoil bank, C Company in close support to the 6th Battalion, and D Company and Battalion Headquarters at Swan Chateau. We remained here till the 25th September, engaged chiefly on fatigue duty at night. All available men were sent forward to carry materials. There were a light tram line and a number of trucks at our service. These were loaded, pushed up hill for a mile or so and unloaded. The material, chiefly mining sets, was then carried up to the tunnels where saps were being driven forward under the enemy line. Several trips were made each night through shell and machine gun fire; then we would get on the trucks and ride home. As it was all down hill, and it was past our bedtime, the pace was very fast, and it was a common experience to be thrown off into the mud. There were, however, no serious accidents.

The 3rd Battalion relieved us on the night of the 25th September, and we came back by train to Dominion Camp, near Reninghelst. Then began the usual cleaning of kit and clothing, training, inspections, etc. A practice alarm was occasionally perpetrated upon us by night, when we would be required on a given signal to turn out in quick time, fully equipped, on the parade ground. We were also issued with the new box respirators, and were instructed in their care and use.

It was while we were here that the Battalion carried out its first raid. A raiding party had been formed sometime before of volunteers under Lieut. J. Bowtell Harris. This party had been specially trained for the raid. The time fixed was the night of the 30th September at 10 p.m. against the enemy trenches opposite portion of the front line we had recently handed over. For some nights previously the wire party (2nd/Lieut. Cowan) had been out in front exploring the enemy wire, and were able to lead the party direct to their destination, when at 9.30 p.m. they crawled from our line. A similar operation was being carried out simultaneously further to the left by the 8th Battalion. Elaborate preparations had been made and all details carefully arranged beforehand. At 10 p.m. our artillery opened on such parts of the enemy front line and supports as we were not concerned with, the wire party rushed forward, pushed in Fritz's parapet, and the whole party followed. 2nd/Lieut. Anderson took his party to the left and penetrated some distance along it, killing all the enemy encountered and throwing bombs down into the deep dug-outs. Sergeant Ball was with this party, and himself killed four of the enemy, and subsequently received a bar to his D.C.M. for his gallantry in the various encounters. Private Stirling who was also with this party as first bayonet man killed two of the enemy before receiving a severe wound in the back, but was able to regain our trenches, and subsequently received a military medal. The right party under 2nd/Lieut. E. J. Hopkins was equally successful and went some distance along the trench, killing the enemy encountered and bombing dug-outs. Private Casey, of this party, was hit in three places in his right leg and once in the left while crawling forward toward the enemy line. Although the wounds were serious, Casey continued with his party and killed one German during the raid. He returned to the trenches exhausted from loss of blood and was subsequently awarded a military medal. None of the enemy would surrender and all were killed. After eight minutes on the pre-arranged signal being given, the whole party returned to our lines guided across No Man's Land by tape laid for the purpose. Our own casualties were three wounded, of whom one, Pte. Mayall, subsequently died from his wounds. In each case the wounded man had carried out his job despite wounds. Lieut. J. Bowtell Harris was subsequently awarded a military cross for his part in the operation. The 8th Battalion's raid was equally successful.

The Battalion remained in Dominion Camp until the 8th October, resting and training. While here we said farewell to our veteran padre, Father Herne, a kindly cultured gentleman, who had been with us ever since we left Australia, and had endeared himself to all creeds and classes by his lovable personality and ready practical sympathy. Here also was established for the first time in France a Battalion Officers' Mess.

On the night of the 8/9th October, we relieved the 9th Battalion at the famous Hill 60, a mere mound, much battered and mined, the spoil from a deep railway cutting which intersected our line on our left boundary. The mud was still plentiful, but the trenches were fairly comfortable. Our line was in parts very close to the enemy's line, approaching in one place to within 30 yards. The enemy was chiefly troublesome with his minenwerfers—great cans containing explosives and shrapnel, which dropped from a great height. Fortunately by day they could always be seen coming, and avoided, but at night they were terrifying. Our breastworks were repeatedly destroyed by them, but always quickly repaired. The Companies supplied men for fatigue nightly. We continued our well-known policy of trench repair and improvement. It was about this time that we commenced our great "Whale-oil offensive" against trench feet. Whale-oil was issued liberally and it was the duty of every officer to inspect his men's feet daily to ensure that they were rubbed with whale-oil, and also to watch for any signs of trench feet. Trench feet was to be treated as a crime, and the officer in whose platoon a case occurred was to be held responsible. These methods continued throughout the winter, and there can be no doubt that they were justified, as cases of trench feet were comparatively rare.

Some mention should be made of the rationing arrangements while here. Not a day passed but the men had at least one hot meal, usually more. The troops whom we had relieved had had cold meat, cooked in the rear areas; we brought up our cookers right into the line, and cooked there. They were scattered and dug well in, and the fires were started before dawn. Food was then cooked as required. False fires were started in harmless places and duly shelled by the enemy. The Canadians across the Canal to our right also began bringing up the cookers close to the line, but took no precautions to avoid discovery. The men would line up in daylight to the cookhouse, but the German artillery soon dispersed them with heavy losses.

We instituted also a system which lasted right on to the end of the war whereby men in the front area could order such canteen supplies as they desired (on a cash with order basis), and they would be forwarded to them in the line. Tobacco, biscuits, chocolates, coffee and cocoa, tinned fish and fruits, soup and custard powders, and condensed milk were the chief "lines" available.

On the night of the 14th October we were relieved by the 21st Battalion, which was unlucky enough to have casualties coming in. We got away safely and returned by train from Ypres Asylum to Dominion Camp, arriving at 2 a.m.

The days spent in the Ypres salient after Pozieres were undoubtedly amongst the happiest of our experiences in France. The conditions were certainly not the pleasantest; mud and water were too plentiful for that; but for the most part the trenches were dry and comfortable—indeed, by comparison with the conditions we were soon to encounter they were ideal, the enemy was peacefully inclined and casualties were light. It was only when we stirred him up, as we did occasionally, that he became at all hostile, for the troops opposed to us were some of those who had been badly handled by the A.I.F. on the Somme, and they were more eager for peace and quiet than we were.

It was to be eleven months before we were again engaged on the Northern front, and then under very different circumstances.

The following day we marched to Steenvoorde, then to Arneke, and on the 17th to Moulle, the last stage being a very severe one. Here we rested among comfortable surroundings for a few days. On the 19th, General Birdwood visited us and presented medals gained on the Somme. On the 21st, we entrained at Arques for the Somme. Detraining at St. Riquier, we spent two days at Bussu, and then were moved by French motor omnibuses to Bray, and marched in the rain to Dernancourt, arriving at night on the 23rd in a dreary, muddy village, where the accommodation was of the poorest imaginable.

CHAPTER 12.

"THE WINTER ON THE SOMME."

Part 1.—The Mud

THE "Winter on the Somme" came upon us rather suddenly, or at least the realities of it did. It began at 5.15 p.m. on the 24th October, when we were marched off the road along which we were marching from Dernaucourt, and led into a quagmire, formerly a German strong-post, used as horse-lines, better known to history as Pommières Redout. Here we were invited to make ourselves comfortable, the whole resources of an acre of mud being placed unreservedly at our disposal. It was a rude shock. We knew we had been brought down from Flanders to the Somme to carry on the offensive which had never been allowed to lapse since we left Poziéres—but we had not counted on the mud. Every inch of this newly won country had been churned up over and over again; it was devoid of vegetation. Here and there, as at Delville Wood, there were gaunt battered tree-trunks, but the earth was simply one brown sea of soft oozy mud, broken up by shell-holes of varying size, giving a realistic impression of wave crests and troughs. The roads were shocking. Besides their muddy, slushy condition, they were almost entirely inadequate to cope with the traffic. Motor lorries, staff cars, horse waggons and limbers crawled at snail's pace along them in two unending streams moving in opposite directions; men, muddy to the waist, wound their way in single file through the wheeled traffic, being spattered from head to foot by splashes from wheels and hoofs. Frequently there were interminable halts for half an hour at a time, while drivers waited with that patience and profanity for which all drivers are notorious, until the next move. The journey from Albert, ten miles away, might take anything up to 24 hours.

There were no kindly sheltering villages, no shelter anywhere. Trenches were simply broad gutters in the ground, deep in water, without even a dry spot to sleep in.

In this country we had to stick for five monotonous months. Occasionally an undamaged German dug-out facing the wrong way provided some shelter, generally for a battalion or company headquarters. The only redeeming feature was that shells buried themselves so deeply in the soft earth that their explosion would deluge us with nothing more deadly than mud. But this is not the place to narrate in detail the horrors of that winter. They are familiar to most. Those who want a good realistic account of Somme mud should read Walter Downing's admirable little book, "The Last Ridge."

The Hun had been driven back on to prepared lines, leaving us the experience of taking up positions in newly won battered country, with no opportunity of preparing for our combat with the elements.

On the 24th, then, we had marched in the rain from Dernancourt, the last village on the fringe of civilisation, and had wound slowly in and out among the traffic, China-man fashion, along worn and muddy roads, and had been spattered from head to foot with slime. At 5.15 we had turned into Pommiéres Redout and invited to make ourselves at home in the ankle-deep mud. We felt we were up against it properly. One could not even sit down and think it over. Trench shelters were found for 250 men, but the remaining 600 were denied even this scanty covering. Private foraging expeditions were promptly set on foot, and the barren desolate countryside out of the debris of battle provided sheets of iron, timber and sundry other material "acquired" (to use a polite word) from goodness knows where. Holes were burrowed in the ground, one man would put his waterproof sheet down on the bottom, his mate would spread his over the top, and the two would turn in together. Next day further shelters were provided, and the following day our needs were fairly well supplied. From here we supplied men for fatigue parties, chiefly for road repair, or the unloading of trucks of ammunition or stores.

Our original Commander, "Pompey" Elliott, visited us, and many of the old Battalion who had gone over with him to the 15th Brigade came across and renewed acquaintance since Egypt and exchanged news of missing comrades. The terrible story of Fromelles was told us in return for our experiences at Poziéres.

Major Hart and Captain Oates left us for duty in England.

On the 29th October we moved out of camp at 4 p.m. towards the line. Our route lay along the crowded roads past Bernafay Wood (where C Company remained) through the famous Delville Wood, sacred to the memory of the South Africans, to a position immediately in front of our 18 pounder guns covering the Guedecourt line, occupying dug-outs in Switch and Gap trenches, where we relieved the remnant of the Border Regiment of the 29th Division. These were reserve trenches, in poor condition, and, of course, very muddy. We supplied numerous fatigue parties and devoted much time to trench improvement. Very little could, however, be done to hold up the muddy sides of the trench, no matter how hard we worked, on account of the fact that such material as there was available was being despatched to the front line.

Heavy rain fell and aided the general cheerfulness! While here there were issued to us sheepskin jackets, which proved invaluable during the coming days. The resemblance of the men to woolly lambs was the subject of many a jest during the winter. We began also to use French chalk as a substitute for whale-oil to prevent trench feet. Captain Scholes, who had been quartermaster since we left Egypt, and had since struggled on despite illness, broke down and was replaced by Lieut. R. J. Hillard, whose organising ability and energy was invaluable in the ensuing weeks.

On the night of the 1st November we relieved the 6th Battalion in the front line at Grease Trench (aptly named), Hilt Trench, and Cheese Trench. B and D Companies were in the line, A in support, and C in reserve, in Bull's Run. Lieut. Rogers was killed by a chance shell just as he left the trench to lead his men forward to the relief.

The state of the ground rendered operations unlikely; nevertheless the Battalion received instructions for an operation in a few days and began preparations. A jumping-off trench was commenced in front of our line, but the constant rain undid all that had been done, causing the sides to fall in. Finally we were informed that the proposed attack was abandoned on account of the weather and the conditions of the ground, and we breathed freely once more. The line ran round the north of Guedecourt, which was on a small knoll some 300 yards in rear. For some reason the enemy disliked the place and used to pump heavy stuff into the unlucky village almost continuously, and naturally it was given a wide berth. We quite approved of the German idea of using it as a target for his spare ammunition, but we often wondered what he did it for, as not a single soldier was located in the place. The few adventurous spirits who did enter the place were obliged to leave hurriedly with their curiosity unsatisfied. Captain D'Alteron led a reconnaissance in search of a reputed monastic tunnel, but could find nothing of interest.

On the night of the 5th, B Company were relieved by C. The same day Sergeant George Ball, D.C.M. and Bar, one of our most fearless and resolute, was killed by a shell. An operation by the 1st Brigade on our left involved us in some artillery fire, and some casualties were sustained. On the night of the 6th November, we were relieved by the 10th Battalion. Unfortunately during the relief we sustained casualties, 2nd/Lieut. Cowen being killed. The night was passed at Switch Trench and Gap Trench, and on the following night we came back to Bernafay Wood, among the heavy guns, where the accommodation was far from satisfactory, but the surroundings were a relief after our front line experience. Here we made acquaintances of two kinds, the first being a couple of naval guns whose bark was terrific, extinguishing all candles for hundreds of yards around; the second the bomb dropping Taube, which came over nightly laden with "eggs" for our entertainment. The whole Battalion was engaged daily on road-repair fatigues in the vicinity of Flers. On the 12th, the Commanding Officer, Lieut.-Colonel C. H. Jess, left to attend a 4th Army Conference at Flixecourt, Major C. H. Swift assuming temporary command.

On the 12th November, we moved back to Dernancourt, and on the 13th to Ribemont. On the 18th, we left by bus for St. Vaast, near Amiens, a comfortable town, but left in a very dirty state by the last occupants. Here we remained until the 30th, engaged principally in training of one kind and another and an occasional visit to Amiens. We saw our first snow here. The chief feature of this rest was that leave was available to Amiens, and our troops made their first acquaintance with the inhabitants of that charming but ill-fated city. It was a good eight-mile walk, and there was not much chance of a lift on the road, but every day the pilgrimage was made. Troops of all units met in the cafes and shops.

or lunched at the best hotels, to the disgust of a few brightly attired gentlemen with red round their caps, who scarcely approved of the intrusion into their exclusive haunts, of ordinary soldiers, and Australians at that. The shops drove a thriving trade in clothing, especially for newly appointed officers, and in souvenirs and postcards destined for Australia, the cafes prospered, and many dainty little ladies contributed to the *entente cordiale*. The Cathedral, although protected by sandbags, was a great attraction. There were merry doings in Amiens in those days, and it is safe to say that the memory of them was a source of inspiration eighteen months later when the hand of the Hun lay heavy upon the city.

The stay in St. Vaast was a very pleasant one. There is no need to say that training was steadily carried out, and that a general all-round improvement was soon noticeable. The surrounding country was exceedingly picturesque and our route marches were always interesting. It was only a short three miles to the Somme at Picqinguy, a place many of us visited later on as it was there that the Divisional School was established. A number of men attended schools while we were at St. Vaast. On the 28th, Lieut. Col. C. H. Jess returned, but took over command of the Brigade in place of Brig. Gen. Antill, invalided sick.

In the army we never ran any risk of missing trains, and our departure was no exception. We left St. Vaast at 2 a.m. on a cold frosty morning, with snow inches thick on the ground. We were at Vignacourt by 6.30 a.m. on the 30th November; our train left there at 11 a.m. Detraining at Burre we camped in huts near the town on the Albert Road, in a most desolate and muddy locality. There we continued the training begun at St. Vaast, the weather being bitterly cold. On the 4th December, we marched forward to Fricourt, Lieut. Col. Jess resuming command, Lieut. Col. (later Brig. Gen.) Heane taking over command of the Brigade. On the 5th, A and B Companies moved to Bernafay "B" huts, and had great difficulty in finding shelter from the heavy rain, as the troops in possession had not moved out as expected. These companies came up next day to the familiar Switch and Gap support trenches, relieving the 14th Battalion, C and D Companies coming to Bernafay Wood. On the 7th, C and D came up to support trenches, and the whole Battalion lay in support to the 5th Battalion until the 14th.

The Brigadier, General Heane, was wounded, and we again lost Colonel Jess, who assumed command of the Brigade, Major C. H. Swift taking over his command.

Working parties were supplied daily and nightly to carry material forward through the mud and rain. Those night fatigues are still a nightmare. The party would proceed to the dump at Brigade, where each man would be presented with a "duckboard," an "A" frame, or a sheet of iron, and the procession would begin, winding up through the mud and slush, slowly and painfully, often in bitter winds and drenching rains, to the 5th Battalion Headquarters, and returning to crawl cold and miserable into our wretched holes in the ground until summoned out for another trip.

It rained every day, and often continuously for days. "Sunny France" became a mockery, and we built up fond illusions about Australia as the land "where the sun shines nearly every day." We had some casualties from enemy shelling which was fairly frequent. Captain Tubb, V.C., returned to us after having been invalided home to Australia from Gallipoli.

On the 14th December, we relieved the 5th Battalion in the right sub-sector of the front line, in our old friend of October, Grease Trench, in front of Guedecourt, A on the right, D on the left, B Company in support at Pilgrim's Way and Pioneer Trench, C Company in reserve in Pioneer, Bull and Possum Trenches. The front line trenches were in very bad condition and constant work was expended upon them. The Hun was fairly passive, confining his activity to shelling and throwing pineapple bombs. As before, he continued to patronise Guedecourt ruins with his attentions, to our entire satisfaction. B Company were engaged nightly in bringing up hot meals to the front line, C in bringing water from Flers and carrying material and improving the front trenches by night. Cold miserable weather continued. On the night of the 18th December, C relieved D and B relieved A. On the 19th, a daylight patrol investigated Lard Trench, close on our left, and found it empty, but saw signs of recent enemy occupation. Scout Moloney, who made Lard Trench his special care, secured numerous small trophies as evidence of his visits. On one occasion he took an officer with him, and as they approached the trench the officer was disconcerted at coming under fire from trenches away to the left. His anxiety was not fully dispelled when

Moloney said, "That's alright, sir. It's only the 8th Battalion!" Lieut. Hill and Pte. Rice essayed a daylight patrol on our right company front. Both were wounded; Hill got back after dark, but Rice received wounds from which he died.

On the 22nd, we were relieved by the 2nd Battalion, and, assisted by the light railway trains, reached Bernafay Wood shortly after midnight. The following day, in a howling wind and driving rain, we came back to Melbourne Camp, where good comfortable "Nissen" huts awaited us. Here we spent our first Christmas in France in some comfort. Our Christmas boxes from Australia were distributed and made very welcome. Additions to our menu provided by the 2nd Brigade Comforts Fund were greatly appreciated; an Australian mail, comprising many parcels, was also received, and in every way the Christmas festivities were a success. New Year was also passed here in some comfort. We remained here until the 7th January, training assiduously. Many men were despatched to schools and leave passes to England came freely. We were at Buire from the 7th to the 13th in poor billets; far more comfortable at Warloy until the 23rd.

Lieut. Col. Jess returned to us on the 13th. After training and living in some degree of civilised comfort, we moved on the 23rd to Albert, and next day to huts in a battered wood at Fricourt Farm, leaving portion of A and B Companies at Meaulte engaged in unloading trucks. This period was intensely cold. The ground was white with snow, ponds were frozen, and a bitter wind swept over the exposed camp. The 26th January was said to have been the coldest day in France for 20 years, and we were content to accept the assertion without verification. The nights were bright and moonlit, and enemy planes came over, bomb-laden, searching for targets. The frozen ground was hard and slippery; skating was a popular, if dangerous, pastime; men going for washing water would take a pick and a sandbag and repair to the nearest shell-hole for raw material to be melted down. Ice was frequently nine to twelve inches in thickness.

On the 10th February we moved to High Wood and Bazentin, and took over various working parties from the 8th Battalion. The Meaulte parties rejoined, and on the 13th we relieved that battalion in the support line, near Flers, and supplied the customary working parties.

Before beginning on the events of the following weeks and narrating the work of the Battalion in the opening phases of the Hun retirement, which eventually enabled us to get out of the mud and stand on firmer ground, it will be convenient to refer to two matters which are intimately connected with our Somme experiences.

The first is the provision made for supplying the front line with hot meals. This was made possible by the issue of food containers which speedily became popular. A container is a sort of glorified thermos flask, made in a shape to fit the back of the wearer and capable of holding sufficient food for 80 men. Each was strapped on to a man's back and, although heavy, was comfortable to carry and left the bearer free to move easily. One container was utilised for tea and another for hot stew. The meals were cooked back at the cookers some miles in rear, and brought up in containers by mules or pack-horses, and then transferred to the backs of the men responsible for getting them forward. There were other contrivances, such as "Tommy cookers" and primus stoves, but it is safe to say that nothing contributed so much to the health and morale of the men during that winter as the hot meals supplied during the night by means of the food container. It should be added that once tried the container was not confined to winter warfare, but became the universal method of supplying the front line troops with hot food until the end of the war.

The other matter relates to trench feet. On Gallipoli the troops had suffered considerably from this trouble and in some cases amputation had been necessary. It was naturally anticipated that the Australians in France, accustomed to a warm climate, would be the greatest sufferers, and at first this was so, but the very greatest attention was given to the problem and, as has been described in an earlier chapter, it was insisted by Battalion Headquarters that the care of his men's feet was one of the first duties of the platoon officer. The first method used was to rub whale-oil into the feet, and to keep dry socks for wear whenever possible. Later, in accordance with the theory of a leading French doctor, who ascribed trench feet to the presence of a germ in the earth, an antiseptic chalk powder was used. Though we favoured whale-oil, both methods were successful. Dry socks were provided nightly in exchange for wet ones, and this proved of great value. The result of these steps was soon seen, for from having the largest percentage of cases in the British Army, the Australians soon had the lowest of all. Considering that we were occupying the very worst part of the whole British front, it is a matter for congratulation that our men carried out instructions so fully and with such complete success, and abundantly disproves the foolish imputations that the Australians possessed only battle discipline.

Reference should also be made to the opportunities afforded by means of schools and leave for a brief respite from the discomforts of the forward area. Certain necessary duties in rear also provided occasional rest for the men detailed to carry them out, usually those least fitted to stand the rigours of the line. But it is to the schools behind the lines, with their comparative comfort, that we are most grateful as they enabled a great many officers, N.C.O.'s and men to enjoy a short holiday; while leave passes, although still infrequent, gave the men with the longest service an opportunity of returning to civilisation for a few bright days.

CHAPTER 12.

"THE WINTER ON THE SOMME."

Part 2.—"The Hun Withdrawal"

ON the night of the 19th February, we relieved the 5th Battalion in the front line, north of Factory Corner, west of the Flers Thilloy Road, C and D Companies in the line, C on the right, B Company and Battalion Headquarters at Factory Corner, and A Company in North Road. The trenches were in a shocking state, being a series of outposts, connected by a muddy and impassable trench. The snow which had lain hard and frozen on the ground for some weeks began to thaw, and the result was mud worse than before. The Battalion right rested on a bank overlooking a sunken road and a valley; on the right flank in the notorious No. 9 post an officer and six men were stationed; by night they kept a constant lookout, but with the first light of dawn they were obliged to crawl into a tiny dug-out and lie cramped and stiff till night. The post was under observation from the enemy so movement would be fatal. But the long days passed in these conditions were agonising in the extreme.

D Company on the left were sheltered behind a bank known as Yarra Bank, but were strafed a good deal by pineapple bombs from nowhere, the enemy line being invisible on the reverse slope.

On the 23rd February A Company relieved C and B relieved D. That same night the excitement began. We were advised on the 22nd that Brigade desired indentification of the enemy units opposite us, and a raid against Bayonet Trench was asked for. On the 23rd a conference of company commanders was held to consider the best method of carrying this out, as four previous raids by other units had all been unsuccessful. It was decided to try and cut out several enemy posts, and plans were discussed.

At 7 p.m. Brigade advised that the enemy were reported as withdrawing in front of the British sector on our left, that the 9th Battalion on our left were attacking that night after 24 hours' bombardment the system of trenches opposite them known as The Maze, and that it was desired that we should enter Bayonet Trench and create a diversion to cover their operations. To alter arrangements at this time was a very difficult task, as the company commanders were somewhere between Battalion H.Q. and their companies, and all preparation as to telling off and assembling parties for the raid previously arranged had been completed. However, patrols were accordingly organised to move down the road on our right to Bayonet Trench and, if possible, enter. The right portion of the front, A and C Companies, was to be under Captain Campbell; the left, B Company, under Captain Hopkins, with D Company, under Captain Oates, in support.

At 7 p.m. patrols were sent out from each company front. Conditions opposite us appeared normal as enemy machine guns and trench mortars were still going. At 8 p.m. the 9th Battalion reported that their patrols had entered The Maze, which the enemy had evacuated. At 9 p.m. the 8th reported having entered Bayonet Trench opposite their front. Our patrols working towards The Maze encountered the 9th Battalion there. At 10 p.m. we were advised that the Butte de Warlencourt, a huge commanding mound opposite the 2nd Division on our left, had fallen. We were ordered to enter and seize Bayonet Trench, as it was believed that the enemy had evacuated. Patrols from our front, however, reported conditions quite otherwise; the enemy were firing machine guns and sending up flares; a careful examination of his wire revealed no opening in its nine feet of thickness. Orders were sent out that the trench must be entered and held, the whole of each company to be used if necessary. Meanwhile, it was reported that the 9th Battalion had passed The Maze and were still feeling forward without opposition. It was very exasperating—the Hun everywhere else had apparently cleared out, but for some reason those opposite to us were still there and ready to fight. Our patrols were fired on from Bayonet Trench, but continued to explore in the hope of finding some weak spot in his defences. The first entrance was not made till after 1 a.m. on the 24th, when Lieut. Booth's patrol on our extreme left gained a footing in Bayonet Trench, and was in touch with the 9th Battalion. Fifteen minutes later Captain Stewart entered Bayonet Trench where it crossed the road on the extreme right. Another twenty minutes and Captain Hopkins reported that he had entered the trench after some opposition, had captured some prisoners, and held about 400 yards of the trench. This made our hold on the trench secure, though these parties did not know of each other's success as yet. The 9th Battalion were in touch with us at times, but were not long constant in any position. Eighty yards to the right we found the 8th Battalion. Patrols were pushed forward to keep touch with the enemy. All our artillery fire had ceased and the latter part of the operation was carried out in a most unaccustomed and unearthly stillness.

By 7 a.m. telephones had been laid on to the captured trench, which was in bad condition. A series of strongposts was organised along it. At 10 a.m., in response to an inquiry as to the condition of the men, Brigade were advised that we neither needed nor desired relief. We were ordered to send patrols forward to Rye and Barley Trenches, the next system of defences. Lime Trench, a small line between Bayonet and Barley Trenches, was occupied. During the afternoon the enemy shelled Bayonet Trench, but did no damage.

At 4.30 p.m. A Company moved forward towards the next objective, but encountered heavy opposition and sustained a number of casualties, particularly in officers, Lieut. Carlyle sustaining wounds from which he subsequently died. Practically leaderless, they dug in between the two lines of trenches until next day. Patrols from C Company moving forward along the road found Barley Trench occupied; being ordered to occupy the trench, Campbell sent additional men forward, and by 4.30 a.m. Barley Trench was entered without opposition and held. About 7 a.m. the 8th Battalion, who had entered on our right, came into touch with us. Great difficulty was experienced on the left. The Battalion on our left had suffered casualties the preceding night, but reported that they were in Rye Trench. Patrols sent out were unable to locate them. It subsequently transpired that they had been in Rye Trench, but had withdrawn to a small trench behind. On the 27th, we were relieved by the 5th Battalion, and came back to supports in our original jumping-off line and finding comfortable dug-outs slept for the first time for three days. We had changed from a raid into an attack in less than two hours and from trench warfare to semi-open, and had penetrated 2500 yards into the enemy territory. Working parties were supplied for various jobs.

On the 2nd March, we relieved the 5th Battalion in the front line, which was now beyond Thilloy, on high clean ground, free from the clinging mud we had been so long accustomed to. B and D Companies were in the line, C in support in a huge mine crater blown on the roadside by the enemy and in Rye Trench, A in Bayonet Trench, and Headquarters at the remains of Luisenhof Farm. Opposed to us was the strong line of Till Trench, which with the Grevillers' line constituted the last defences of Bapaume. C Company relieved D on the 5th, and on the following night the 18th Battalion relieved us. We came back to Bendigo Camp, Bazentin, and Mametz Camp. On the 13th, we moved to Dernancourt. Major Swift assumed command in place of Lieut. Col. Jess, who went to England on duty, having been selected as an instructor to the Senior Officers' School of the British Army at Aldershot. He was the first Dominion officer to be selected for a post such as this. It might be mentioned here that whilst serving with the 7th Battalion Lieut. Col. Jess was awarded the D.S.O. and the Serbian White Eagle. Training ensued under Major Swift. On the 21st, we came to Buire and continued to train vigorously in cold bleak weather on a muddy hillside.

Brigade operations were performed and freely criticised by brigade and divisional commanders. On the 31st March there arrived George Gautier, who was to be our French interpreter for many months to come.

After we left the front line the Hun retirement was very rapid. Bapaume was evacuated, and he fell back on his great Hindenburg Line, a prepared position some miles beyond the town. A party of two officers and 200 men was sent to Le Sars, on the Bapaume-Albert Road, for the purpose of repairing the road, which was now the main artery for this part of the front, and had to carry heavy motor and horse traffic. On the 8th, we moved to Villers-au-Flos as reserve battalion to the 1st Division. The accommodation here was very limited and of poor quality.

The following day B and D Companies were sent to occupy the Corps Main Line, and on the 10th were at Fremicourt, and on the 11th back at Villers-au-Flos. Heavy falls of snow made these apparently purposeless movements very trying. On the 15th March we were ordered to Fremicourt again, the Hun having attacked at Lagnicourt, but he was easily repulsed. Later in the day

—a very wet day it was—we moved to Beaumetz and relieved the 29th Battalion in supports. The following night we relieved the 10th Battalion in the front line opposite Pronville, near Bullecourt. It was a dark night with heavy rain, the guides were lost, and relief was not complete until 4.30 a.m. The disposition was B on the left, D in the centre, and C on the right, with A Company in supports. The line was a system of outposts and pickets, and despite bad weather the work of consolidation proceeded. On the 20th B Company advanced their line about 600 yards to cut out a salient. On the 22nd a raiding party attacked an enemy post and drove them out. The 8th Battalion sustained casualties, and bombs, tools and stretcher-bearers were sent across. On the 23rd we were relieved and occupied sunken roads in supports. Fine warm weather followed and the troops revelled in the first days of spring after a terrible winter. Clean dry ground covered with green grass, sunny days and a general atmosphere of peacefulness was a welcome change from the ordeal of mud and discomfort. While here the vote for the Federal elections was taken. From the 25th April we were attached to 2nd Division for the purposes of the attack contemplated by them on the Hindenburg Line at Bullecourt. On the night of the 1st May we relieved the 5th Battalion in the front line, as Right Battalion of the Right Brigade of the 2nd Division. C Company with two platoons of A Company were on the left, D Company and one platoon of A on the right, the remainder of A Company and B Company were in support. There was no continuous trench, but a line of outposts. The enemy line was the Hindenburg Line, about 1000 yards distant, between us and Queant, near Bullecourt. On the 2nd, we were advised that the attack by the 2nd Division was timed for 3.45 a.m. next morning.

The night was quiet and calm, but precisely at 3.45 a.m. the whole sky behind us lit up with the flash of a thousand guns—it seemed an age till the first sound was heard—then it was like a thunderclap. The point of attack was about a mile to our left, but the screech and roar of the shells, and the crash as they burst were deafening. Machine guns crackled, and the Germans gave their customary pyrotechnic display—red flares, green flares, white flares, singly and in clusters. It was quite five minutes before the German barrage was properly down, and it included our front, but did no damage. By 6 a.m. our front was quiet, but on our left the battle was waged all day, and dense smoke obscured our view. Later in the day reports reached us—the 61st Division on the left of the 2nd Australian Division had largely succeeded, and the 2nd Division also had taken most of their objectives and pierced the Hindenburg Line—but Bullecourt still remained in enemy hands, and, in fact, resisted capture for three weeks.

During the night our patrols were very active in expectation of an enemy attack. At 3 a.m. he barraged our right company, and we prepared to meet an assault, but he did not come. At 3.45 a.m. the 2nd Division renewed the attack. We were able to observe throughout the day enemy movement in the vicinity of Quéant, evidently reinforcing there. At night our patrols again were very active in No Man's Land, and the Right Company were again subjected to a barrage, but no attack followed. On the night of the 5th we were relieved by the 2nd London Regiment, who had not previously been engaged on the Western Front, and amused us considerably by their naiveté. One officer wished to know where he could put his saddle, which he had brought to the front line. Another asked if we had water laid on. At Headquarters another complained that there was no messroom. However, we departed. We came back to the Bengny-Ypres trenches several miles in rear, and left them to find these things out for themselves.

On the 7th, we moved forward again, heading for Bullecourt. We relieved the 23rd Battalion that night in the ruined village of Noreuil, behind Bullecourt. The accommodation here was very poor and very crowded, and conditions were rendered very unpleasant by heavy rain. Enemy shelling was frequent. The men were employed carrying ammunition and material forward. We remained here till the 9th, expecting to be thrown at any time into the battle which still raged for the possession of Bullecourt, where attack and counter-attack followed in quick succession and bombing encounters caused heavy casualties.

On the 9th, however, we were relieved by the 60th Battalion, and came back to a camp of tents on a hillside at Biefvillers, near Bapaume, where hot stew, an Australian mail and sleep soon made us oblivious to the trials of war.

With our arrival at Biefvillers our campaigning was ended for the present, though we did not know it. We had raged a hopeless and terrible warfare with mud and cold, and only the grim determination of the men carried them through. They were beyond praise. No one who was there will deny that no part of the whole four years of war was so severe as those months on the Somme; there was none of the exultation of victory, none of the excitement and novelty of battle, just one long uninspiring drudgery, when one could only live on the hope of better days.

Then had come the German retirement, enabling us to drag ourselves out of the mud and stand on clean dry ground, following the Hun into new scenes where grass was green and trenches inhabitable, for pleasanter warfare, but strenuous and exacting for men who had been subjected to the ordeal of the mud.

And so it was a tired, listless Battalion which rested on the hillside at Biefvillers. How soon we recovered and how we fitted ourselves to play once again a prominent part in offensive warfare the latter chapters will show.

Lieut.-Col. E. E. HERROD
C.M.G., D.S.O., V.D.

CHAPTER 13.

THE SUMMER OF 1917.

" Rest and Training "

AT Biefvillers, we lost no time getting to work, training and smartening up. We received 164 reinforcements, including a number of officers, and 64 of our old men back from hospital. Our strength now was 46 officers, 1054 other ranks. On the 11th May there rode up to the camp the Divisional Commander, Major-General Walker, with our new Commanding Officer, Lieut.-Col. E. E. Herrod, from the 2nd Battalion. Major C. H. Swift, who had acted as Commanding Officer since the departure of Lieut.-Col. Jess, handed over command. The new Colonel at once made an impression. His task, coming from a "foreign" battalion, was not an easy one, but he soon established a firm hold over the Battalion and a sure place in the affection of the men. Lieut.-Col. Herrod commanded us until the end of the war. General Sir William Birdwood paid an informal visit. B and C Companies took over portion of the Corps second line near the camp, lived there, and improved it. We spent a good deal of our time at sports, and played football matches with the 8th Battalion, which we lost, and with the 59th Battalion, which we won. On the 24th May we moved to Ovillers, rather a long march. We left early the following morning for Henencourt, where we were billeted in huts in a wood in a very pleasant locality.

Our stay at Henencourt is probably the brightest spot in the history of the Battalion. Our quarters were good, the country was charming, dense wood near the camp, green fields all around, glorious summer weather, plenty of sports and games, leave to Amiens and liberal leave to England, schools and rest camps, and, of course, a certain amout of work.

On the 6th June we were visited by General Birdwood and Mr. Andrew Fisher. Inter-company footracing resulted in a win for D Company. A Battalion sports meeting was held in the parade ground below the camp on the 9th June, a Brigade sports meeting on the 11th June, and a Divisional meeting on the 12th and 13th June. The Divisional meeting was especially successful, embracing not merely athletic events, but horse jumping events and transport displays.

Major Swift on his Jim (Colonel Jess's old horse) secured first prize for the best officer's hack, Colonel Herrod got second prize for tent-pegging, and the Battalion also secured first prize for the best water-cart. There were various side-shows and booths where good beer was obtainable. A number of comic costumes gave a touch of gaiety, and there were some excellent make-ups. Evidently the troops were on good terms with the madamoiselles of the district. One digger, arrayed as a staff officer with much gold and red tabs about him, evidently a travesty on "Birdy," caused much amusement; and when the two orderlies who were attending him made an arch of their lances, and a bugler struck up the general salute, the crowd roared its delight. However, it was not all play here, and we were soon back at work again. On the 18th June, leaving early in the morning, we marched to country once in the war zone, and, after successfully capturing Bolton Camp, at Mailly-Maillet, we were allowed to occupy it. Here for some days we practised open warfare operations. On the 24th we moved to Engelsart Camp, Engelbelmer, a dirty camp. From here we captured the deserted village of Auchonvillers, and engaged in a night operation. On the 28th we returned to Henencourt. The same day our Adjutant, Captain H. G. Bastin, M.C., left us to join the Staff of the 1st Brigade. Several interesting gas demonstrations were attended. On the 8th July 4 officers and 68 men attended at Pozieres the unveiling of the 1st Division monument to the men who had fallen; the ceremony took place in heavy rain.

On the 12th July we lined the Albert Road to cheer His Majesty King George V. as he passed.

A series of football matches were played, in which we defeated the A.M.C., Cyclists and 6th Battalion, but were defeated by the 5th Battalion, and by 8th Battalion in two matches out of three, and by the Pioneers. A number of cricket matches were also played.

On the 4th July we moved to Bray, on a wet morning. Here strenuous training was continued. Our proximity to the Somme gave us facilities for swimming, which were eagerly availed of. Route marches with full packs were inflicted on us. Lieut. Oliver Harris was appointed Adjutant, a position he occupied until the end of the war.

On the 24th we moved to Meaulte, and entrained at Aveluy on the 27th, arrived at Caestre, up north again, and marched to billets at St. Marie Cappell. Our stay at St. Marie Cappell was a very pleasant one. The billets were good and the inhabitants very kind and friendly. There was a good deal of rain while we were here. On the 4th August we had an informal visit from "Birdy."

Some assistance was rendered to the farmers in getting in their crops, a pleasant duty for those who assisted.

On the 8th a most memorable and severe march of 18 miles brought us to the vicinity of Bailleul, near our first resting place in France. We were comfortably billeted at farmhouses scattered over a wide area of country. German aeroplanes frequently came over at night, and were engaged by machine guns. One night four bombs were dropped in the Battalion area, but did no damage. The civilians were considerably scared; we, of course, were quite unconcerned—to outward appearance that is.

A sports meeting held on the 3rd September was very successful. A beginning was made while here with the Battalion band, which lasted until the end.

B and D Companies represented the Battalion in a march past before General Plumer, the 2nd Army Commander. On the 13th September we moved to Berthen, leaving behind 11 officers and 55 men, who remained at reserve at the Reinforcement Camp, Caestre. The Battalion reached Berthen about lunch time. Great difficulty was experienced, as the inhabitants were quite hostile to us, and it was only after much cajoling and threatening, in which our interpreter, George Gauthier, played a prominent part, that we secured the billets reserved for us. On the 14th we moved to Scottish Lines, Reninghelst. Orders for the forthcoming operation were issued, and a plan of the country, fashioned out of sand, was carefully studied.

On the 18th we were at Chateau Legard, and the following day at Zillebeke Bund, ready to move to the attack. Our training was completed, and, as fresh troops, we were now to be involved once more in big fighting.

CHAPTER 14.

INTERNAL ORGANIZATION.

" Domestic Economy "

BEFORE proceeding to follow the fortunes of the Battalion in the Passchendaele operations, it will be convenient to pause for a while and consider certain matters important to a proper understanding of this history. A battalion, though a small and almost insignificant unit in the scheme of the army, is a most intricate and delicate organization.

The normal strength of a battalion is 1,000, but on active service might be anything down to 300 or 400. But a large proportion of these men are not to be reckoned as "bayonets," that is, their duties, although onerous and dangerous enough, do not actually take them into action against the enemy.

A battalion consists of a commander, a headquarters and four companies, each company having an officer commanding and a second in command; each company consists of four platoons, each being under an officer; a platoon should be 50 strong, but in fact never was; each platoon contains four sections, commanded by non-commissioned officers. The section is thus the fighting unit, and embraces about 8 to 12 men. In addition, in each company headquarters were the company sergeant-major, quartermaster sergeant, clerk, gas N.C.O., two batmen, four cooks, four stretcher-bearers, signallers, runners, scouts, etc., totalling in all about 20 men, necessary for the conduct of operations, but not in fact combatants.

At battalion headquarters an even larger number of "details" was necessary; there was an orderly room staff of clerks; signallers and runners to keep up communication with companies and with brigade by telephone, by bicycle, or on foot; scouts, whose job included the location of any position from a given map reference and guiding parties to required destinations—patrol work, sniping, enemy observation, etc.

The head of the battalion was its commanding officer, with the rank of lieut.-colonel. It would be idle to attempt any definition of his duties, save to say that he saw to everything and was immediately responsible to the brigadier. It was the personality and ability of the "colonel" which gave a battalion its reputation, and we were exceedingly fortunate in our Commanders—Elliott, Jess and Herrod.

Next to the commanding officer came the second in command, who, in addition to acting as a deputy or understudy to the colonel, so as to be ready to replace him should the occasion arise, was directly concerned with those things most nearly touching the welfare of the men, such as meals, canteen, sports and amusements. The most prominent man in the unit was undoubtedly the adjutant, who might best be described as the colonel's staff officer. He was the mouthpiece and secretary to the colonel; his duties were many and arduous and would defy any attempt at enumeration.

Usually, if an officer could be spared, there was an assistant adjutant. The adjutant's immediate concern was the supervision of the orderly room staff. While the personality of the adjutant counted for much, especially in the case of such men as Bastin and Harris, his chief attributes must be efficiency and a genius for organization.

Pioneers, the handy men of the battalion, doing odd jobs out of the line, and responsible for the burial of the dead when in action; a medical section, in charge of the regimental medical officer, who was a doctor; a quartermaster's staff to supervise the issue of clothing, rations and materials; and a transport section to carry the impedimenta and to bring our supplies up. A few words should be added about each.

The orderly room comprised the orderly room sergeant and that most important person, the pay sergeant, and several clerks; they kept records, furnished returns, and generally, under the adjutant, performed the extensive clerical work of the battalion.

The signallers were a most essential section. They fitted up and kept maintained the telephone services, a perilous job at many times, when wires were apt to be blown up by enemy shelling and must be mended at all costs; carrying messages between companies and headquarters often through heavy barrages; cycling back to brigade with urgent despatches. Theirs was not an idle life nor a safe one.

Then there were the scouts. The scouts were first formed soon after our arrival in France, when Lieut. James gathered together the bravest men and the best shots of the Battalion. Under enterprising and gallant officers they became a wonderfully efficient body. In the line they patrolled No Man's Land; with the aid of special periscopic rifles they were responsible for the sniping department of the Battalion; they established an observation post and reported enemy movements; they acted as guides to incoming units, and on other occasions as required. They were expert in map and compass work, possessed a keen sense of direction, and were enthusiastic explorers of No Man's Land. They were in everything, those fellows—never a company carried out an operation but the scouts were there with them. They attained fame as souvenir "kings," and the famous Maloney was the shining light in this department, and could produce a desired article within 24 hours, whether it be an enemy helmet or cap, revolver or bayonet. He was quite uncanny, but unfortunately was killed later on.

The pioneers, we have said, were the handy men. "Joe" Rutherford gathered together a collection of the roughest and toughest—men who could do anything. They made latrines, dug trenches, did odd jobs, and, in the line, buried the dead. "Joe" had records of every man he had buried, from the Gallipoli landing onwards, records which proved of great value when the others were lost or mislaid. They always earned the extra "tot" of rum they somehow got, the pioneers.

The A.M.C. were under the Battalion doctors—Gutteridge, Campbell and Barlow were the best known. "Doug" Barlow came to us in the mud of the Somme, and left us only at the end. Merciless towards "lead-swingers," he was a most conscientious and loyal servant to the troops; he won his M.C. for his gallantry in tending the wounded under fire at Passchendaele; he was immensely popular and respected throughout the Battalion for his courteous bearing and upright character. With the Doc. was a small staff from the 2nd Field Ambulance, who assisted him in ministering to the sick on sick parade and treating the wounded in the line.

"Bobbie" Bates, who was wounded while with us, was a splendid sample of the men they were. They were fiendishly fond of chlorinating our water supply—a process which they said was necessary from a health point of view, but imparted a beastly flavour. They were not stretcher-bearers—the stretcher-bearers were with the companies, and of their devoted and gallant work everyone knows. Many a man has had reason to bless "Jock" Hardie and his fellows.

The battalion quartermaster was naturally an unpopular person—he never could possibly have enough for everybody. He and his staff drew and distributed rations, clothing and material; his department included the despatch and receipt of mail, the canteen, tailoring, bootmaking, rifle and machine-gun repair, salvage of everything that could possibly be turned to use, cooks and cookers, war trophies, in short, a thousand important matters—but not, as the disappointed were wont to assert, the periodical issue of decorations.

The transport were concerned with the horses and vehicles. It is characteristic of the A.I.F. that the "hardest doers," the roughest diamonds, all seemed to gather round the horses, and our transport was no exception. Headed by an officer and a sergeant, the transport section were entrusted with the care of horses, vehicles and harness; their job was to go wherever a pack horse, limber or a wagon could go, whether it were to bring the rations from a distant dump; to take supplies forward to the troops in the line, often amidst heavy shelling; or to follow the troops into action leading the ammunition pack mules, as was so gallantly done on the 9th August, 1918. They served as targets for enemy aircraft and long range guns. When we went into the line they remained some miles in the rear, but made the dangerous trip through airbombs, shells and machine-gun fire every night. And never once did they fail to deliver their loads. The transport never let us down.

There were one or two other "spare parts" at Battalion Headquarters. There was first the padre, with no special job beyond the Sunday morning church parade, but yet never idle. In the line he was to be found near the regimental aid post, helping the doc., dispensing hot coffee or cigarettes, or perhaps advice or consolation. All honour to the padres, older men than most of us, but enduring gamely what we endured with often far less patience. And double honour to that fine old man, Father Herne, who was our first and dearest padre.

At Battalion there were also the gas-sergeant, responsible for the condition of our respirators and the supply of fresh ones when required; a Lewis gun sergeant and a bomb sergeant; sometimes a musketry sergeant and a physical training and bayonet fighting sergeant, each with his special role to play. And then there was "Bill" Baker, the regimental sergeant major, with duties too numerous to mention, the chief being the instruction of young subalterns in their duty as "orderly officers," and the frequent and violent "roaring up" of the N.C.O.'s of the Battalion. There was nothing slack about "Bill," and his popularity testifies to his efficiency.

Two other departments must be mentioned. Bombs and Lewis guns. At first a bombing section was attached to Battalion Headquarters, Captain "Bow" Harris training them till their eyes looked wild; at Poziéres they proved their value, but later on they went back to their platoons and there they remained.

One section of the platoon was trained in the bomb and rifle grenade, and made good use of their skill on many occasions. A Lewis gun platoon also existed for some time, being lent out to companies a bit at a time. Later, each platoon was given a gun of its own and trained to use it, and the Lewis Gun Company broke up. A second gun was allotted to each platoon later on, and crews were trained in their parts. The use of both these weapons demanded some ability. It was easy enough with practice to throw a bomb or discharge a grenade, or fire a gun with accuracy; just as it is easy enough to kick a football straight; but to know when to use it and how best to use it was a matter of tactics, even as a game of football is a matter of tactics that required considerable training and perception to realise—but the troops showed many times, notably on the 9th August, 1918, how well they understood these things.

So much for the composition of the Battalion. Some general account of its activities should be added. Out of the line the daily routine did not vary much—training and games all day, the evenings being spent variously—perhaps sitting round a brazier of "salvaged" coal swapping yarns or discussing events and persons, or, most often, places and doings in Australia; perhaps reading, playing cards or writing letters by the light of a flickering candle; there may be a concert or a picture show on at the Y.M.C.A., or in a village some distance away; an "estaminet" may attract others, or a "cafe" in some stone kitchen where the womenfolk displayed a wonderful ability to interpret our curious language. In the line we were scattered in a series of posts, anything from 10 to 100 yards between each group; by night we worked, trying to dig our trench deeper or make our dug-outs stronger, or patrolled No Man's Land, or put up some fresh wire in front; at dawn and dusk we "stood to," there being a tradition that that was the most favourable time for an attack, when the light obscured movement, but yet gave some assistance to the attackers; by day we slept or read or cleaned our arms; one or two men would remain on duty with eyes on the periscope for two hours, until relieved.

Hot meals were supplied once, and frequently twice, nightly by means of hot food containers, of which some account has been given in Chapter 4. In these the meals were brought up—stew and tea generally—and served hot in the line.

Daily, reports were sent back as to the situation and the enemy attitude, and more frequently if necessary. We generally came into the line without packs, though in quiet sectors they would be taken up; but if there were any operations to be undertaken our packs would be dumped until our return, and we would take up a haversack only, with a waterproof sheet. The hat was replaced by the heavy steel helmet when we went into action.

It was early established that the whole Battalion should never go into the line, but that a small proportion should remain behind not as a reserve to be called on if necessary, but as a nucleus for the re-forming of the Battalion should some disaster annihilate us. In practice, the "nucleus," as it was called, served as a depot on which commanding officers could call for officers and N.C.O.'s to replace casualties. It afforded, moreover, an opportunity for giving a rest to each in turn, according to the length of continuous service. It was by no means a much-coveted favour, and many a man has appealed earnestly to his company commander to be allowed to go with "the boys" when an operation has been contemplated.

Leave to England, Paris and other places served as a useful restorative for tired troops, but unfortunately not to be had when most needed, that is, while operations were being carried out. Army, corps and divisional schools for officers and N.C.O.'s also afforded opportunities for recovering lost vitality and for learning the very latest about the weapons we had to use.

It may be desirable to say something of the soldier away from his battalion. A man might be separated from his unit by one of many causes; he may be evacuated to hospital, sick or wounded; he may proceed on leave to England or Paris; he may be sent to a rest camp or school in France or England; he may be sent away on some special duty, such as escort for prisoners, or for service at corps or army headquarters. There were always large numbers of men coming and going behind the lines in this way. The man on leave, at the expiration of his furlough, would rejoin his battalion direct, being guided to it by means of the information circulated to R.T.O.'s (railway transport officers); but the man who had been to hospital would, if he had been to England, receive fourteen days' leave (and possibly a convalescence period as well) and would be sent to a depot on Salisbury Plains to wait, usually for a fortnight or so, until a draft was leaving for France. This draft would be sent to Le Havre, again to wait until troops were being sent up the line to his unit. These periods in camp, whether in England or France, were so exasperating that men commonly endeavoured to "wangle" it back to their units direct, and deserting to the front line was quite a common offence, but, of course, was never punished. The task was, however, not easy of accomplishment, as proper passes were required of troops travelling by rail. It was a well-known fact that once men became in any way separated from their battalions their one desire was to get back. The battalion was the home of the men, where all their friends were, and where they were employed in much more interesting occupations than forming fours.

Of the leave periods nothing need be said here. The troops appeared to penetrate to every part of the United Kingdom and to every corner of Paris, and their exploits are well known. The hospitality everywhere received did much to hearten them in the long days of toil and warfare.

CHAPTER 15.

THE BATTLES OF PASSCHENDAELE.

September-October, 1917

ON the 19th September, as we have described, we arrived at Lillibeke Bund and organised for the attack to be delivered on the following morning. At 11 p.m. we left after a hot meal, and moved forward in the inky darkness through steady rain by a boggy and slippery track. A and C Companies had to carry a quantity of ammunition, etc., which rendered their task still more difficult. It was unfortunate that it should rain that night after weeks of such perfect weather. By 4.45 a.m. we were in position on the tapes, waiting for the attack to commence. The hour fixed for the attack was 5.40 a.m.

The plan of attack was as follows. The front line was being held by the 1st Brigade. The enemy was holding his line, not by a continuous system of trenches, but by means of a series of isolated posts and concrete blockhouses, or "pill-boxes," scattered at intervals. There were to be three objectives; the "red" line," to be taken by the 6th Battalion; then the "blue" line by the 5th Battalion; and the furthest objective was the "green" line entrusted to the 7th and 8th Battalions, the 7th being on the left in touch with the 3rd Brigade, the 8th Battalion being on the right. B and D Companies were to form our first line of attack, A and C in support, D being on the right, and B on the left of the first line; C on the right and A on the left of the second line. The Battalion was to follow 100 yards behind the 5th Battalion, and the second line 100 yards behind the first. On the capture of the blue line by the 5th, we were to go ahead and get as close under the barrage as possible, and reorganise during the two hours for which the barrage was stationary; then to advance with it to the green line, the front platoon advancing in line, the remainder in small columns in file; A and C were to "mop up" or clear all enemy from the country between the blue and green lines. Separate parties were detailed to attend to special strong-posts. On

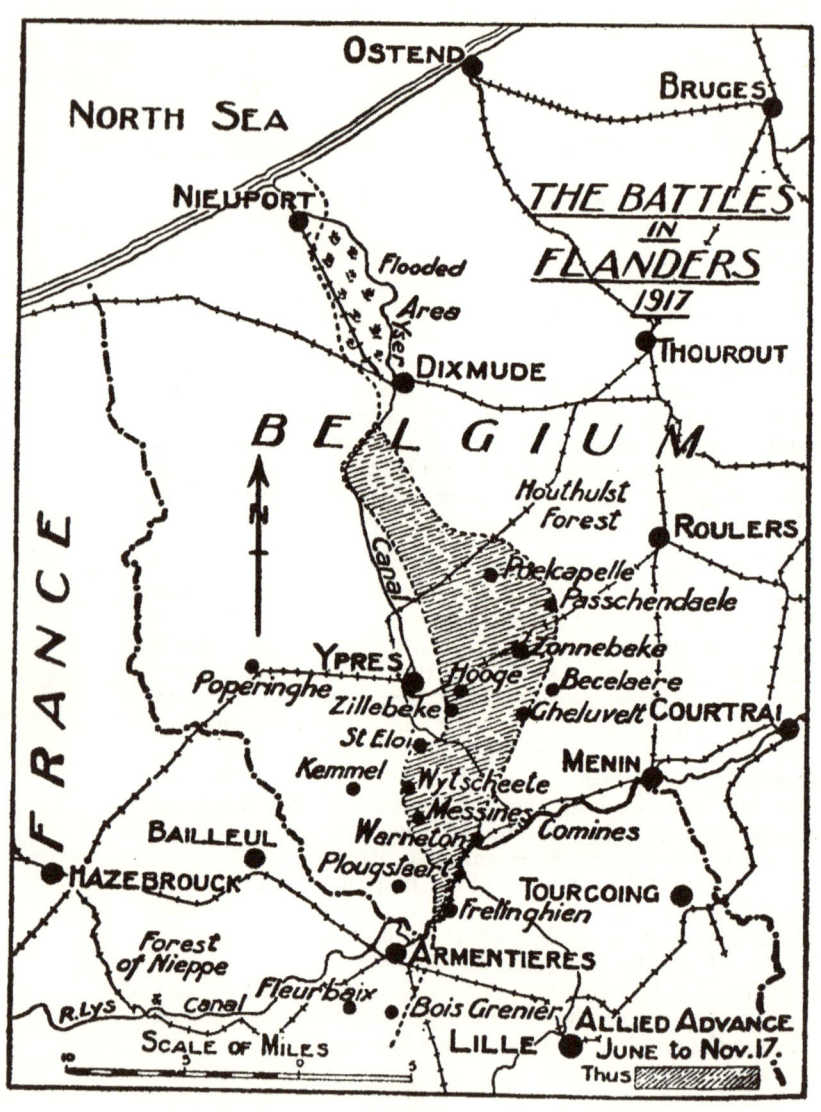

YPRES

the capture of the final objective the line was to be pushed forward and consolidated. All ranks had carefully studied the maps and aeroplane photographs of the country to be advanced over, and the plan prepared in sand. For the purpose of keeping the exact direction officers were detailed to march on compass bearings. The dress was to be, as usual, fighting order (that is, without packs); each man to carry 48 hours' rations, 2 bombs, 2 grenade rods, 220 rounds of ammunition, 2 ground-flares for signalling to aircraft, and 2 filled water bottles, which made us veritable human camels.

The artillery time-table was shown by means of special maps issued to us. At zero the barrage was to be put down 150 yards in front of our line, then it was to advance at the rate of 100 yards every 4 minutes, and later 100 yards every 6 minutes; halt at the red line for 1½ hours, and at the blue line for 2 hours to allow reorganisation, and finally finish and remain stationary 200 yards in front of the final objective to cover consolidation. Thus, by keeping close up to the barrage, we should be able to advance with a minimum of opposition.

At 5.40 a.m. down came the barrage and we went forward under it. The whole of the attack proceeded as arranged, right up to time-table, and almost without incident. Prisoners soon began to trickle back, dazed by our barrage. Battalion Headquarters occupied a pill-box recently vacated, where they found breakfast spread and a candle burning. Some little time later Lieut. Moloney looked into a pill-box alongside and dug out some 20 prisoners. Messages came back from the forward company giving locations, and reporting O.K. The first and second objectives were duly captured and we reorganised prior to going forward. The only difficulty experienced was that some of our own guns were firing a little short and causing casualties.

About 10.30, according to the time-table, we moved forward towards the green line. In response to a request from the 10th Battalion on our left, two platoons were extended to the left to assist them, and two platoons from A Company were sent to B Company. At 10.55 our final objective was taken. Major Tubb, V.C., was seriously wounded just as we arrived here while attacking a pill-box. C Company came up to assist D, and the line was made good. At 11 everything was reported O.K. We had gained our objective and were in touch with both flanks. The enemy could be distinctly seen getting his guns out, and we had some excellent targets. No counter-attack developed on our front, but the enemy could be seen attacking the 2nd Division to our left, and throughout the day enemy movement about the Polygon Butte was noticed. The enemy shelled our rear and communications consistently throughout the day; at night rations were sent forward, but no hot meal was available. Our line was strengthened and improved. Continuous shelling lasted through the 21st, and about 7 p.m. this developed into a heavy barrage along our rear areas, cutting all communications. An S.O.S. signal was sent up from the units on both our flanks, drawing down a barrage from our artillery. For some time it was not known what was happening on our front, but no attack developed, and our positions were intact. About midnight we were relieved by the 3rd Battalion.

Our casualties were:—

Killed	3 officers	29 men
Died	2 ,,	11 ,,
Wounded	5 ,,	155 ,,
Missing	— ,,	5 ,,
Total	10 ,,	200 ,,

Major Tubb, V.C., evacuated wounded, died of wounds in hospital, the other officers who lost their lives being Lieuts. O'Connor, Sara, Attwood and Foers.

Our captures were 2 machine guns and 93 prisoners. It is estimated that 500 enemy were found dead during the advance, and that another 200 were killed after the advance was completed.

Special mention should be made of the work of the 2nd Light Trench Mortar Battery who were attached to us for the operation and performed valuable work. They were especially serviceable after our final objective was gained. The 2nd Machine Gun Company was likewise of great use, and were with us right through the piece. Great difficulty was experienced in obtaining sufficient stretchers and stretcher-bearers to cope with casualties, and some hardship and suffering resulted. The troops were enthusiastic about the excellence of our artillery barrage. A certain amount of short shooting was inevitable, but the destruction inflicted on the enemy must have been tremendous.

After relief we came out to Dickiebusch, where hot meals were served. Later in the day we were taken by bus to Steenvoorde and comfortably billeted. The reserve from Caestre rejoined, and rest and training were mingled during the next few days.

On the 1st October we were moving forward again—by bus to Dickiebusch, leaving behind, as was usual, a nucleus of officers and men at Caestre. The following night, after a long heavy march, we relieved the 11th Battalion at Westhoek Ridge. Our fighting strength was 28 officers and 530 men. The day was spent in trenches on the Ridge, preparing for the operation of the following day. After dark Lieuts. Pollock and Crowe and N.C.O.'s went forward to lay the tapes for the assembly of the Battalion. Just before midnight a stray shell landed at the entrance to a pill-box used by C Company as headquarters and wounded Captain Campbell and two of his officers, necessitating hasty arrangements to replace them. At midnight we were advised that the tapes had not been laid. This we found later was caused by the death of Lieut. Pollock, who was killed by a shell.

At 1.45 we moved forward to our assembly positions. It was pitch dark, the track was bad, and the enemy shelling a good deal, but we reached our positions safely and soon were crouching on the ground, waiting with chattering teeth till zero, which was fixed for 6 a.m.

The plan of the attack was very similar to that of the 20th September, excepting that we had only two objectives instead of three. The 5th Battalion were already holding the front line, and would remain there. The first objective, the red line, was to be captured by the 8th Battalion, the second objective, the blue line, by the 6th (right) and 7th (left). The 6th Brigade, 2nd Division, were on our left. The inter-battalion plan was two companies in the line, C right and B left, D in support (right) and A in support (left). The troops were to carry the usual equipment of ammunition, rations and material. The artillery barrage was similar to that of the 20th, a steady advance to the red line; a halt of one hour there, and then on to the blue line, remaining stationary 200 yards ahead of it.

At 5.20 a.m., as we lay crowded on our assembly positions behind our front line, an intense enemy barrage descended on us, and continued to play on our lines until zero. Considerable losses were sustained, but to have attempted to escape would have upset the order of attack and resulted in inextricable confusion. There was nothing to do but lie low and hope for the best. Never were minutes so carefully watched, never was time so slow, never was sound more welcome than the opening of our barrage. At length it came. With the first burst from our guns we rose—those who were able—and moved forward out of the zone of shell-fire into the peace and safety of No Man's Land. As it was, we became mixed with the 8th, and all advanced together. The first objective was taken by the 8th, and we formed up in rear to await our phase of the attack. A great many prisoners taken from pill-boxes en route were sent back to the rear. At 8 a.m. we moved forward behind the barrage up the slope towards our final objective. We were well in touch on our flanks, and opposition melted as we advanced. Some trouble was experienced in keeping well under the barrage owing to the risk of shorts. Captain Hopkins took charge and led the attacking wave forward, at times he was fifty yards ahead of us all, right under the barrage. Over Broodseinde Ridge we went, and down the gradual slope beyond, with Becelaere visible beyond us, and the enemy retreating as fast as they could before us. Many excellent targets were presented, and every advantage was taken of them. By 8.40 we were on our objective. Patrols were pushed forward, strong-posts established, and the work of consolidation proceeded. We were in touch with the units on our flanks, and ready to resist any counter-attack. None, however, developed. The day and night passed quietly. There was heavy shelling of our communications, but no damage was occasioned. On the night of the 5th October, we were relieved by the 11th Battalion. Owing to the relieving battalion being lost while coming in, we were very late getting away, but finally reached Swan Chateau at 6 a.m. the following morning.

Once again we owed much to the work of the Light Trench Mortars and Machine Guns, who were with us right through, and scored off all targets that offered. The barrage again was good, and earned the admiration of the troops. Our captures were estimated at about 220 prisoners, 4 machine guns, and 1 field gun. In addition some 300 enemy dead were found in our lines, and 150 it is estimated were killed after the advance.

	Officers.	Other ranks.
Killed (Lieut. Pollock) ..	1	15
Wounded	13	177
Missing	—	53
Total	14	245

Our total casualties for the two offensives were 480, or about 50% of our strength. A great many of the wounded were, fortunately, only slightly wounded, and able to return to us within a few months.

These two battles, known generally as the battles of Passchendaele, constituted the most notable achievements of the Battalion in France so far. They were what Sir John Monash described as "set piece" battles, that is, everything goes according to a rigid and carefully prepared time-table. It used to gall us a good deal to be unable to follow up a success of this kind. Having reached our objective we were bound to stay there, and not able to exploit our attack as we should have liked, and as we did in the closing battles of the war. In each of these operations we simply followed our barrage, and cleaned up as we moved forward. The elaborate preparation expended upon these offensives, the careful co-operation of infantry, artillery, engineers, pioneers, transport of every kind, and all other branches of the army, each with its special job, reduced the element of uncertainty to a minimum and assured our success.

It is worthy of note that in both these operations the 7th was detailed to capture the final objective, and in both it accomplished everything asked of it.

CHAPTER 16.

"THE WINTER IN BELGIUM."

AFTER the battles of Passchendaele we were withdrawn from the line and came back to Shrapnel Corner, now a somewhat healthier spot than it had been prior to the recent advances. On the 11th October we moved to Reninghelst, and on the 15th to Halifax Camp, where we began a period of training. On the 22nd we moved to Ypres and encamped beneath the ramparts in Esplanade Gap, and the details and reserve nucleus went back to Caestre. On the 23rd we moved forward to Anzac Ridge and at night relieved the 16th Battalion in the line.

Our disposition was A and B in the line, C and D in support. There was some artillery activity, and, as usual, patrols explored No Man's Land. We received the operation order for an offensive on the 26th, but our front was not immediately involved; beyond keeping an active lookout for signs of enemy action opposite us, we were not concerned. We had one man killed in an encounter between one of our patrols and an enemy party. A German aeroplane flew over the transport lines and dropped bombs, killing 7 horses and wounding 4. The personnel luckily escaped casualties.

On the 30th October we were relieved by the 11th Battalion, and came back to rest near Belgian Chateau, where we occupied huts. The weather was cold and showery, but training was steadily carried on, and fatigue parties were sent to Ypres. On the 12th November we left the line behind, and, entraining to Arques, near St. Omer, marched by stages to Desvres, where we were billeted comfortably among a very hospitable and kindly people. The month we spent here in rest is probably the pleasantest we ever spent in France, many friendships were formed among the madames and ma'moiselles of the town, and long after we had departed letters to and from Desvres commonly passed through the postman's hands, and many a digger on leave found time to call at Desvres before he rejoined us.

The time was profitably spent also in training solidly. The weather was fine and the health of the troops good. A number of men who had been slightly wounded in the recent fighting began to straggle back. But all good things must end, and the 11th December found us swinging out of Desvres, and the 13th brought us by train to Rossignol Camp, Kemmel. The following night we were in the line again in the sector beyond the variously pronounced Wytschaete.

As this sector, commonly known as the Ravine, was the scene of our labours many times during the next three months, some description of it should be given.

It was some way to the right of our last positions, round Passchendaele, and was between Ypres and Messines. The front line consisted of a series of posts with no protected communication along the front. The enemy opposed to us was occupying several pill-boxes dotted along the front. Behind our line there was a protected communication trench running back over a hill to a deep ravine behind where forward Battalion Headquarters was situated. A duckboard track led back through battle-scarred and often snow-covered flats to the gaunt relics known as Denys Wood, where there were a number of comfortable dugouts, the home of our Reserve Company; a mile of duckboard ran back to Onrael Farm, another collection of shattered timber, where rear Battalion Headquarters was accommodated in pill-boxes of enemy construction. The support company occupied an unhealthy locality to the right of the Ravine in another matchwood forest known as Ravine Wood. The whole country was very rough and broken by previous battles, but duckboard tracks gave good communication. The chief feature of the sector was the system of light railways. Rations, ammunition and material were brought up by motor power to Clarke's dump and there transferred to other trucks which were pushed forward right up to the Ravine. The carry from there to the line was not very severe. A great economy of men and animals was effected through the agency of these tramways; occasionally an enemy shell would blow up a few yards, which meant that the trucks must be unloaded, carried over the break and reloaded; but the repairs were soon effected.

The Hun was fairly passive opposite us. His one venture, into which he was probably goaded by some blood-thirsty commander back towards Brussels, was in this wise:—On the 16th he sent out a strong raiding party to cut out the left post of the 8th Battalion on our right. In this they succeeded. With five prisoners and a Lewis machine gun the party was making its way back when it came under observation from our right post. Fire was opened and the raiders went to earth. Word was sent back, and Sergeant Charville was sent up to cut the party out. Charville left our lines with eight men, and Lieut. Grant with two men. Under covering fire from our posts these parties closed on the enemy, killing four, capturing five, recapturing three men of the 8th Battalion who were being carried off as prisoners, and enabling a fourth to make his escape back. It is believed that not one of those raiders returned to the enemy lines. The success of this little skirmish was due chiefly to the resource and skill of Charville. The following messages were received later and show the extraordinary interest taken by "Birdy" in the doings of the boys:—"Congratulations on excellent stunt. Prompt counter-attacks nearly always mean success.—Birdwood." "Hearty congratulations on successful defence of post.—Hobbs." For this exploit Sergeant Charville was awarded a D.C.M. and Pte. Reade a M.M.

We had some bitterly cold snowy weather. Christmas Day was a perisher. The Hun celebrated Boxing Day by concentrating his artillery on a bombardment of Denys Wood, then occupied by D Company, with mustard gas. There was no wind, and the poison penetrated the dugouts and hung about the wood for days before finally evaporating. Company Headquarters was in an underground dugout beneath a pill-box and suffered worst. Seven officers and 34 men were sent away gassed and practically all the rest of the company suffered some effects of it, and many were eventually sent to hospital. On the night of the 31st we were relieved, and a long march down a frozen, slippery road where no one could walk without falling brought us to the comfortable huts at Rossignol Camp.

Here we remained until 7th January and "dealt with" our Christmas mail, including the boxes sent by the Lady Mayoress' League.

Working parties were supplied nightly. On the 7th we relieved the 8th Battalion in support to the 1st Brigade at Chinese Wall and Irish House, and continued to send parties forward every night for work.

On the 15th January we relieved the 11th Battalion to the right of our last position. It was a memorable relief. Heavy soaking rain fell continuously; if the roads were bad the trenches were shocking. Mud and water everywhere were thigh high, and came in over the tops of our long rubber trench boots. Dugouts were flooded, and the trenches in a bad state of repair. We had a few short intervals of fine weather, and got to work to improve matters, but were not sorry to be relieved by the 11th Battalion on the 23rd. The Hun apparently was as busy as we were contending with the elements and left us alone.

Back to Rossignol Camp we came, and on the 29th, to our great relief, we moved back to Locre, where we occupied huts for the next few weeks; trained as usual, and performed the numerous fatigues allotted to us, principally road repair work.

The officers' mess was re-established, and an officers' club in the town, to which was attached a tennis court, was a great boon. Locre was soon to become No Man's Land, but luckily for our peace of mind we did not then know it. It still held civilians, who lived chiefly by ministering to the wants of the troops at famine prices.

In a brigade test in connection with army platoon rifle competitions, No. 16 Platoon (Lieut. Gaulton) won first place, and each man received a bronze medal.

On the 28th February we moved a few miles to Murrumbidgee Camp, La Clytte, and were again established in huts.

It was about this time that we heard the first definite expectations of an early enemy offensive. How we prepared to meet it, and what transpired are reserved for the following chapter.

CHAPTER 17.

THE GERMAN ATTACK—FEBRUARY-APRIL, 1918.

For many weeks the English papers had been prophesying a monster German offensive for the early spring. For weeks G.H.Q. had been passing down "screeds," to which each lower formation had added improvements of its own, relating to defensive methods. It did not come easily to troops who had been accustomed to train always for the offensive to find themselves imbibing the principles of a branch of warfare they had hitherto scorned even to contemplate. But there was no mistake about it. The enemy were reputed to be preparing an offensive, and it was equally obvious that we were not.

The daily programme at this time is instructive. Our camp at La Clytte was some five or six miles from the line. Working parties, comprising everyone not required in camp, were despatched daily to the forward area, when under the guidance of pioneer officers and men they were employed to construct defence posts to meet the threatened onrush.

The journey up was made by special train leaving Kilmarnock siding at 7 a.m.—a narrow gauge train made up of open trucks. One's teeth chattered on these cold mornings, sitting in an open truck, as our tiny engine dragged us on laboriously, round the Dickiebusch Lake, through woods, and, as we approached the line, over shell-pocked ground, then across the long since stagnant canal to our destination. Then a long walk to the job, a good day's work, and back by train, leaving about 3 p.m. Cooks accompanied us, and provided hot tea at midday.

Many an officer's heart quailed within him as he checked his picks and shovels at the dump on his return, for they had a strange knack of disappearing, despite careful supervision, or, at best, the heavy picks which some men took to the job would come back as shovels, which were comparatively lighter, the exchange being easily effected at some forward dump.

In due course all these posts were ready for occupation. Then a decision was arrived at which occasioned much comment by the troops.

Each platoon was allotted a post in this support area, and each post was manned by two men as "nucleus garrison," water and ammunition were placed in them, every officer and N.C.O. was sent to reconnoitre the route to his particular post and to study his "arcs of fire" and prepare "range charts." On an alarm being given the Battalion could then move quickly and quietly into their prepared positions and await developments.

On the 13th March we moved to Seddon Camp, about two miles nearer the line, and continued the same programme.

Our billets were in old wooden huts, comfortable enough, and, except for isolated shots which came over searching at random for stray targets, were safe from shells. A few poor civilians still hung on in the straggling village, eking out a precarious livelihood by ministering to the needs of the troops. But the general expectancy was uppermost in every mind. For a couple of weeks before the launching of the offensive we were awakened before dawn every morning by the sounds of an artillery barrage somewhere on the front.

The German policy was to make a demonstration along the whole line so that none might know where the blow would fall. As we lay awake and listened to these bombardments we wondered when the order would come to go up and man those strong-posts so recently constructed. But the blow was not dealt at us. When it fell it was the unfortunate Somme which had once again to bear the brunt of heavy fighting, thus proving wrong all those strategists amongst us who ridiculed the idea of the Germans choosing such broken country to advance across. The immediate result was that those early morning outbursts entirely ceased, and the enemy on our front became as gentle as a lamb.

The next development was the disappearance of our sister divisions from the front, gone south to stop the gap. On the 24th March we were again in the front line in the well-known Wytschaete sector, just beyond the

Ravine; the whole Brigade in the line, without supports and without reserves—unless the Chinese Labour Corps, who were reported to be some miles behind us, could be counted as moral support.

It was a thin line to oppose to the foe, but our position down south was desperate. But the Boche was as amiable as could be desired. One could not suspect him of any mischief as one gazed over his peaceful lines on those sunny March days; while away on the Somme he was massing a tremendous army, and advancing by sheer weight of numbers. Our hearts were with those other Australian divisions who had left us to join the battle on that front.

Our turn was not long in coming. On the night of the 3rd April we were relieved by the 21st Division, who had come from the Somme. They had met the German onslaught that first day, and told us of the deadly slaughter wrought by their machine gunners, of no avail against the countless masses of the enemy.

Since leaving the Somme they had been reinforced by some of those boys of eighteen, who had been gathered up from the training camps of England and hurried across to France to fill the depleted ranks of famous regiments. Their appearance and their lack of equipment alarmed us, for they appeared to be ignorant of warfare; they had lost all their machine guns, all their telephones, and most of their equipment in the retreat—though their officers were gleeful about a piano they had secured from some deserted village. We left with the fervent prayer that the Germans would leave them alone.

So down to the Somme we scurried. Entraining at Strazeele in the early morning of the 6th April, we left the northern front. We detrained at Hangest sur Somme at 5 p.m. The Y.M.C.A. was waiting for us with hot coffee, and then we set out through heavy rain along ten miles of sloppy roads to Pernois, where we arrived at 11 p.m., and soon settled down to sleep in overcrowded billets. Great crowds of refugees from the villages which had been brought into the figthing zone had filled the town, and had brought stories of the great retreat, which had hardened the heart of the villagers against the British. It was in vain to explain that we were Australians.

Stray odds and ends of innumerable English regiments were billeted here also, drawing rations from heaven knows where. Many of these were evicted to make room for our men. At 10 a.m. on the 9th we were on the move again, and the troops scored an important victory—for all packs were carried for them by motor lorry. The Battalion spent the night poorly accommodated in Coisy and Cardonette. On the 10th we moved to Bussy, where good accommodation was found, the majority of the civilians having departed. At night a startling rumour gained currency to the effect that the Germans had begun an offensive on that northern front from which we had just been withdrawn, but no confirmation or denial could be obtained. George, our volatile interpreter, was very despondent, and asked the colonel to shoot a certain officer who had sped the rumour on its way. "In our army we do it, colonel," he pleaded.

Next day the bad tidings were confirmed. The enemy had broken through on a wide front to a depth of several miles. Following on this news came the intimation that we were to return to Hazebrouck immediately. Consternation seized us as we called to mind those defence schemes we had so carefully elaborated and those outposts we had so laboriously constructed. It appeared that they had fallen without a blow. Possibly there had been no men to man them. However, there was no use complaining—up north we must go.

We were to leave St. Roch station, at Amiens, at 10 p.m. As we approached the station after dark, along the magnificent avenue which skirts the inner city, we could hear shell after shell screaming overhead to work havoc in the town. To us who knew it so well in happier days, a sort of little Paris, behind the lines, with its magnificent old cathedral, the pity of it all came home very forcibly. Some of these shells fell in the station yard prior to the arrival of the Battalion, during the difficult task of entraining the transport; these caused casualties and confusion. Four men were killed and thirteen, including our Regimental Q.M.S. Brown, were wounded. When all was quiet and the Battalion did come in and entrain it was discovered that the French train crew had made off to safety and had not returned. And so we sat for hours, in constant dread lest the enemy should renew their bombardment. Had they done so, the consequences would have been disastrous, not to ourselves alone, but to the northern front, where a few hours' delay would have meant that we should not have arrived at all.

The enemy would have had the railway in their possession and there would have been no troops between them and the coast. Fortunately we were not then aware of the desperate crises to which our forces were brought. We finally left at 1.30 a.m. and reached Hazebrouck at 2 p.m. the same day—12th April. Along the line we saw many evidences of the disaster which had overtaken our arms. Stations had been bombed, but luckily the line was intact. Our train was attacked by aircraft but escaped. Along every road civilians were pouring back in a pathetic and continuous stream. Every manner of vehicle had been pressed into the service to carry off a few household goods, while women and children and old men trudged wearily beside them. It was a sight that touched the hearts of the most callous, and if anything were needed to arouse the resolution of our men to a desperate defence it was provided here. It was just a week since we had entrained at Strazeele station. Strazeele and its surrounding farmhouses were then peaceful places, where peasants tilled the soil, caring little for the great struggle some twelve miles away. Now they were in flight. Those farmhouses, where we had slept a week before, were now in flames. Our coming restored the confidence of the folk wonderfully. When our big hats were seen, they exclaimed, "Les Australians," in great relief, and quite a few of the people of Hazebrouck, who had begun to pack their belongings, commenced to unpack. Could we justify the confidence?

The extent of the retreat alarmed us. In a few days the whole of a vast tract of country hitherto peaceful had fallen into enemy hands. It included many districts and villages almost sacred in the minds of the men. There was the area round La Creche, the Battalion's first resting ground in France; L'Hallabeau, where we next sojourned; Fleur Baix, where we first were in the line in France and were schooled in trench warfare; the trenches round Ypres, where we had licked our wounds after the Somme; Polygon Wood and Broodseinde Ridge, which had been won by us at great loss in that short-sighted offensive of the autumn of 1917. Doulieu and its pleasant neighbourhood, where we had prepared for that offensive, and made many friends among the simple peasantry; Ballieul, where we had shopped and dined and flirted and drunk vin blanc or vin rouge—all these, with the graves of many of our comrades, were in German hands; Caestre, Meteren and Hazebrouck, the popular leave centre, were being shelled to pieces; St. Marie Cappel, where we had spent such a happy fortnight in July of 1917, among a kindly populace, was threatened; and St. Omer, the Amiens of the northern front, with its busy streets, its big hotels, its splendid gardens and the painted harpies "of No. 4" was being shelled by long range artillery, and was gradually being deserted. At Hazebrouck the situation was, to say the least, obscure. The colonel reported immediately to Brigade Headquarters. The Brigadier handed him a map (for sometime it was the only one in the whole Battalion) with a blue line ruled across it running through the forest of Dieppe, near La Motte village. His instructions were to occupy that line, and dig in and stick there. If the Germans had that line we were to take it. The line was four miles long. The seriousness of the situation was undoubted, and we can picture the anxiety of the C.O. and adjutant as, having made hurried arrangements for transport and nucleus, they rode forward ahead of the Battalion to reconnoitre. As they moved up the news of the fall of Merris reached them. Merris was on our left and only about four miles from Hazebrouck. As we moved up we passed scattered bodies of troops moving to the rear. The sum of the information they could supply was "Jerry's coming, choom." One of them enquired whether we had seen any of his regiment. "Stiff luck, chum," replied a digger; "the last of them———has just dived off Calais pier."

At the Headquarters of the 31st Division we found everything ready for flight, and only the most meagre information could be gleaned. Quite frankly, they were glad to be off and leave the miserable business in our hands. On the heads of the luckless Portugese descended all the obloquy and responsibility for the retreat; none of the troops we passed were Portuguese.

The Battalion found its allotted position and dug in as instructed. Ahead of us were the remants of the Grenadier Guards, who, having fought a magnificent defensive battle, had engaged to hold the line till we arrived. Our own line was four miles long; behind us were the 5th Battalion who had arrived shortly after us. The 8th Battalion were expected during the night, and the 1st Brigade in the morning. The anxiey of that night cannot be overstated, as we were spread out in a long thin line, the only bar in the way to Hazebrouck.

With the arrival of the 8th Battalion, and later of the 1st Brigade on our left, we were enabled to shorten our front considerably.

An incident which occurred on the morning of the 13th, after the most critical night in the Battalion's history, is worth recording. The colonel and adjutant were discussing the critical situation at Battalion Headquarters with officers from other units; maps were spread on the table, and in the midst of the conference there entered an English colonel and his staff, behind them were several orderlies laden with all the requisites for a hearty meal. The visitor desired permission to spread his breakfast on the table and use it for his repast. Our colonel, usually the mildest of men, rose to the occasion in fine style, and, under a fire of withering abuse, the visitors withdrew to more civilized regions, and the business of the war was resumed.

On the 13th vigorous enemy attacks were pressed against the 8th Battalion and the 1st Brigade on our left, but were all repulsed. On the 14th we relieved the remnants of the gallant Guard's Brigade, which had fought so doggedly for several days, despite heavy losses and the defection of flanking units.

An enemy attack against D Company was driven off with loss, leaving a prisoner in our hands. Two Huns leading a donkey laden with loot pursued their search too far and walked into our lines. By the time we left the line—on 19th April—the front had become stationary, and the construction of defences was well in hand. Both sides had brought up artillery, and the ordinary incidents of trench life were resumed.

There were several extraordinary incidents connected with this period. The peasants for the most part had evacuated their homes in good time; in one case, however, two old ladies refused to leave their home, but were removed by our men. The following morning their home was destroyed by enemy shells. In another case an officer wrote from the front line complaining that a house near him was occupied by an old couple who were a source of danger by reason of the fires they kept up by day and the lights they showed by night. These, too, were evacuated by us.

A good deal of criticism subsequently descended upon our heads because the pretty little village of La Motte had suffered from the depredations of looters. We were called on for a report. This was furnished and set out that the village was not in fact occupied by us, but had been a resting place for stragglers from a great many other units, and was full of these men before we arrived; and further, that it was abundantly clear that the nature of our work in the restoration of a line of resistance was such that we had neither time nor inclination for such pursuits as were alleged against us. General Plumer told our commanding officer subsequently that he was entirely satisfied that we had no share in the looting of the village. The calumny was often repeated by English troops, but the refutation is easy.

We were relieved by the Irish Guards and the King's Own Yorkshire Light Infantry on the 19th April. We were able to hand over a defined series of well-constructed outposts, and the front was perfectly stable. The Hun blow was spent, and conditions were normal. From the moment of the arrival of the 1st Division on the front, the line moved only one way—back towards Germany.

Our casualties had been fairly heavy during this strenuous week—27 killed (including 2nd Lieuts. Meyer and Trotman) and 73 wounded. The ground had never previously been fought over, and consequently was clean and pleasant, but it had this drawback, that it had no cover from shellfire.

CHAPTER 18.

"THE RETURNING ASCENDANCY."

It may be stated that by the 19th April the line had become stable along the front between Ballieul and Estaires.

When the Battalion came out of the line on that date, we handed over a series of unconnected but well-constructed defences. From this time until the beginning of August the Division was never out of the front line, holding sometimes a one brigade front, sometimes a two brigade front. The line stabilised and resumed the ordinary incidents of trench warfare. This may be termed the period of recovery—but it was more. The general situation did not warrant the resumption by us of an offensive, but it did not discourage what has been styled the "wearing down" process. Battalion vied with battalion and brigade with brigade in nibbling away at small portions of the line opposed to us—a few hundred yards at a time or in carrying out informal little raids with great daring. The result was the improvement of morale among our own ranks and the deterioration of the morale of the enemy. This went on to such an extent that our men carried out some very audacious daylight patrols, returning frequently with prisoners more numerous than their captors. The most notable exploit was that of the 1st Battalion, which advanced their line several hundred yards, and captured over two hundred prisoners in one day with one casualty. The standing crops between the lines facilitated stealthy approach to the enemy trenches. By night our patrols scoured No Man's Land, but rarely encountered any enemy. It was said that No Man's Land had ceased to exist, and that our territory ended only at the enemy's trenches. We captured documents which made it clear how far this told on the nerves and spirits of the enemy. Troops taken from this sector were reproved by their generals for their continual loss of ground. The troops who suffered the reverse alluded to above, when over two hundred prisoners were taken by day, were men who had been specially chosen to go in and resist the constant pressure of the Australians.

The line on the 19th April ran from Ballieul, west to Meteren; round the west of Meteren, then in a south-easterly direction, just west of Merris and east of Strazeele station, then south towards Merville. Thus the Germans were in a deep salient, of which the front opposite us was the most advanced part.

As soon as it was clear that the position had stabilised, arrangements were made to give each brigade in succession a regular rest. The routine, though varied, ran for the most part like this—a week's line work, a week in supports and a week in rest. The rest area was near Sercus, a prettily situated village about ten miles from the line. Here troops were encamped in a field, and combined inevitable training with various sporting activities. The week's rest was always very pleasant and acceptable.

A feature of the early part of this period deserves mention. The inhabitants in their flight from the invaded regions had left behind great quantities of live stock and a good deal of furniture, etc. Such of the live stock as could be removed, consisting principally of cows, were driven back and collected by the French authorities on behalf of the owners. In this way we gathered in eighty-four head of cattle. But pigs, poultry, pet rabbits, etc., could not be similarly dealt with, and instead of being allowed to die off were killed for food. Several amateur butchers were discovered, the Battalion draughtsman being an expert. Eggs were plentiful. Each company kept a cow. When a unit moved, anyone who happened to wander along a little-used back road frequently came on a couple of "cook's offsiders" in charge of the Battalion's milk supply. A valuable discovery was a supply of flour, which in the hands of the cooks was transformed into puddings and pies, to the great satisfaction of all concerned.

Pianos rescued from the ruins were also in demand, but woe betide any unit found in possession of one. All sorts of devices were availed of to hide their presence when the brigadier came round.

Messes were fitted out with sound crockery, to be broken by the carelessness of batmen at the first shift.

In Pradelles, Battalion Headquarters were in a large cellar beneath a factory, protected on the side facing the enemy, but with windows on the side away from him. To this place were carried beds and a supply of clean sheets, chairs, carpets, tables, a roll-top desk, large mirrors to hang on the walls, and many other articles, till the place resembled the lounge of a fashionable hotel. Many serviceable articles of clothing were found, and many the wearing of which made their new owners appear grotesque. The troops voted retreat better fun than advances. So much for the general characteristics of this period. We must now deal in detail with the doing of the Battalion in this somewhat novel kind of warfare.

On the 19th April, then, we moved across from our first position around Dieppe Forest, and occupied a railway camp, from which the owners had fled leaving a comfortable home behind them; this was near Barre. Here the nucleus, who were left out when the Battalion went into action, rejoined, and fresh personnel joined the nucleus. On the 22nd April we moved to support positions behind the 5th Battalion, who were in the line. Deserted farmhouses made comfortable billets, though the enemy had a tendency to use them as targets. From here companies went forward at night to improve the defences of the area. On the 29th we relieved the 5th Battalion in the line, south of Meteren, in the vicinity of Moolenacker. An incident of the tour is instructive. The Army Commander desired identification of the units opposed to us, so he asked each of the four Australian Battalions in the line to try and obtain prisoners, and each of the Battalions was successful. Our party, under Sergeant Charville, raided an enemy listening post, killed three of the enemy and brought back a wounded prisoner. This gallant N.C.O. was wounded himself by one of our own bombs. Following is a report of this patrol:—

"PATROL REPORT."

"Patrol left our lines at X. 25 C. 41. They crept up to an enemy listening post about X. 25 C. 70. The night was very dark and observation difficult. Bombs were thrown into the post, which was then rushed.

"There were four men in post, all of whom were wounded by bombs. The patrol endeavoured to get all these men away, but they would not come, and made a great noise calling to their post behind them. The men in this post answered them, so that it was necessary to get away as soon as possible. Three of the enemy were killed and the fourth was carried out on a stretcher lying near the post. The wounded prisoner belonged to the 1st Eisatz Bn. 23rd J.R. 3rd K.

"The Patrol Leader, Sergeant Charville, was wounded by pellets from one of our bombs and evacuated."

Relieved on the 4th May, we moved back to positions at L'Egerneist, where we bivouacked until the 13th May, when we moved to the area around Pradelles in supports. From here working parties were despatched nightly to the forward area. Enemy shelling of the billets of C and A Companies caused some casualties, 2nd Lieut. Mettam being killed.

On the 19th May we moved a short distance back to the area near Rougeboix, where we occupied scattered farmhouses. Occasional shells fell in the vicinity of our billets but did no damage. On the 25th May the explosion of a lamp resulted in the severe burning of two signallers, one of whom subsequently succumbed to his injuries. The Battalion suffered a heavy loss in the departure for India of Major H. E. Bastin, M.C., and Capt. J. Bowtell Harris, M.C., officers whose service with the Battalion was the subject of a commendatory letter which is appended to the end of this chapter.

It was apparent to us shortly after our arrival on this front that 2nd Army and 15th Corps, to which we were attached, had us "in the bag." We were trusted nowhere. The only villages not out of bounds were those in the firing line, and this was the subject of many a bitter jest. It was commonly asserted that the entrance to a certain village bore this legend, "Out of bounds to Chinese and Australians." When we moved back to Sercus on the 26th May, the experiment was tried of opening the town for the first time. Other towns followed, to the intense disgust of little town majors and A.P.M.'s, and eventually the stigma was removed. It is hardly necessary to add that this policy was justified.

A persistent rumour gained currency that a huge German attack was expected on the 25th May, but the day passed off uneventfully. On the 26th May we moved out for our first rest—a seven days' spell in the picturesque district around Sercus. Various sporting events were held. At a brigade sports meeting on the 31st May an enjoyable day was spent. The Battalion team easily won the brigade championship with 45 points, the next team scoring only 14 points. A concert was held at night. A cricket match against the 8th Battalion was won by 29 runs.

On the 3rd June we moved forward again, and the following night relieved the 12th Battalion in the front line, astride the railway line, just east of Strazeele station. In continuation of a successful operation by the 12th Battalion two nights previously we advanced our line slightly. A local operation had been planned for the night of the 11th June, but as the English Division on our right—the 29th—had planned a gas attack for that night we had to postpone our affair; instead, we evacuated our trenches to allow the gas to go over, but owing to unfavourable wind it did not transpire. We were due for relief on the night of the 12th, which would have meant that the incoming battalion would work on our plans and carry out the operation themselves. Relief arrangements were actually completed, but at the special request of the companies concerned, Brigade were prevailed on to postpone the relief for 24 hours to enable our operation to be carried out on the night of the 12th/13th. Arrangements were made for the 3rd M.G. Co. to barrage enemy back areas, and with medium and light T.M.'s to bombard the position to be attacked. Zero was fixed at 1 a.m. The attack was carried out by C and D Companies and was a great success. Our line was advanced south of the railway line about 500 yards on a front of 650 yards. About 50 enemy were killed and 47 taken prisoners; nine machine guns and one trench mortar were captured. Our casualties were 2 killed and 17 wounded. Second Lieut. P. Edgoose was severely wounded. For his gallantry and initiative in leading at a critical time Lieut. P. H. Smedley was awarded a Military Cross. Divisional and brigade commanders congratulated the troops on a neat little success. Much of the success was undoubtedly due to the preliminary reconnaissance and careful planning of our Intelligence Officer, Lieut. E. G. Robb. The affair also reflected great credit on the company commanders concerned, Capt. W. R. D'Altera and Lieut. E. W. Hill. We were relieved by the 5th Battalion on the following night and came into supports about Pradelles. The chief feature of the following days was the very bad attack of "wind up" which afflicted the higher powers. They gave it out that there were excellent reasons for believing in a powerful German offensive on the morning of the 16th June; consequently, instead of moving back to rest area, the 3rd Brigade were kept in the vicinity. We were employed feverishly strengthening the support lines by cutting standing crops in front of the trenches. There was a general confidence among the men in the issue of any encounter that could not fail to impress us. The enemy would have had a very rough time had he done what was expected of him. But no attack came, and in due course we again moved to the Sercus area for a brief rest.

Throughout this period we remained under orders to move at two hours' notice should the expected enemy attack develop. Each battalion in turn was inlying picquet, ready to move by bus on half an hour's notice. Twice special warnings for readiness were issued. Officers were required to make themselves familiar with the roads leading backwards towards the coast. In short, somebody "higher up" was suffering from "nerves," and our rest was rendered less beneficial by the constant state of preparedness.

Nothing transpired, however, and we moved forward on the 26th June and took over once again the Moolenacker sector, just south of Meteren. A quiet spell followed. There was much patrol activity and enemy posts were frequently bombed. A party of Americans, comprising four officers and eighteen men was attached to us to gain experience. Fine fellows they were, and very eager to learn, and our men spared no pains to teach them. After a short stay they left, and were replaced by others, expressing themselves as delighted with their visit.

A party of officers were standing together at a forward post one night when an enemy minenwerfer fell among them, passed through the arm of Capt. R. McG. Stewart, inflicting a serious wound, and fell harmlessly to the ground. Had it burst—as these things usually did—our loss would have been serious. The "minnie" was secured for the War Museum. On the 3rd July 2nd Lieut. Tucker ("Gorrie") was wounded on a daring daylight patrol and could not be brought in till night. Subsequently he died from his wounds. He was a member of the original Battalion, and had only recently been promoted from sergeant to 2nd lieutenant. One of the bravest and coolest of soldiers, he had won a D.C.M. for his magnificent work at Pozieres, when, with Captain Oates and others, he had fought a bombing fight which had saved for us a newly won trench. His loss was greatly deplored.

On the 5th July news of the Hamel success reached us, and that evening we were withdrawn, relieved by the 5th Battalion. We came back into supports until the 13th, during which period we supplied nightly working parties for the forward areas. On the 14th we marched to Racquinghem for a fortnight's spell. Here we were camped in tents on low ground and not very comfortable. However, we went in largely for sports and games. We were handy to the Neuf Fosse Canal and swimming was popular. Musketry was carried out on a miniature range near by. As usual we were under orders to move at two hours' notice. Leave to St. Omer was granted, and many a man trudged the long road home in a state of unsteadiness, unable to pick up a lorry on the way. Many of the officers established friendly relations and got on visiting terms with the Australian sisters at a casualty clearing station at St. Omer. A swimming carnival on the 25th July was a huge success. At a church parade General Birdwood presented medals and addressed the troops in the well-known "Birdwood" style. Inter-company and inter-battalion cricket matches were played. We defeated at cricket the Pioneer Battalion, Brigade Headquarters and the 6th Battalion, the last match being won by six runs, thanks to a fine innings by Lieut. W. H. G. Smith. On the 26th July we marched out several miles in the rain to be reviewed by General Plumer, and got wet through; as it was too wet for the general to come the troops returned in high spirits.

The news from the south deserves mention. Reports continued to come in of the success of our sister divisions on the Somme—the Hamel victory was welcome news. Then came tidings from the French front—where the German offensive seemed to be converted into a retreat. We felt it was time we left this front. The divisions on our flanks were given periodical rests, but our Division had held the front continuously. The popular belief was that 2nd Army knew that as soon as we were taken out of the line our own corps would claim us. It was generally felt that that day was not far off.

On the 29th July we again moved forward, and the following evening were in the line again. B Company got a prisoner the next night. On the night of the 2nd

August we were relieved and left this sector for good. We had been first in the line in this sector in April, and now were the last to leave it. They had been four months of strenuous work, of much anxiety and constant strain. We had been thirty-five days in the line, forty-three in supports and twenty-eight in rest.

Our casualties for the period were:—Officers, 4 killed, 6 wounded; men, 44 killed, 178 wounded; and our prisoners totalled 49. The total number of prisoners for the Division was just 19 short of the 1000, well up to the average of the divisions on the Somme, which, by reason of more constant fighting, had perhaps had greater opportunities.

After a few days near Lynde we entrained at Arques on the 6th August, and detrained once more at Hangest at 8.30 that night; after the customary Y.M.C.A. coffee we marched to St. Omer, arriving about 12.30 and were soon in bed. The following evening at 8.15 we embussed and after a long drive through the night debussed at 2 a.m. on the morning of the 8th. A tired battalion marched into La Motte Brebière at 4.30 a.m. just as the outburst of artillery fire which shook the earth and illuminated the sky told of the opening of the great offensive a few miles away, and the beginning of the greatest battle in which Australian troops had been engaged.

AN APPRECIATION.

Major H. E. Bastin, M.C.
Capt. J. Bowtell-Harris, M.C.
Capt. A. Oates, D.S.O.

On the 25th day of May, 1918, the Battalion bade farewell with infinite regrets to two of its most capable and brilliant officers in Major H. E. Bastin, M.C., and Capt. J. Bowtell-Harris, M.C., who left that day en route to England and India to take up appointments in the Indian Army.

Among the lists of distinguished officers of the Battalion, probably there are none more highly esteemed and honoured than these two officers. They enlisted in the ranks with the original Battalion, both went through all the hard work and stress of training at Broadmeadows and in Egypt; both rose to N.C.O. rank, and sailed with the Battalion for Gallipoli; both took part in the historic landing, Major Bastin as a platoon sergeant, and Capt. Harris as a headquarters signaller.

At Helles, Steele's and Quinn's Posts and at the immortal action of Lone Pine these officers served brilliantly with the Battalion. They both obtained their commissions on Gallipoli, and their respective absences from the Battalion have been remarkably short.

Major Bastin was wounded at Lone Pine while acting as adjutant. Many of those present at Lone Pine and still alive assert that hardly bare justice has ever been paid Major Bastin for his very gallant and courageous work. Major Bastin returned to the Battalion again on the 28th November, 1915, and remained with the Battalion from that time on until his departure for India (save for a short period as staff trainee on 1st Australian Brigade). Major Bastin again took up the duties of adjutant at Tel-el-Kebir on the 10th January, 1916, and was appointed adjutant on the 7th February, 1916, holding that position until the 1st September, 1917, when he received his well-earned majority; subsequently he acted as a company commander and at times was second in command of the Battalion. Associated with the Battalion during every action and tour of duty in the line in France, his ability and courage, coupled with a genial and merry temperament, could not but make a deep and favourable impression on all with whom he was brought into contact. As adjutant he was able to set a high standard for the officers of the Battalion, and to deeply impress on all that the 7th Battalion must and should be all in all to those who wear its colours.

In all this, at all times, and under all circumstances no officer of the Battalion more zealously and effectively aided Major Bastin than Captain Bowtell-Harris. Friends from the inauguration of the Battalion, they both were never weary of working for and upholding the honour and fame of the 7th Battalion.

Capt. Bowtell-Harris served the Battalion successively as platoon commander, bombing officer and company commander, and in each capacity succeeded in more than ordinary measure. Present at and taking a leading part in the Battalion's work in the evacuation and its work on the Suez Canal, at Serapeum, and again in France, particularly at Pozières, his name will also be associated with that of another 7th Battalion officer, Capt. A. Oates, D.S.O., in the memorable bombing stunt of sixteen hours at Pozières on the 19th July, 1916, for which Capt. Oates was deservedly awarded the D.S.O. No officer has paid a finer tribute to another than the generous and manly terms in which Capt. Oates has always referred to the bravery and devotion of Capt. Bowtell-Harris in that bombing attack.

Subsequent to Pozières Capt. Bowtell-Harris won his M.C. with the greatest courage and dash in a successful raid which he organized and led on the German trenches at Ypres on the 30th September, 1916. Again, when the Hun retirement commenced before Bapaume, the skill and knowledge of Capt. Bowtell-Harris were of the greatest value and service to his battalion commander. Of the many valuable services jointly rendered by these officers probably their joint work at Factory Corner, near Bapaume, in the Hun retirement in March, 1917, ranks as highly as any because of the manifold difficulties successfully faced and overcome by them during the advance of the 7th Battalion. The name of Capt. Bowtell-Harris is and always will be associated in the Battalion with deeds of daring carried out with more than ordinary coolness and skill.

It is given to few men so young as these officers to have in such a marked degree obtained so great and unquestioned an influence over their fellow soldiers, and in whom so marked a confidence was always placed by all ranks under all circumstances both in and out of the firing line.

It is but just, in the interests of the Battalion and its future history, that there should be placed on record some short resume, however far it falls short of doing justice, of the careers of these two officers who have so profoundly and so beneficially impressed their respective personalities on their Battalion.

Their love for the Battalion is proverbial, and no officers have ever commenced their military career in any sphere with more generous and more earnest good wishes and respect than Major Bastin and Capt. Bowtell-Harris carry with them on the commencement of their careers in the Indian Army.

In writing of Major Bastin and Capt. Bowtell-Harris it is impossible to separate their names and the name of Capt. A. Oates, D.S.D., who left the Battalion for the Indian Army on the 12th February, 1918. Captain Oates enlisted in the 8th Battalion, and came away with the original 1st Division, was transferred to the 7th Battalion in the early stages of the Peninsula Campaign and soon rose to commissioned rank. He was present at and displayed much ability and courage in every action in which we were engaged on Gallipoli. Capt. Oates came to France with the Battalion as a company commander, and soon became noted for his skill and courage. He and his company especially distinguished themselves at Pozières on the 19th July, 1916, when his company led by himself, and Capt. Bowtell-Harris, carried out a fierce bombing attack which lasted sixteen hours. For his work on this occasion Capt. Oates received the D.S.O.

On many subsequent occasions his work was of a very fine standard, notably in the retirement of the enemy before Bapaume.

Apart from his actual skill and bravery in the line, Capt. Oates' work in the Battalion has been of particular value to the Battalion in the excellent stamp of N.C.O.'s and men he trained while acting as company commander. It has been noticed frequently what fine work has been done by the N.C.O.'s whom Capt. Oates trained, and how worthily they have carried on the system and kept up to the standard he laid down.

A man whose word was his bond, known far and wide as a man of the most scrupulous honour, Capt. Oates left the Battalion amidst the deepest regret of his comrades of all ranks, but with their assured belief in his success in whatever work he undertook in the Indian Army, and that he would still further add to the laurels of his old Battalion.

(Signed) E. A. Herrod, Lieut. Col.

O. Harris, Lieut. Adjutant.

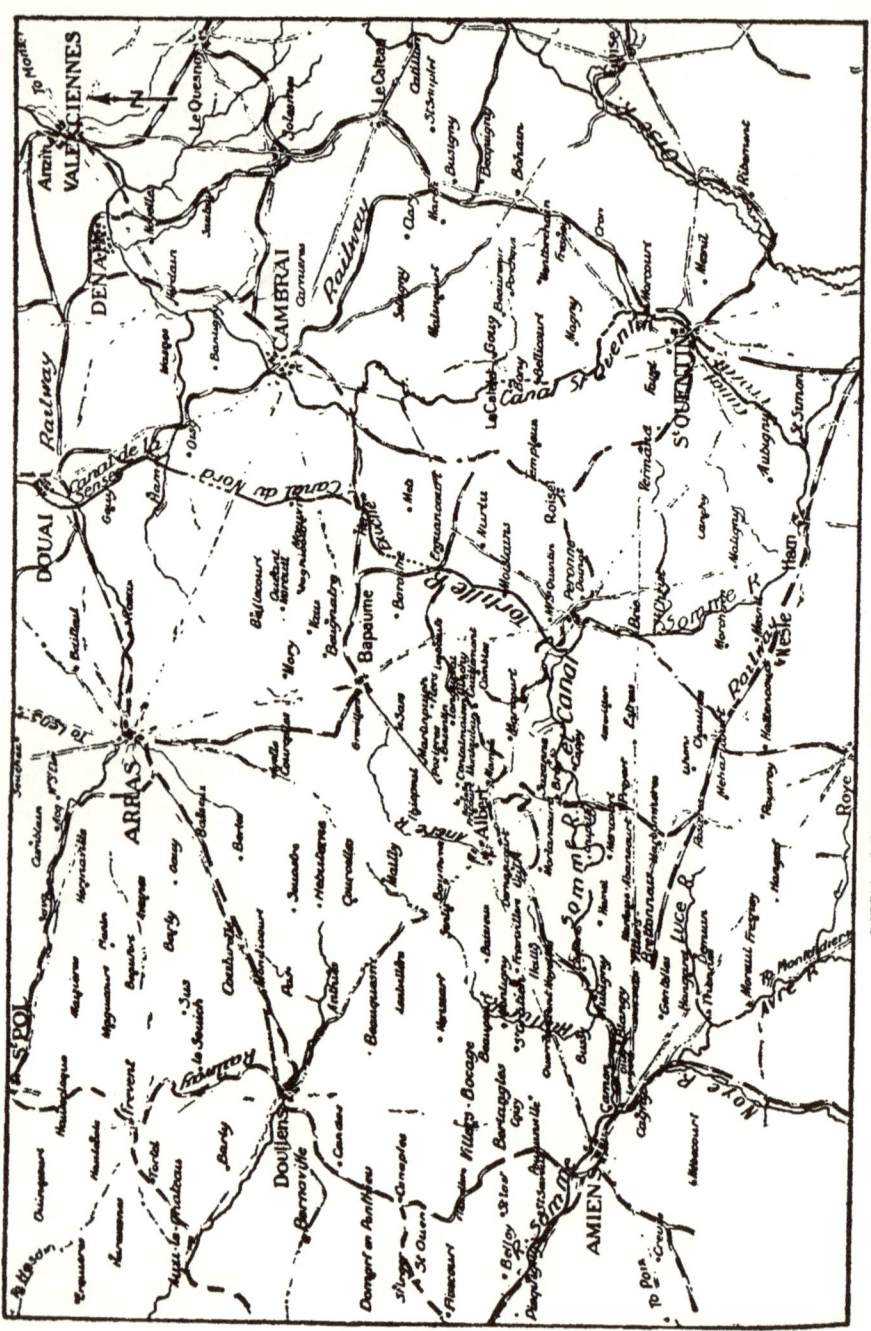

THE SOMME TO ST. QUENTIN, 1918

CHAPTER 19.

"THE GREAT OFFENSIVE."

WE had a shrewd suspicion that we had not been brought down to the Somme for an outing. Just prior to our departure from the north the writer met an English staff major. After referring to our projected move and expressing his admiration for our work, he said, "But surely your corps will give you a rest now." He was quite surprised to learn that we entertained no such expectation.

The first definite news we had of what was coming was during a halt in our march from where we had debussed on the early morning of the 8th August. As the troops rested on the roadside, officers by the aid of electric torches read to them Monash's now famous order. It was vague, but inspiring; and it thrilled us to think that at last we were taking a lesson from the enemy and launching an offensive on a grand scale. We saw the flashes later which announced the opening of the play, and chuckled to think how Fritz must be dancing to our music.

We reached La Motte Brebière, a poor desolate shattered spot on the Somme, at 4.30 a.m., dog-tired with our night's travelling. The village afforded poor accommodation, but we would sleep anywhere. At 4 p.m. we were on the move again. Leaving the nucleus behind with our spare kit, we marched to our camping ground at Aubigny, not far from Corbie.

At 4.5 a.m. on the 9th, we received word to be prepared to move at 6 a.m. if required. This message had left Division at midnight, but all communications were by despatch rider, as it was impossible to erect telephone lines. At 7.30 Brigade issued orders to move at once, 7th and 8th Battalions leading, to a position about Harbonnieres. At 8.30 we moved out in column of route.

We must revert for a moment to the doings of the previous day. The attack was on a wide front. On the left, north of the Somme, was the 3rd Corps; in the centre the Australian Corps, and on the right the Canadian Corps, who joined with the French. The 2nd and 3rd Divisions were entrusted with the opening of the attack for our corps, with the 5th and 4th Divisions behind them. The operation proceeded according to plan. The 2nd and 3rd Divisions easily took their objectives by 7 a.m. The 4th and 5th Divisions, going through them, likewise gained their objectives. Casualties were light and captures both of men and material enormous. The German front had been pierced to a depth of about six miles. A staggering blow had been inflicted, as Sir John Monash had confidently predicted. North of the Somme the 3rd Corps had not been very successful, but on our front the victory was complete. But it was not to be allowed to rest there. Our Division was to be thrown in to exploit the success, and to drive a still deeper wedge into the enemy's defences, in conjunction with the Canadians. By midday on the 9th, as we had not been able to arrive in time, the 5th Division had begun the further advance and had captured Vauvillers. They were resting here, preparing to carry the attack still further in the event of our being delayed, when we overtook them, as will be seen hereafter.

At 10.45, while we were on the march through territory won the preceding day, the C.O., in response to a verbal message, proceeded to Brigade. The Brigadier, Brig. General J. Heane, had been motored to Division for instructions, and had just returned. Before leaving us, the C.O. instructed us to continue to advance as far as Bayonvillers, where he would rejoin us, in echelon of companies. At Brigade he received instructions to continue the advance from the green line, south of Harbonnieres, and held by the 15th Brigade, to the red line. We were allotted six tanks, a section of the 2nd Machine Gun Company, and two 18 pr. field guns. At 12.15 the C.O. rejoined us at Bayonvillers. The transport was parked, and each company drew its Lewis guns from the limbers.

At 12.30 we resumed our march in artillery formation, B and A Companies in front, C and D behind, each company having with it its pack horse laden with 2000 rounds of ammunition. At the appointed spot, south of Harbonnieres, we assembled for the battle. Company commanders received their instructions, the situation was explained, boundaries and objectives defined, and tanks and artillery received their orders. The 8th Battalion were on our right, and we got in touch with them.

The ground over which we were to advance was a gentle slope for the first half mile or so, when we passed over a low ridge; then almost flat for the remainder of the distance, rising sharply to the red line—our objective—about 4000 yards off. This last rise gave the enemy a perfect view of our movements during the whole advance, and was, moreover, a difficult spot to attack. It contained a network of trenches and gunpits, and marked the spot where the line had run prior to the German offensive in March. The whole battlefield was covered only by short grass, except for an occasional copse; many old trenches served as cover for the defenders, but gave no assistance to the attackers. The position would be a formidable one to attack at any time, but we were to advance against it with no artillery barrage.

On our left was the 2nd Division. It was expected that they would co-operate with us and advance on our left. The attack was originally timed for 11 a.m., but as we could not possibly arrive by then it was postponed. When we did advance we found that our left was entirely unsupported, and our left flank was in the air all the way. How much trouble this occasioned will be seen.

Having completed our assembly we began the advance at 1.50 p.m. It was a warm dusty day, and the troops had had a long march without rest. The plan of attack was to send on in front a thin line of scouts about 100 yards apart; 150 yards behind them came the tanks, four in front and two behind; 150 yards in rear of the tanks, B and A Companies in artillery formation (B on the left), each with two platoons in front and two behind; 500 yards behind were C and D Companies in echelon of platoons; Headquarters were between the attacking and supporting companies. As soon as we moved, the two artillery officers (they were not Australians), who had been ordered to keep with Battalion Headquarters, disappeared, and were not seen again. Consequently, we were deprived of the use of our two field guns. We soon came under artillery fire, and were attacked by six aircraft, but our extended formation prevented us from suffering many casualties. South of Vanvillers we passed through troops of the 15th Brigade, and immediately encountered heavy machine gun fire from the front and from the left. This was unexpected, as we had reckoned on covering fire from a line of the 15th Brigade still further ahead. These troops were mistaken as to their actual position, and were

1000 yards behind the green line. The tanks had worked too far to the right, and the troops tended to follow the tanks soon left us altogether. To counteract this, C Company was brought up and put in on the left. This caused the enemy to retire, pursued by our machine gun fire. C Company seized the opportunity and pushed forward. Heavy opposition was again met with, particularly from the left, where the enemy, having no troops in front to worry him, harassed our flank with machine gun and rifle fire. A copse afforded him good cover, but he began to evacuate it a few men at a time by means of an old communication trench. We assaulted the copse and captured it. At 4 p.m. we continued the advance by short rushes against heavy fire, and succeeded in reaching the foot of the hill which was our objective. Here we were held up. The hill was a mass of trenches and old gun-pits, and afforded ample cover to the enemy. We were on open ground and exposed to galling fire. The left flank was experiencing especial difficulty. A Company on the right had captured a German hospital, but had suffered heavily and expended their rifle grenades. D Company was pushed forward to assist them.

By the skilful use of volleys of rifle grenades we got a footing in old gun-pits. Advance over the open was impossible, as the Hun was resisting determinedly and his machine guns and snipers were holding us up. Here the old trenches were of some use, and by bombing our way along them we gradually made headway. Eventually, seeing us creeping on, the enemy took fright and bolted. Machine guns were on him in an instant and many were shot down. With a rush we were up the last pinch and on our objective and the enemy driven out. Posts were established along this line and the position consolidated. We still had to suffer machine gun fire and the enemy were still strong. Our left, still short of the objective, was fired at from the flank and from the rear, from Germans occupying positions in the still uncaptured ground opposite the 2nd Division, but gradually they, too, advanced and made good the position, a much weakened and exhausted company. At 6 p.m. Brigade were advised that the red line was ours. At 6.30 a determined counter-attack withered before our fire. Just in front of us was an enemy battery which had been firing till the last. The Germans made many attempts to limber the guns and get them out, but they and their horses were shot down.

A graphic description of the advance is given in Downing's "To the Last Ridge." As an eyewitness' account of the action it is interesting.

Extract from Downing's "Last Ridge."

"At 11 o'clock a new attack was made along the whole line. The 1st Division . . . . was coming through. If it could not arrive in time we were to go over. . . . . The time drew near. We were twice ordered to prepare to attack; twice the advance was postponed. At last the 58th and 60th, who had been following us through the fighting, lined our trench. Over they went. . . . . There was hot fighting. We were mounting the parapet to follow, when a runner hurried through the trench. 'From Captain ―――― to old platoon sergeants. Don't go over.' We wondered. Then we looked behind us.

"And there was the 1st Division, in artillery formation, dotted over the ridge a mile behind. The waves in their regular patterns stretched backward for thousands of yards, and sideways for miles. . . . . On they came. They passed over us. It was twenty minutes before the last wave went through.

" 'Best of luck, 8th Battalion.'

" 'Thanks, boys.'

"Their fresh faces contrasted with ours, that were unshaven, and grimy, and wan. They strode on, and on, and on. Shrapnel eddied and flashed and puffed above them, bullets ripped through their formation. As one man fell, another stepped into his place, without slackening, without hurrying, outwardly calm.

"They extended into single lines and swept forward to Lihon's Wood. Then they advanced by short rushes. We saw them charge with the bayonet far away. They reached the wood, tiny dots, as tiny as when we first saw them, a long way behind. Parties of men came and went with stretchers. Batches of prisoners shambled through. Motor ambulances rolled along the road by our trench as the sun was setting."

At 7 p.m. we gained touch with the 8th on the right, but our left was still in the air. A Company from the

5th Battalion, who had followed our advance, was sent across to form a defensive flank on the left. Even then this flank was exceedingly vulnerable. It was not until 8.45 p.m. that the 25th Battalion came up on our left and got touch. Even then, they were short of the red line, and were too far to the left, our troops being well into 2nd Division territory. How much this lack of co-operation between the divisions had cost we know too well. It was 2 hours 50 minutes after our attack commenced before the flank moved forward; had we begun together the enemy on our left would have been far too busily engaged in front to have harassed our flank. The comparison is forcibly brought out by the casualties. Our losses were:—

	Killed.	Wounded.	Missing.
Officers	6	8	1
Men	52	169	2
	58	177	3

the total being 238. The casualties sustained by the 25th Battalion totalled 19. Such incidents are inseparable from big offensives, but we may be pardoned the regret that we should have been the victims.

Of the achievement of that day we make no apology for being proud. On a hot dusty day troops who in the eleven nights preceding had had but two nights' rest, had marched twelve miles without a halt, and gone straight into action. Let the official report continue:—"The mere statement of facts on paper does not convey any idea of the severity of the task. The position assailed overlooked the whole field of battle, the Battalion advanced and fought over the field in broad daylight, without assistance from other arms of the service, against an enemy who fought determinedly, and enemy in strongly entrenched positions, with enemy field guns firing over open sights; fought and advanced with an open and exposed flank, against machine gun fire of fierce intensity, on a hot day; and at the conclusion of a long, tiring, dusty march.

"The 9th August is sacred to the men of the 7th Battalion as the anniversary of their famous Lone Pine fight, and the deeds of that day were worthily emulated by the men of the present 7th Battalion."

Our prisoners numbers 100. Booty captured included 2 9-inch Howitzers, 1 6-inch Howitzer, 1 3-inch Howitzer, 2 granatenwerfers, 4 heavy machine guns, 14 light machine guns, and a German hospital with much equipment.

Of our losses we hardly cared to think. Our total casualties were 238. We had had killed six fine officers —2nd Lieut. J. H. Hamblett, M.M.; Lieut. W. Poole; Lieut. R. B. Purbrick; 2nd Lieut. J. Caddy, D.C.M., M.M.; 2nd Lieut. T. V. Harris; 2nd Lieut. T. J. Ross, and eight others wounded. All our company commanders had fallen early. In addition many splendid N.C.O.'s and men, including Sgt. Milgate, an original, and Sgt. Cumberland.

That night passed without incident. Hot food was got forward to us. At 8 a.m. next morning the 3rd Brigade passed through us and carried on the attack. We were then relieved and withdrawn to support positions a little further back, where for several days we remained, occupying old trenches, and except for shellfire comparatively quiet.

On the 10th we were ordered to send a company to assist the 8th Battalion on the following morning. D Company, under Lieut. W. H. G. Smith, was sent. The 3rd Brigade were to attack on the left; the objective was 500 yards beyond Lihons. Tanks and artillery were to cooperate. D Company were 200 yards behind the centre of the 8th Battalion. The attack began at 4 a.m. The ground was very difficult, being intersected by many deep trenches, which in the darkness were not easily crossed by men burdened with all the impedimenta of battle. They pushed forward, however, and encountered heavy machine gun fire. The advance was made a section at a time, and they established themselves in a trench with a company of the 8th on the right; and, after bombing their way along the trench the left company was also found. A party was sent to "mop up" Lihons. At 4.30 p.m. determined enemy counter-attacks were beaten off. That night the Company was relieved and rejoined us the following morning. Their casualties were 2 killed, 15 wounded,

2 missing. A letter from the commanding officer of the 8th Battalion evidence the work they had performed:—

Headquarters,
8th Battalion, A.I.F.
14th August, 1918.

To Commanding Officer,
7th Battalion, A.I.F.

Dear Sir,

I am desirous of conveying to you my appreciation of the splendid work done by your D Company under command of Lieut. Smith during the recent operation in which the Company was attached to this Battalion.

The work of the Company, officers, N.C.O.'s and men was of the very highest order, and I consider it an honour to take such a fine Company into action.

Their dash, combined with the skilful leading of their officers, was of tremendous assistance to the Battalion during the advance, and the courage and determination which they displayed in repelling the enemy counter-attacks was well in keeping with the traditions of your grand old Battalion.

If at any time in the future operations render it necessary for other troops to be attached to this Battalion, I sincerely hope that we will again have the good fortune to have such troops as these with us.

J. W. Mitchell, Lieut. Colonel,
Commanding 8th Battalion, A.I.F.

While in support area we were subjected to a good deal of hostile shelling, and lost three young officers killed—2nd Lieuts. Grant, Summers and Kelly.

On the 15th August the Division was relieved and came back to Cerisy, on the Somme, where we sought shelter in dugouts and bivouacs. There was a road near by and the constant traffic raised a dust which was very unpleasant. Fortunately the Somme was handy, and swimming was a universal attraction. The nucleus rejoined and all our spare gear was sent up from La Motte Brebière. By night enemy aeroplanes dropped bombs along the road.

On the 18th we moved back via Hamel to Hamelet, just across the Somme from Corbie. The town was sadly damaged and accommodation was poor. On the 21st the nucleus left for Corbie and we were on the move again at 8.40 p.m. We came up to the support area, about 1½ miles south-east of Proyart, and about 2 miles north of Lihons. On the 22nd the C.O. attended a conference at Brigade Headquarters and received instructions for an attack early next morning. That night after a hot meal was served we moved forward to our assembly positions.

The plan of attack was as follows:—The 5th and 6th Battalions were to attack, and we were to follow and support the 5th, who were on the left flank. We were to form up 500 yards behind the Framerville-Proyart Road and to follow the 5th at a distance of 1000 yards, unless required by them to assist in the attack. We were to clean up all trenches and dugouts in the conquered territory. Fifty men were to be sent up to the final objective with material necessary for consolidation. We were to construct a support line previously marked down, in which the 1st Pioneer Battalion were to assist us. D and A Company led our advance, with B and C in support. The 1st Brigade were co-operating on the left and the 97th Imperial Brigade on the right.

We were in position in artillery formation at 3.45 a.m. At 4.45 a.m. the attack began and we moved forward through the enemy barrage. The dense smoke and dust prevented our seeing more than 100 yards ahead. We reached St. Martin's Wood and came under machine gun fire. The 5th had passed through ahead of us, and D and A Companies proceeded to mop up. Three officers and 65 men were captured; also 1 7.5 cm. field gun, 5 heavy machine guns and 24 light machine guns. Each company then dug strong-posts on the line allotted to it. At 8 a.m. heavy shelling of a gully forward of the wood compelled us to move forward to escape it. That night we were again shelled heavily and early next morning a gas shell bombardment began, lasting several hours. The men wore their respirators, but could not keep them on permanently, and the gas hung about the wood all day. At night we relieved the 5th Battalion in the line. It rained heavily and relief was rendered difficult by reason of the slippery nature of the ground. After an unpleasant 24 hours, we were relieved by the 30th Battalion, and were brought back by motor bus to Hamel, where we were bivouacked comfortably in a gully before dawn on the 27th.

Our task in the operation had not been a major one, but had been very heavy. We had suffered intense shellfire; ours was a difficult and dangerous job in mopping up the woods, but D and A Companies had performed it thoroughly and quickly. Our losses were:—

	Officers.	Men.
Killed	—	12
Wounded	2	31
Gassed	2	88
Missing	—	2
Total	4	133

The Pioneers and Engineers rendered valuable service, and assisted materially in the construction of our strong-posts. As usual we received the congratulations of General Birdwood and other commanders.

This operation was known as the "Souvenir Stunt," as in the course of "mopping-up" the wood we collected a great many trophies. One soldier was seen with a sandbag into which he threw watches as he gathered them. As each one went in he would name the recipient for whom he intended them, and his monologue was something like this: "Here's one for old Bill, who is left with the nucleus; here's one for Marie, down near Abbeville; here's one—a bit slow—give that to the sergeant; here's one to send home," and so on. Many revolvers were similarly acquired. The prisoners gladly parted with everything except their gas-masks.

We remained about ten days in the gully near Hamel, while other units crossed the Somme, captured Mont St. Quentin, and continued to carry the line forward. We were reorganised on a three company basis, A Company being disbanded; each company consisted of three platoons instead of four. This was necessary as our ranks had been considerably depleted, and our strength was just about 400. On the 8th September we left, and were brought by motor bus through interesting recently-won territory to Mont St. Quentin. Here we were bivouacked in trenches and a partially destroyed hospital, and were occupied in salvage work on the field of battle. On the 10th we moved to Tincourt, where we remained till the 15th. R.S.M. Baker and 12 others left for Australia on six months' furlough.

On the 15th we marched out at 7 p.m. and relieved the 4th Battalion in the front line near Loisel. The weather was becoming very bad, and there was a good deal of rain. The enemy artillery was fairly active, and aeroplanes dropped bombs on our supports; 12 fell on Battalion Headquarters, doing a lot of damage to our records and to the typewriter, but causing very few casualties. On the morning of the 18th the 1st Brigade attacked through our lines. Three nights later we went forward and relieved them in the positions they had gained, near Hangicourt, but were not actually in the front line. On the 23rd the 59th American Regiment relieved us, and we came back to Tincourt. From here we entrained to Longpre, and marched to Ailly-le-Haut-Clocher, near Abbeville, for, we hoped, a complete rest. A rumour that we would not see any further fighting caused considerable amusement; but in fact, though we did not know it, we had seen our last shot fired. Lieut. Colonel Herrod, Lieut. Robb and four N.C.O.'s remained behind with the Americans for a few days to assist them in their operations. This party did excellent work and well earned the thanks which were accorded them.

We rested at Ailly for six weeks. Leave was reopened and training resumed. A splendid rifle range afforded facilities for musketry practice. Sports, concert parties and lectures helped us to spend an enjoyable time. The mornings were devoted to drill, the afternoons to games. At a sports meeting held on the 27th October and attended by a number of Australian sisters from No. 3 A.G.H., led by our first R.M.O., now Lieut. Col. E. W. Gutteridge, D Company won the championship with 32 points, C Company scored 30½, B Company 17, Transport 16, Headquarters 7. The championship went to Pte. "Red" Wyatt 7 points, the others being Pte. Crowley, Capt. Wright and Pte. Davey 6 points each, and Cpl. Henshall 5½. Lieut. Swift won two of the other events and was second in three. At a divisional rifle competition Capt. H. H. Young secured eighth place. Platoon, company and battalion teams competed, but without much success in the various events.

Day leave to Abbeville was plentiful; but it was a long walk home, and on the road might be seen any night belated parties of revellers trudging unsteadily homewards, stopping only to sing at each kilometre post, "There's a friend in every milestone." The result was that by the time home was reached everybody was quite sober.

On the 8th November we entrained at Port Reney at 7 a.m. on a very cold morning, and by midnight were in huts at Tincourt. On the 9th we moved by bus to Brazieul. On the 11th we marched to Favril, preparatory to moving forward to continue the advance. Then came the message, "Hostilities will cease at eleven hours 11th November. There will be no intercourse with the enemy until receipt of further instructions which will be issued." And so the war ended.

The news was quietly received—how else could it be in such a desolate spot? It seemed too good to be true—after the years of campaigning and apparently unending warfare. We moved back to Bazieul on the 13th, forward to Bohain on the 14th, Mozinchien on the 22nd, Prisches on the 23rd, Boulogue on the 24th, and Sars Poteries on the 26th, where we were billeted in a huge factory, from which the Germans had removed every vestige of useful machinery and destroyed the rest.

CHAPTER 20.

IN BELGIUM.

The Battalion Breaks Up

The concluding story of the Battalion may be shortly told. After 3½ years of warfare we had suddenly reached a condition of affairs which we had often imagined and speculated upon, but had never dared to hope for. It was known that it would take many months to get us home, but that did not displace the general desire to get home at the earliest possible moment. Already the original members of the Battalion had departed on well-earned furlough, and the rest of us were anxious to get away. The great problem was how to interest the men, to keep them contented and out of mischief. Obviously it was necessary to keep some drill for the sake of discipline, and equally obviously it was futile to attempt battle training of the old kind. The education service made a big endeavour to fill the gap and some account of its work deserves mention.

The education service was launched by Bishop Long, who formulated the details of the scheme. The suddenness of the termination of hostilities robbed it of any opportunity of preparing for this period beforehand, and consequently inevitable delay occurred in organisation. Classes in elementary and technical subjects were formed in the Battalion and worked well for some time. An education officer was appointed. Corps workshops at Jeumont aimed at instructing men in a variety of technical subjects and men were sent there for courses. Army workshops throughout France did the same, with varying success. Arrangements for non-military employment in England were made, but it was some time before they were properly established.

We were about three weeks at Sars Poteries, whose wretched populace, having been deprived of everything during the German occupation, were now living on rations sent up by army lorries, meagre enough, but liberal by comparison with the starvation of the last four years. A series of sports competitions were organised. The general hope and expectation was that we were to go to the Rhine to form part of the Allied Army of occupation. While at Sars Poteries we lost our little interpreter, George Gauthier, who had been nearly two years with us, and was a universal favourite. He carried with him the best wishes of all for his peace pursuits, and he assured us he was coming out to Australia to see us all some day. He had some queer ideas about Australia, one of the most deep-rooted being that Bendigo was the capital, and the Bendigo "Advertiser" the chief paper in the Commonwealth. But then the adjutant hailed from Bendigo—and what Bendigo man doesn't think Bendigo the first city of the Southern Hemisphere!

Just before Christmas we moved up to Belgium. We were three days on the roads. The first day we marched 18 kilos. along good roads in light rain; the Prince of Wales inspected us on the march. We spent the night at Solre-St.-Gery—in country unscarred by the war. A 21 kilo. march next day along muddy and rough roads brought us to Thy-le-Chateau, and the third day we covered 12 kilos. to Couillet, a suburb of Charleroi. We had passed through pleasant country, in striking contrast to the barren areas behind. Couillet was a kind of promised land, and as we swung down the main street behind the band crowds lined the streets and we felt that all our troubles were past.

The men were accommodated in comfortable billets and proceeded to establish themselves on familiar terms with the populace. Unlike the people of France in the war zones, these folk could speak no English, and all conversations were carried on by means of our scanty French resources with remarkable success. Many men were taken into private houses, given good billets and treated almost as "one of the family." The search for men for fatigues and guards used to drive orderly corporals to despair. The civilians took us to their hearts very quickly. The first example came on Christmas Day. It was decided to have a Battalion dinner. Tables and forms were provided and set in a big hall; the inhabitants lent us table linen, ornaments, flowers, flags, cutlery and crockery. The Battalion cooks supplied the dinner. The waiting was done by the officers and sergeants. A three-course meal was served, washed down by bottles of good beer and a rum issue. Our civilian friends crowded in to admire. The Brigadier visited the men at dinner and wished them the compliments of the season. The season was likewise amply feted in the officers' and sergeants' messes later on.

Soon afterwards the mayor held a reception to the Australians. The 6th and 7th Battalions marched past a saluting point where the Brigadier was standing with the mayor and councillors. Refreshments were served to officers and addresses of welcome were delivered and replied to. A series of dances was held by the civilians, to which our men were admitted, and by officers' and sergeants' messes, and also by the Battalion. As was inevitable the young men of the town resented the familiarity with which we fraternised with the girls, and we had to exclude them from our dances.

However, the thoughts of all men were turned eagerly homeward. The first contingent to leave said farewell to the Battalion on the 19th January, leaving behind many temporarily broken hearts among the young ladies of the town.

The arrival of reinforcements in January created much merriment; but the vast majority were boys only just old enough to enlist, and they settled down cheerfully to the routine and duties of the Battalion from which the older men were largely released. These were the first reinforcements which had come to the Battalion since January, 1918, and during the strenuous campaigns of the past year the Battalion had had to rely on the return from hospital of men who had been evacuated ill or slightly wounded.

While waiting liberal leave was given to visit Brussels and Waterloo, a privilege eagerly availed of. A few men paid quite unofficial visits to Cologne.

During February men waited anxiously for the departure of the next quota, but as a direct result of the coal strikes in England demobilisation was delayed. The date of departure was deferred from time to time till men were tired of waiting. At last, on the 1st March, they left, leaving behind, as the last had done, many sad hearts among the girls of Couillet.

The next quota finally left on the 5th March. On the 5th March we were thrown into mourning by the sudden death from influenza of Lieut. K. G. Banks, a loyal-hearted and popular young officer whose record of service with us had been long and valuable. He was accorded a military funeral. In March the 6th and 7th Battalions amalgamated and in April the 5th and 8th joined us to form the 2nd Brigade Battalion. In due course these also were sent over to England and finally reached Australia.

There is no need to follow the men through the camps of England, where there were interminable and exasperating delays, broken only by short furloughs to bid farewell to friends in England, nor to trace them homeward on their boats, nor speak of happy reunions on Australian soil. But we can truthfully say that our joy at setting our faces towards home was not unmingled with a pang of regret to be leaving for ever the Battalion that had been our home so long.

So we have traced the glorious story of our dear old Battalion. After years of strife and buffeting, changing from day to day as old identities passed away and new arrivals came, the Seventh had held on its path. We who were privileged to serve with it know what a famous regiment it was. No true member of it but did not feel when he was separated from it that he was away from home; and when he rejoined it after absence, it was with a thrill of joy, as at a homecoming. Many gallant comrades have fallen to make its history; its record is written in letters of blood. And what a record! Memories of the Landing, of Helles and Lone Pine, of Pozières, of Ypres, of Guedecourt and Flers, of Ligny-Thilloy, of Polygon Wood and Zonnebeke, of Wytschaete and the Ravine, of Hazebrouck, of Harbonnieres and Lihons, of Martin's Wood and Roisel come crowding in on us—a story of victory and triumph, with never an inch of ground yielded or a task unfinished. How can we help but be proud of it!

Roll of Winners of Decorations

V.C. (4)
Cpl Burton, A. S.
A/Cpl Dunstan, W.
Capt Symons, W.
Major Tubb, F. H.

D.S.O. (3)
Lt-Col Herrod, E. E. (and C.M.G.)
B/Gen Jess, C. H. (and C.M.G., and 2 M.I.D., and Serbian W/Eagle).
Capt Oates, A.

M.C. (15)
Capt Barlow, D. L.
Major bastin, H. E.
Capt Harris, J. B. (and Bar)
Lieut Harris, O. J.
Capt Fowler, J.
Lieut Graham, R. J.
Capt-Chap Hearn, J.
Capt Hillard, R. I.

Capt Hopkins, J. W. (and Bar)
2/Lieut Phillips, D. G.
Capt Piercey, R. L.
Lieut Reynolds, O. G.
Lieut Smedley, F. J.
Lieut Smith, W. H. G.
Lieut Teare, A. M.

D.C.M. (21)
L/Sgt Anderson, F. B.
Sgt Ball, G. (with Bar)
Capt Barker, H. A.
Sgt Binell, W. H.
2/Lieut Caddy, J.
Sgt Charville, J.
R.S.M. Deacon, G. L. W.
L/Cpl Hardie, A. G.
Sgt Hogg, J. H.
Pte Jones, R. J.
Pte Lynch, J.

C.S.M. McDonald, F.
Cpl McDonald, J. W.
C.S.M. Stanton, J.
Cpl Thomas, J. R.
Sgt Tinney, L. H.
L/Cpl Tracey, W.
Lieut Tucker, W. L.
Sgt Walters, J. F.
Cpl Webb, H.
Lieut Wraight, H. T.

M.M. (77)
L/Sgt Anderson, D. C.
Pte Andrews, N. J.
Sgt Bailey, A. D.
Pte Ballack, W. F.
L/Cpl Barnard, V. A.
L/Sgt Bates, R. (and Bar)
Pte Belsey, B. R.
Cpl Bissett, G. F.
L/Cpl Blythe, H. (and Bar)
Lieut Burrows, F. A.
2/Lieut Caddy, J.
Pte Cain, H.
Pte Casey, A.
Dvr Cook, P. E.
Cpl Cornish, L.
L/Cpl Cox, W. J.
L/Cpl Croshaw, H. G.
Pte Cummins, J. W.

L/Cpl Cummins, W. J.
Cpl Cunning, F. A.
Dvr Currie, D. H.
Pte David, M. T. R.
Pte Davies, H.
L/Cpl Faulkner, F. W. G.
Pte Feltman, C.
Pte Fenton, H.
Sgt Foley, W.
Lieut Fryberg, L.
Pte Garvan, C. J.
L/Cpl Gasson, E. W.
Pte Gibbons, A. H.
Pte Glasspool, W. H.
L/Sgt Gray, A. J.
L/Cpl Gray, A. H.
Cpl Grimble, C. F.
Sgt Gunther, H. V.

M.M.—(Continued)

Sgt Guthridge, J. F.
L/Cpl Hambly, P. E.
L/Cpl Hardie, A. G.
Pte Harwood, O. J.
Pte Hempel, J. (and Bar)
Sgt Hicks, T. H. (and Bar)
Pte Hill, R. S.
Cpl Hodgson, R. J.
Sgt Holland, G. W. F.
Cpl Jenkinson, F. H.
Pte Keating, M. M.
Sgt Kerr, M. J.
Pte Kidd, H. C.
Sgt Laird, F. A.
Pte Larsen, A. H. S.
Sgt Laycock, R. S.
Pte Lee, A. G.
Cpl Maloney, C. E. (and Bar)
C.Q.M.S. McCallum, R.
Sgt McCormick, D.
Sgt McDonald, A. R.
C.S.M. McIntyre, N. A. R.
L/Cpl McNeil, G. J.
Pte Paice, M. M.

Pte Palliser, W.
Cpl Peach, W. E.
Dvr Price, R. A.
L/Cpl Reade, G. P.
L/Cpl Reid, N. S.
L/Cpl Robertson, G. G.
Pte Robinson, A. (and Bar)
Lieut Robinson, R. C.
Pte Rolls, W. G.
L/Cpl Schumann, J. D.
Pte Scott, A.
Cpl Self, W.
L/Cpl Smith, J. H.
Pte Spall, A. R.
Cpl Stevenson, W. R.
L/Cpl Stirling, R.
Sgt Swindells, R.
Pte Tatti, H. M.
Cpl Thorpe, H.
Pte Tiller, A. T.
L/Cpl White, W.
Pte Whitehead, J. F. R.
L/Cpl Wignell, C. W. (and Bar)
Lieut Wraight, H. T.

Mentioned in Despatches

Lieut Anderson, C. R.
R.S.M. Baker, W.
Cpl Burton, A. S.
2/Lieut Caddy, J.
Sgt Ball, G.
Capt Anthony, H.

R.Q.M.S. Brown, W.
Capt Campbell, W. D.
C.S.M. Carey, J. L.
Pte Ellis, O. J.
Capt Fowler, J.
B/Gen. Jess, C. H. (2)

Meritorious Service Medal (4)

R.S.M. Baker, W.
Sgt Cumberland, J. W.

R.S.M. Deacon, G. L. W.
Cpl Moore, J. L.

C. de G. (Belgium) (3).

R.Q.M.S. Brown, W.
C.M.S. Carey, J. L.

Cpl Davey, S. W.

Med. Mil. (France)

Sgt Milgate, F. M.

Serbian White Eagle.

B/Gen Jess, C. H.

Award Statistics

(exclusive of Mentions in Despatches)

V.C.	4	D.C.M.	21
D.S.O.	3	M.M.	86
C.M.G.	1	M.S.M.	5
Serb. W. Eagle	2	Belgian C. de G.	3
M.C.	19	French Med. Mil.	1

Total - 145

ENGAGEMENTS IN WHICH WON.

Engagement.	V.C.	D.S.O.	M.C.	D.C.M.	M.M.	Belg. C. de G.	Fr. Med. Mil.	M.S.M.
Anzac, 25/4/15	—	—	—	1	—	—	—	—
Helles, 8/5/15	—	—	—	1	—	—	—	—
Lone Pine, 9/8/15	4	—	—	2	1	—	—	—
Messines, 30/6/16	—	—	—	1	—	—	—	—
1st Pozieres, 25/7/16	—	2	—	4	7	—	1	—
2nd Pozieres, 18/8/16	—	—	2	1	2	—	—	—
Raid, 30/9/16	—	—	1	1	2	—	—	—
Ligny-Thilloy, 24/2/17	—	—	1	—	1	—	—	—
21/4/17	—	—	—	—	—	1	—	—
Polygon Wood, 20/9/17	—	—	1	—	12	—	—	—
Broonseinde, 4/10/17	—	—	4	2	14	—	—	—
17/12/17	—	—	—	1	1	—	—	—
Strazelle, 13/6/18	—	—	1	1	—	—	—	—
Aug. 9, 1918, Vauvillers	—	—	2	2	23	—	—	—
Aug. 11, 1918, Lihon	—	—	2	2	8	—	—	—
Aug. 26, 1918	—	—	1	1	7	—	—	—
Sept. 16, 1917	—	—	—	—	—	—	—	1
General .. 1 C.M.G.	—	1	4	2	6	—	—	4
	4	3	19	22	84	1	1	5

CAPACITIES OF WINNERS.

	Infantry.	Signallers.	A.M.C. Stretcher-Bearers.	Transport
V.C.	4	—	—	—
D.S.O.	3	—	—	—
M.C.	18	—	1	—
D.C.M.	18	2	1	—
M.M.	42	23	11	7

Principal Engagement Casualties

	OFFICERS.		MEN.		
	Killed.	Wounded.	Killed.	Wounded.	Total
Landing, 25/4/15	4	13	184	327	528
Helles, 8/5/1915	6	7	82	172	267
Lone Pine, 9/8/15	1	13	78	293	384
1st Pozieres, July, 1916	2	10	52	265	329
2nd Pozieres, Aug., 1916	2	8	76	151	241
Ligny-Thilloy, 25/2/17	1	2	14	36	53
Polygon Wood, 20/9/17	5	6	56	149	216
Broonseinde, 4/10/17	3	13	92	171	279
Ravine, Dec., 1917 (gas)	—	10	5	81	96
Hazebrouck, April, 1918	2	3	30	73	108
Hazebrouck, June, 1918	—	2	6	47	55
Vauvillers, 9/8/18	10	5	78	169	263
August 25, 1918	—	6	12	128	146
September, 1918	—	2	3	32	37

TOTAL CASUALTIES OF THE BATTALION

Gallipoli (8 months)	14	52	400	957	1422
France (2½ years)	33	77	523	1653	2286
	47	129	923	2610	3708

NOMINAL ROLL
7th Battalion, 2nd Infantry Brigade, A.I.F.
1914-1918

Indicating Reg. No., Rank, Name in Full (with Honors) and Casualties.

A

74 L/Cpl Abbey, Fredk. Brien
  D.O.W. Cairo, 30/4/15
814 Pte Abbot, Wm. (stated to be Young, Geo. G.)
1901 Pte Abbott, Wm. James
2838 Pte Abell, Samuel
75 L/Cpl Aberdeen, Norm. E.
  K.I.A. Anzac, 25/4/15
1907 Pte Ackman, W. (stated to be Stead, Charles)
  D.O.W. at sea, 13/8/15
1501 Pte Acott, Thomas Richard
3001 Pte Adams, Henry H. E.
3542 Pte Adams, Henry Joseph
510 Pte Adams, John Knox
  K.I.A. Anzac, 25/4/15
1903 Pte Adams, Morgan
4126 ER/Cpl Adams, N. W.
6211 Pte Adams, Percy
3226 Pte Adams, Reg. Chas.
1966 Pte Adams, Roderick McL.
684 Pte Adams, Wm. Thomas
  K.I.A. Anzac, 25/4/15
2554 T. Cpl Addison, Harold G.
4128 L/Cpl Adkins, Roland E.
  K.I.A. France, 4/3/17
2776 Pte Agger, Arthur
768 J./Cpl Agnew, Roy James
6952 ER/Sgt Ahern, Maurice
7197 Pte Ainslie, Brodie
299 Pte Ainsworth, C. J.
1305 Pte Ainsworth, Wm. Ed.
6950 Pte Aiston, Percy Alfred
  K.I.A. France, 9/8/18
3002 Pte Akers, Joseph
  K.I.A. Belgium, 4/10/17
6215 Pte Alberry, Arthur W. F.
3005 Pte Alderson, Walter A.
1302 Pte Aldred, John
5027 Pte Aldridge, Harold
514 Pte Alexander, Archibald
  K.I.A. Anzac, 26/4/15
— Lieut Alexander, Eric C.
7591 Pte Alexander, Marshall G.
2556 Cpl Alford, Geo. Thomas
  K.I.A. Belgium, 4/10/17
4129 Pte Allen, Alexander
4132 L/Cpl Allan, Archie
  K.I.A. Belgium, 4/10/17
847 L/Cpl Allen Albert Ed.
  D.O.W. France, 10/5/17
2552 Pte Allen A. E. (M.M.)

7436 Pte Allen, Andrew J. P.
747 Pte Allen, Arthur Thomas
3543 Pte Allen, Alfred Wm.
818 Pte Anderson, Charles
— Lieut Anderson, Chas R. (M.I.D.)
3455 Pte Anderson, David
2502 Cpl Anderson, Donald C.
5646 L/Sgt Anderson, D. C. (M.M.)
7438 Pte Anderson, Donald R.
  K.I.A. France, 9/8/18
5247 L/Sgt Anderson, Fredk. B. (D.C.M.)
3004 L/Sgt Anderson, Geo. F.
  K.I.A. France, 13/4/18
772 Pte Anderson, James
  K.I.A. Anzac, 25/4/15
1303 Pte Anderson, John Ed.
  K.I.A. Anzac, 25/4/15
1904 Pte Anderson, John H.
2061 Pte Anderson, James N.
2558 Pte Anderson, John Thos.
6954 Pte Anderson, Leslie Alex.
  K.I.A. Belgium, 4/10/17
2485 Pte Anderson, Norman
3228 Sgt Allcorn, Herbert Ed.
201 L/Cpl Allison, John
1712 Pte Allshorn, Frank
4130 L/Cpl Amiet, Leonard A.
532 Dvr Allen, Ernest Robert
60640 Pte Allan, Francis
462 Pte Allen, John
  K.I.A. France, 24/7/16
3227 Pte Allen, James
2840 Pte Allen, John Reginald
5330 Sgt Cook Allen, Rchd. P.
391 Pte Allan, Wm. Henry
1611 Gnr Allen, William James
3006 Cpl Anderson, Arthur F.
  K.I.A. France, 18/8/16
— Lieut Anderson, G. (stated to be A. G. Anderson)
9 Dvr Anderson, Arthur P.
6456 Pte Anderson, Nairne E.
1905 Pte Anderson, Oswald B.
  K.I.A. France, 9/8/18
— Lieut Anderson, Roy
  Died Melb., 14/1/19
738 Pte Anderson, Robert
  K.I.A. Anzac, 25/4/15
805 Pte Anderson, Rasmus

139

804 Cpl Anderson, Rueben G.
2556 L/Cpl Anderson, Wm. A.
819 MT Dvr Anderson, W. H.
2554 Andrews, C. H.
    Died Etaples, 6/8/16
6211 ER/2/Cpl Andrews, E.
1503 Sgt. Andrews, George
    K.I.A. France, 19/7/16
4131 Pte Andrews, Norman J. (M.M.)
820 Pte Andrews, Roy
3678 Pte Andrews, Richard C.
6703 Pte Angus, George B.
516 Pte Angus, John Sinclair
    K.I.A. Anzac, 25/4/15
439 Dvr Anlezark, John Alex.
6457 Pte Annand, George
6214 Pte Annear, John William
55556 Pte Answerth, George H.
— Capt Anthony, Hugh C. (M.I.D.)
12 Pte Anthony, Wm. John
— 2/Lieut Appleton, Wm. T.
    K.I.A. France, 24/7/16
1504 Pte Apps, Alfred
6458 Pte Archbold, Stanley
680 Cpl Archer, Walter
2841 Pte Archer, William
7439 Pte Argall, Edward
5971 Pte Argyle, Wm. John M.
5972 Pte Armistead, Henry
    Died Boulogne, 13/2/17
202 Pte Armour, John
    K.I.A. Anzac, 25/4/15
329 Pte Armstrong, Alfred
    K.I.A. Gaza, 19/4/17
60639 Pte Armstrong, Alfred
5032 Pte Armstrong, Ernest
    K.I.A. Belgium, 5/10/17
6213 Pte Armstrong, James
2778 Pte Armstrong, Leonard
    K.I.A. France, 19/7/16
212 Sgt Armstrong, P. R.
2103 L/C Armstrong, T. H. W.
7110 Pte Armstrong, Thos. M.
55558 Pte Arnold, Arthur Mason
807 Pte Arnold, Norman Chas.
1216 C.S.M. Arroll, Geo. Chas.
77 Cpl Arroll, John Duncan
6951 Pte Arthur, Thomas Ed.
3007 Pte Ash, Alfred Allen
3008 Pte Ashby, Henry Walters
2779 Sgt Ashton, Ernest
    (C. de G., Belgian)
822 Pte Ashton, Francis H. G.
2559 Cpl Ashton, Sylvester
309 L/Cpl Aston, Francis T.
— Capt Aspinall, Wm. Robt. (R.M.O.) (M.C.)
    K.I.A. Belgium, 20/7/17
3229 Gnr Atkins, Fredk. Chas.
1107 Pte Atkins, Herbert Jos.
    K.I.A. Anzac, 8-9/8/15

26 Pte Atkins, Stanley James
    K.I.A. France, 9/8/18
2560 Pte Atkinson, Geo. Thos.
60641 Pte Atkinson, Thomas B.
5334 T/Sgt Atkinson, William
— 2/Lieut Attwood, Henry
    K.I.A. Belgium, 20/9/17
3233 Pte Attygale, Chas. Ed.
33 Pte Auchinachie, William
    D.O.W. Anzac, 9/5/15
1506 Pte Augustine, John
3009 Pte Audsley, John Donald
865 Sgt Ault, Edwin Joseph
    K.I.A. Anzac, 25/4/15
1906 Pte Austin, Arthur John
2066 Pte Austin, Harry
434 Dvr Avard, Carlton
2553 Pte Avery, George
    K.I.A. France, 25/7/16
5034 Cpl Axen, Charles Oscar

B

5033 L/Cpl Bacon, Bertram S.
3234 Pte Bailey, Alfred
2562 Sgt Bailey, Archibald D. (M.M.)
2578 Dvr Bailey, Allan Stewart
2563 Pte Bailey, Charles Henry
    K.I.A. France, 25/7/16
2561 Pte Baillie, Wm. McD.
60646 Pte Bain, Malcolm James
660 Pte Baird, David
    K.I.A. Anzac, 25/4/15
15 Pte Baker, Chas. Malcolm
3017 Pte Baker, David Arthur
    Died France, 19/2/19
2566 Pte Baker, Ernest
    K.I.A. Bel., 25-26/10/17
3521 Pte Baker, Eric Jack
6218 Pte Baker, Harry Hector
372 L/Cpl Baker, Harold R.
    D.O.W. Gal., 10/5/15
1908 Pte Baker, John Geo. V.
2564 Pte Baker, John Spink
3016 Dvr Baker, Leonard Geo.
2104 Pte Baker, Leonard Henry
    Died Cairo, 19/4/16
290 R.S.M. Baker, William (M.S.M., M.I.D.)
105 Dvr Baker, Wm. Thomas
473 Pte Balchin, Horace Robt.
2781 Dvr Balchin, Wm. Charles
1909 Pte Balderson, John
    K.I.A. Anzac, 8-9/8/15
900 Pte Baldwin, Alfred
    K.I.A. Anzac, 25/4/15
6718 Pte Baldwin, Albert Ed.
    K.I.A. France, 9/8/18
1012 Pte Baldwin, Ed. (stated to be Baldwin, Ed. M.)
    K.I.A. Gallipoli, 8/5/15

479 Pte Bale, Charles
   K.I.A. Anzac, 25/4/15
651 Sgt Ball, Albert (stated
   to be Ball, Alfred Albt.
881 Sgt Ball, George
   (D.C.M. and Bar, 1
   M.I.D.)
   K.I.A. France, 5/11/16
509 Pte Ball, Philip
4730 Sgt Ball, Robert Ernest
6617 Pte Ballagh, William
   Fleming (M.M.)
6217 Pte Ballantine, Henry
5983 Pte Ballard, Alfred E.
1623 Pte Ballard, Chas. H. S.
2564 Pte Balmain, Ivor
   K.I.A. France, 11/12/16
1620 Pte Bamford, H. W. R.
— Lieut Banks, Kenneth G.
   Died France, 4/3/19
6717 Pte Bannerman, Victor
   D.O.W. Belg., 22/9/17
2209 Pte Barker, Wm. Thomas
   K.I.A. Anzac, 8-9/8/15
3236 Cpl Barkla, Joseph Harold
   Died after discharge
— M.O. Capt. Barlow, Douglas L. (M.C.)
5473 L/Cpl Barnard, Victor A.
   (M.M.)
   K.I.A. France, 9/8/18
565 Pte Barnes, George
   K.I.A. Anzac, 26/5/15
6470 Pte Barnes, George
2896 Pte Barnes, Harrie H.
   K.I.A. France, 8/8/16
2229 Pte Barnett, Allan R.
   K.I.A. Anzac, 8-9/8/15
5036 Pte Barnett, Frank Jessell
610 Pte Barnett, Victor
   K.I.A. Gallipoli, 8/5/15
6719 Pte Barr, James Edward
3237 Cpl Barr, Stanley Howard
2565 Pte Barrand, Richard E.
611 Pte Barratt, Charles
7443 Pte Barrett, Alf. Leonard
76 Pte Barrett, Edward
   Died after discharge
2567 Pte Barber, George F. T.
   D.O.W. France, 5/8/16
3014 Pte Barber, James Maxwell
7092 Pte Barber, Roy Alex.
10 Dvr Barber, William
3012 Pte Barber, Wm. Ernest
   D.O.W. France, 19/7/16
7198 Pte Barbor, Samuel James
3999 A/Sgt Barbour, William
849 Pte Barclay, Roy A.
   K.I.A. Anzac, 8-9/8/15
5336 Pte Barclay, Thos. H.
   D.O.W. Belgium, 4/10/17
512 Pte Bardioux, Joseph
   D.O.W., Alex., 30/4/15
5337 Pte Barfoot, Thomas

7442 Pte Barker, Frank
— Capt Barker, Harold A.
   (D.C.M.)
5656 Pte Barker, Jesse
1308 Pte Barker, James Gristy
   K.I.A. France, 19/7/16
5338 Pte Barrett, John Leonard
6229 Pte Barrett, Norman H.
5653 Pte Barritt, Frederick
3231 Pte Barrkman, Harry
3003 Pte Barrow, William Jas.
6216 Pte Barry, Albert
358 Pte Barry, John Francis
   D.O.W. Alex., 11/5/15
381 Pte Barry, John Gerald
   K.I.A. France, 21/8/16
1118 Dvr Barry, Martin A.
564 Pte Barry, Richard
1910 Pte Barry, Rupert Allen
736 L/Cpl Bartlett, Albert
   K.I.A. France, 18/8/16
1313 Pte Barton, Anthony N.
   K.I.A. France, 18/8/16
6963 Pte Baster, John Horton
— Major Bastin, Hector E.
   (M.C.)
60643 Pte Bastion, John Francis
3260 Pte Batch, James
7344 Pte Batchelor, Harold G.
7202 Pte Bates, Ernest M.
375 L/Sgt Bates, Robert B.
   (M.M. and Bar)
1307 Cpl Bateson, George
3238 Pte Batten, Ernest
1019 Spr Batten, Richard J. V.
2582 Pte Battersby, John Henry
6230 Pte Battley, William
1866 Pte Batty, John
   Died after discharge
7446 Pte Batty, James
6722 Pte Baxter, Leslie L.
   K.I.A. Belgium, 20/9/17
1658 Pte Baxter, Thomas Wm.
   K.I.A. Belgium, 20/9/17
203 Pte Bayles, Frederick
   K.I.A. Gallipoli, 8/5/15
— 2/Lt Bayntun, Arthur Rolt
   D.O.W. France, 30/6/17
2580 Pte Bayson, George Ellis
1312 Cpl-Capt Bazeley, E. T.
   (M.C., M.I.D., 2)
882 Pte Beachley, Hubert G.
   K.I.A. Gallipoli, 25/4/15
1315 Pte Beadle, Ernest John
   K.I.A. Gal., 8-9/8/15
2565 Pte Beal, Cyril
7112 Pte Beal, James
55561 Pte Beale, Geo. H. (stated
   to be Burridge, Geo. H.)
4146 Pte Beard, Fredk. Arthur
   D.O.W. Eng., 30/7/16
6706 Pte Beard, Thomas
5340 Pte Beard, Thomas Robert
5341 Pte Beasley, Robert

5978	Pte Beattie, William	127	Pte Bible, Harold
2562	Pte Beattie, Wm. Stanley	6220	Pte Bickerton, Geo. Wm.
4135	Pte Beck, Norman R.	9	Sgt Bier, Eli William
190	Pte Beckensall, Walter H.	652	Pte Biggs, Bertram H.
	K.I.A. Gal., 25/4/15	3241	Pte Biggs, Herbert Alfd.
6619	Pte Beddell, George		K.I.A. Belgium, 4/10/17
	K.I.A. Belgium, 4/10/17	1513	Pte Biggs, Lionel
—	Lieut Beech, Albert E.	3243	T/Cpl Bignell, Jack Wilfd.
1509	Pte Bees, John Francis	133	S/Sgt Billinge, Francis R.
6962	Pte Begley, Arthur A. A.	2561	Pte Billington, Robt. Hy.
3254	Pte Beinke, Edward Emil	7103	Pte Binch, Arthur
78	Cpl Beith, John Humphrey	—	Lieut Binder, Harold A. L.
	K.I.A. Gallipoli, 12/7/15		(M.C.)
6956	Pte Bell, Arthur	673	Pte Binning, Albert
3239	Pte Bell, Algernon F.		D.O.W. Cairo, 17/5/15
	D.O.W. France, 24/7/16	566	Pte Bird, Albert Clarence
829	Pte Bell, Allan Ross	2581	Sgt Bird, Edward James
	K.I.A. Belgium, 4/10/17		K.I.A., France, 6/11/16
2585	Cpl Bell, Charles	6463	Pte Bird, Sydney Clarence
2587	Pte Bell, Charles Henry	725	Pte Birkin, Conrad
1717	L/Cpl Bell, Frederick T.		D.O.W. France, 17/4/18
1116	Pte Bell, John Charles	3244	Pte Birkin, Fred Percival
	K.I.A. Anzac, 25/4/15		D.O.W. France, 6/5/16
79	Pte Bell, Wm. Richard	695	Sgt Birrell, William H.
3004	Pte Bellas, Harry		(D.C.M.)
2563	Pte Bellesini, Andrew		K.I.A. Belgium, 4/10/17
2669	Pte Bellesini, Joseph	1719	Cpl Bishop, John
	D.O.W. Eng., 13/3/17	5976	Pte Bishop, Sydney
2560	Pte Bellingham, Phillip J.	6959	Pte Bishop, Thomas Ross
	K.I.A. France, 19/7/16	5984	Cpl Bisset, George Fredk.
1718	Pte Belsey, Bertie Robert		(M.M.)
	(M.M.)	2561	Pte Bisset, George W.
1510	Sgt Belsey, John Robert	55569	Pte Black, Albert
	K.I.A. Anzac, 9/8/15	2564	Pte Black, Lawrence J.
1436	Pte Benham, Frederick R.	2568	Pte Black, Mathew W.
	K.I.A. France, 27/4/18	5985	Cpl Black, Robt. L. C.
3018	Pte Benham, Hector A.		K.I.A. France, 9/8/18
3690	Pte Benham, Herman C.	2933	Pte Black, Thos. Jas. M.
2579	Cpl Benjamin, Leslie J. W.	1514	Sgt Blackburn, Francis
	D.O.W. France, 16/8/18		(M.S.M., M.I.D.)
3240	Pte Bennett, Clyde James	597	Pte Blackburn, Jack
	K.I.A. France, 19/7/16		K.I.A. Gallipoli, 25/4/15
2106	Pte Bennett, Geo. Henry	49	Cpl Blackman, Percy O.
1912	Pte Bennett, John		(M.M.)
6219	Pte Bennett, Peter John	3008	Pte Blackmore, R. W. E.
	D.O.W. France, 11/3/17	28	Pte Blackney, Wm. John
5342	Pte Bennett, Royden L. C.		D.O.W. France, 25/12/16
	K.I.A. France, 18/8/16	1515	C.Q.M.S. Blackwood, R.
7200	Pte Bennett, William	5041	Pte Blaikie, William
1511	Pte Bennetts, Fred James		K.I.A. France, 18/8/16
1310	ER/Sgt Benson, E. P.	2109	Pte Blain, John
3261	Dvr Benson, James	80	Sgt. Blair, Reg. Thomas.
1512	Pte Bentley, William	6707	Pte Blake, Francis Thos.
653	Sgt Benton, John	6958	Pte Blake, Sydney
1186	Pte Bergman, Gustave H.		D.O.W., Belg., 4/10/17
384	L/Cpl Berriman, Edward	403	L/Cpl Blake, Sydney L.
770	Pte Berry, Reginald James	6715	Pte Blake, William Chas.
17	Pte Besemeres, Howard V.	2558	Spr Blakey, Harold
1618	Pte Betts, George Victor	6946	Pte Blanche Edwd. Jas.
1119	Pte Bevan, Albert Ernest	204	Pte Bland, Lawrence
310	ER/2/Cpl Bevan, G. H.	688	Pte Blannin-Ferguson, Daryl Gardner
81	Pte Bevan, Herbert R.		K.I.A. Gallipoli, 8/5/15
5038	Pte Beevan, James Patk. (stated to be Bevan, James Patrick)		

687 Pte Blannin-Ferguson,
       Lance Sisca
       K.I.A. Anzac, 25/4/15
1721 Dvr Blay, William Hy.
5343 Pte Blencowe, Francis T.
       K.I.A. France, 31/10/16
— Mjr. Blezard, Ivie
— Lieut Blick, Leslie Colin
       K.I.A., Anzac, 25/4/15
7343 Dvr Bligh, William Hy.
3245 Pte Blowes, Walter H.
6221 Pte Blundell, Howard D.
4136 Pte Blundey, Edward
       K.I.A. France, 25/7/16
1724 L/Cpl Blythe, Henry
       (M.M. and Bar)
7207 Pte Boak, William J.
2575 Pte Boase, Thos. W.
205 L/Cpl Boase, William V.
       K.I.A. Gallipoli, 8/5/15
3246 Pte Bohan, Patk. Leo
612 Cpl Bohun, Harry
       (M.M.)
773 Pte Bolitho, Arthur
30 Pte Bolton, Chas. Henry
340 L/Cpl Bond, Reg. Rupert
       K.I.A. Gallipoli, 25/4/15
2559 Pte Bond, Ralph Richard
       K.I.A. France, 19/7/16
501 Pte Bone, Alfred Wm.
1306 Pte Bonham, Roy
       K.I.A. Gallipoli, 25/4/15
4137 L/Cpl Bonner, Percival C.
       K.I.A. Belg., 4/10/17
4144 L/Cpl Bonney, Francis J.
— Lieut. Bonney, Leslie
1845 Sgt. Bonning, Leslie C.
       Died after Discharge
654 Sgt Bonser, Ruben Jas.
       (M.S.M.)
6222 Pte Bonuda, Wm. Joseph
956 Pte Boot, Arthur
       D.O.W. at Sea, 27/5/15
6223 Pte. Booth, John
— Lieut. Booth, William
       K.I.A. Belgium, 4/10/17
1913 Pte Booth, Thomas
       K.I.A. Gall., 8-9/8/15
6620 Pte Borbridge, James C.
       D.O.W., Belg, 5/10/17
6224 Pte Borella, Charles
— 2/Lieut Borrowman, J. K.
— Capt-Chap Bossence, I. E.
       (M.C.)
1674 Pte Bott, Alfred
4737 Pte Bottomley, Edwd. E.
25A Pte Boucher, William J.
       K.I.A. Anzac, 25/4/15
2576A Sgt Bourke, Chas. E.
2578 Pte Bourke, Dom. V. M.
405 Cpl Bourke, Lawrence J.
885 Pte Bourke, James A.
       K.I.A. Anzac. 5/7/15
7448 Pte Boveird, Robert A.

59 W.O. Bowden, Henry
       Died after Discharge
3248 L/Cpl Dvr Bowen, D. J.
820 Pte Bowling, F. B.
1517 Pte Bowers, C. G.
229 Pte Bowers, L. W.
1210 Pte Bowes, W. E.
5043 Pte Bowles, Owen Viv.
— Lieut Bowman, Frank S.
       (M.I.D.)
55567 Pte Bowring, George A.
— Capt Bowtell-Harris, J. F.
       (M.C.)
861 C.S.M. Box, William R.
       (M.S.M., M.I.D.)
4138 Pte Boyd, Daniel Douglas
       Died after Discharge
6225 L/Cpl Bovd, James
771 L/Cpl Boys, Frederick
1114 Pte Bracy, Philip Henry
2577 Pte Braddish, Watson H.
539 Pte Bradley, Robert C.
       K.I.A. Anzac. 25/4/15
2565 Cpl Branagan, Bernard F
5345 ER/Cpl Brand, Andrew
342 Pte Brander, Alex.
2107 Pte Brauer, Ludwig L.
3249 Artif. B/Smith Bray, J.
5045 Pte Bray, William
2326 Pte Bray, William Roy
       K.I.A. France, 15/7/16
7452 Pte Breakey, Stanley E.
4439 Pte Breen, Percy John
7453 Pte Brenchley, Geo. S.
7191 Pte Brennan, Fredk. Geo.
6725 Pte Brennan, Peter
2557 Pte Brennan, Timothy
       Died at Sea, 9/8/17
2583 Cpl Brennand, Francis M.
       D.O.W. France, 11/2/1:
1914 Pte Breslin Thomas
       K.I.A. France, 19/7/16
4139 Pte Brewer, Samuel T.
4148 Pte Bride, Benj. Wm.
5347 Pte Bridges, Ernest Amos
7454 Pte Brien, Archibald J.
       K.I.A. France, 6-7/6/18
3250 Pte Brierley, Chas. West
36 Pte Briggs, Henry C. W.
3009 Pte Bright, Bertram L.
4133 Cpl Brighton, Arthur P.
       K.I.A. France, 17/4/18
2108 Pte Brighton, Ernest C.
1654 Pte Brilliant, James
1518 Pte Brilliant, Neil
2327 Pte Brinckmann, H. C.
       K.I.A. France, 19/7/16
6666 Pte Brinkhurst, Benj. J. R.
2842 Pte Brittain, George
60649 Pte Brittain, William
2586 Pte Brittingham, Hy. H.
206 Pte Brock, Horace Harold
       D.O.W. Alex., 10/5/15

83 Pte Brock, John Alexander
    K.I.A. Anzac, 2/9/15
7455 Pte Brodie, Andrew C.
6232 L/Cpl Brodrick, A. MacK.
6233 Cpl Brodrick, John H.
3693 Gnr Bromilow, Thorold J.
207 ER/S/Sgt Bromley, C. E.
4746 Dvr Bromley, Walter G.
883 Sgt Bromyard, William
— Capt Brookes, Leslie R.
    (M.I.D.)
389 Pte Brookes, Vernon T.
    K.I.A. Anzac, 25/4/15
3316 Pte Brooks, Frank Sydney
4442 Pte Brooks, Robt. Joseph
    K.I.A. France, 25/9/1;
2110 Sgt Brooks, Thos. Victor
2567 Pte Brooks, William
— Lieut. Brooksbank, W. H.
    (M.M.)
2874 Pte Broom, Wm. George
1723 Pte Brown, Albert Edwd.
454 Gnr Brown, Alfd. John T.
2584 L/Cpl Brown, Alex. M.
    K.I.A. France, 19/7/16
6709 Pte Brown, Alfred Victor
    D.O.W. France, 15/4/18
89 R.Q.M.S. Brown, Chas. G.
    (C. de G., Belg., M.I.D.)
6961 Pte Brown, Duncan R.
    K.I.A. Belg., 5/10/17
2844 Pte Brown, Ernest
55571 Gnr Brown, Edward
681 Pte Brown, Francis G.
3265 L/Cpl Brown, George E.
1311 Pte Brown, Harry
2587 L/Cpl Brown, Henry
3266 Pte Brown, Herbert D.
    K.I.A. France, 26/1/17
2105 Pte Brown, Herbert E.
    Died France, 26/3/17
— Lieut Brown, Henry J. T.
    K.I.A. France, 25/7/16
5975 Pte Brown, Horace Wm.
    K.I.A. France, 6/3/17
2574 Pte Brown, Joseph
1021 Sgt Brown, Stanley
3251 Pte Brown, Stanley R.
60650 Pte Brown, Thos. Ernest
3254 Pte Browne, Walter F. S.
3253 Dvr Brown, Walter
4145 Cpl Brownlie, Matthew
    D.O.W. France, 1/3/17
2780 Pte Bruce, Douglas
    (M.M.)
2703 Pte Bruce, Robert
1865 Pte Bruce, Robert John
    K.I.A. Anzac, 1/9/15
2568 C.Q.M.S. Brunning, P. J.
884 Pte Brunton, Fredk. F.
1720 Pte Bryan, William
6965 L/Cpl Bryant, Herbert E.
6711 Pte Bryant, Thomas
1916 Pte Bryning, Arthur H.

3255 Gnr Brydon, Lindsay C.
    (M.M.)
4143 Pte Buchanan, Eric Thos.
    K.I.A. France, 25/7/16
2590 Cpl Buffrey, George
7456 Pte Bugden, Richard C.
— Lieut. Buggy, Raymond
3256 Pte Bull, Edward Leslie
    K.I.A. France, 19/7/16
3268 Pte Bulling, Thomas Wm.
84 Cpl Bullock, Jas. Norman
5652 Sgt Bulmer, Edward C.
7457 Pte Buls, James
— Lieut. Bunbury, Austin E.
— Capt Bunbury, H. L. A.
45 L/Cpl Bunning, Robt. A.
    K.I.A. France, 25/7/16
208 L/Cpl. Bunting, Albert E.
1852 Gnr Burgan, Thomas
55570 Pte Burge, Thomas
1917 Pte Burgess, Joseph
    D.O.W. at Sea, 10/8/15
837 Pte Burke, Edward M.
1519 Pte Burn, Alexander
5651 Pte Burrell, George
2569 Pte Burrett, Ernest Geo.
— Lieut. Burrow, Sydney V.
— Lieut Burrows, Fredk. A.
    (M.M.)
55566 Pte Burrows, Fredk. H.
1240 Pte Burrows, Thos. Hy.
    D.O.W., France, 24/8/18
— Capt Bursey, T. F. McL.
    (M.C.)
210 Pte Burt, William George
    K.I.A. Anzac, 25/4/15
384 Cpl Burton, Alex. Stewart
    (V.C., M.I.D.)
    K.I.A. Gall., 8-9/8/15
— Capt Burton, Clerke C.
    Died England, 13/12/18
2570 Cpl Burton, David Robt.
2572 Pte Burton, Francis Robt.
40 L/Cpl Busch, Stanley F.
3267 Pte Butler, Arthur
    K.I.A. France, 19/7/16
55574 Pte Butler, Alfred V.
2112 Pte Burnes, Frederick
    K.I.A., Belg., 4/10/17
2325 Pte Burns, Allan
6468 Pte Burns, Alex. Eric
209 Pte Burns, David
    D.O.W. at Sea, 7/6/15
1120 Cpl Burns, John Rogers
2030 *K.I.A. France, 3/5/17*
6622 Pte Burns, John Walter
2113 Pte Burns, Peter Robert
    K.I.A., Gall., 8-9/8/15
7205 Pte Burns, Peter Raymond
599 Pte Burns, Robt. C.
6623 Pte Burns, William
    D.O.W. France, 15/8/18
1314 Pte Butler, Herbt. A. K.
    K.I.A., Gall., 8/5/15

6714 Pte Butt, Arthur Thos.
    K.I.A. France, 27/4/18
423 Pte Butt, Richard
    K.I.A. Anzac, 25/4/15
421
25813 Cpl Butler, John Francis
326 Pte Butler, John Patrick
3264 Pte Butler, William
2573 Pte Butterfield, Arthur J.
886 L/Cpl Butterworth, E. T.
86 Sgt. Butterworth, John A.
55564 Pte Bye, Alfred
1853 Pte Byrne, Charles M.
    Died Dublin, 4/11/18
— Lieut Byrne, Evelyn S.
1117 Pte Byrne, Gerald
    D.O.W. Alex., 12/8/15
— Lieut Byrne, John Blane
1918 ER/2/Cpl Byrne, John J.
398 ER/2/Cpl Byrne, R. J. M.
    K.I.A. Anzac, 25/4/15
1722 Cpl Byrne, Thomas
    K.I.A. France, 17/6/18
56 Pte Byrne, William B.
2329 Dvr Byrnes, George
841 Dvr Byron, Abraham J.
537 Pte Birkill, Archibald
    K.I.A. Gall., 8/5/15

C

6240 Pte Caccianiga, C. V.
1668 Cpl Caddy, Frank B.
    D.O.W. Malta, 20/8/15
— 2/Lieut Caddy, James
    (D.C.M., M.M., M.I.D.)
    K.I.A. France, 9/8/18
4166 Pte Cadger, William R.
4160 Pte Cadwallader, H. T.
    K.I.A. France, 18/8/16
1634A Pte Cahir, Michael P.
    K.I.A. France, 16/12/16
3259A Pte Cain, Albert
4167 Pte Cain, George Phillip
    K.I.A. France, 22-25/7/16
1646 Pte Cain, Herbert
    (M.M.)
4162 Pte Cairns, James
887 Cpl Cakebread, Thos. M.
474 L/Cpl Calcutt, Gerald
    K.I.A., Gall., 24/5/15
7459 Pte Calder, Edward L.
3282 Pte Calder, John Alex.
1669 Gnr Calder, Robert McI.
851 Pte Caldwell, Fredk. H.
1629 Pte Callaghan, Albert
3269 Pte Callander, Thos. A.
613 Pte Callaway, William
402 Sgt Calley, Francis Alex.
2352
5051 Spr Cambridge, E. G. H.
7463 Pte Cameron, Alex. T.
5661 Pte Cameron, Gordon D.
88 L/Cpl Cameron, G. P.
    K.I.A. Gall., 12/7/15

1260 Pte Cameron, James
2618A Pte Cameron, Norman
    K.I.A. France 19/7/16
723 Cpl Cameron, Wm. Hugh
4155 ER/S/Sgt Camm, P. E.
55575 Pte Campbell, Andrew
1919 Pte Campbell, Colin
— Lieut Campbell, Fredk. C.
    (C. de G., Belg., M.I.D.)
912B Lieut Campbell, John B.
— Mjr Campbell, John C.
    (D.S.O., M.I.D.)
    Medical Officer
4170 Pte Campbell, John R.
3270 Pte Campbell, James S.
    D.O.W. France, 13/6/18
— Lieut. Campbell, James W.
1637 Pte Campbell, William
— Capt Campbell, Wm. B.
    (M.I.D.)
1632 Pte Campfield, James
    Died after Discharge
2118 Dvr Canna, Ray
1023 Pte Cantwell, Robert
888 Pte Cantwell, Wm. R.
    K.I.A., Anzac, 25/4/15
3286 Pte Cardwell, R. W.
    D.O.W., France, 20/8/16
1728 Pte Carew, James
    D.O.W. Anzac, 5/8/15
2116 Pte Carey, John
880 C.S.M. Carey, John Leslie
471 Pte Carless, James N.
    K.I.A. Anzac, 25/4/15
— Lieut. Carlile, Edward K.
    D.O.W., France, 28/2/17
— 2/Lt Carmichael, T. McL.
    D.O.W., Gall., 8/5/15
6235 Pte Carney, James
    K.I.A., France, 25/2/17
4153 Pte Carnie, Thomas Fdk.
    D.O.W., France, 1/11/16
1735 Pte Carpenter, Claude
    K.I.A., Belgium, 4/10/17
488 Cpl Carlile, Joseph
— Lieut Carlisle, Algernon H.
7461 Pte Carlsson, Sven Eugen
2604 L/Cpl Carlyon, H. R.
1311 Pte Carmody, Matthew
2270
1670 Sgt Carnaghan, John E.
— Lieut Carne, Percival R.
3010 Cpl. Carne, Thomas
457 Pte Carroll, M. D. E.
2117 Pte Carroll, Michael F.
    D.O.W. at Sea, 12/8/15
1324 Pte Carroll, Patrick
    K.I.A., Belgium, 4/10/17
55581 Pte Carroll, Wm. M. I.
1869 Cpl. Carruthers, David
603 L/Cpl Carson, George R.
6741 Pte Carswell, Percy John
6472 Pte Carter, Edward V.
    K.I.A., France, 12/8/18

2592 Sgt Carter, Frederick (M.M.)
2570 Sgt Carter, John
5052 Pte Carter, Leslie M.
    D.O.W., Belgium, 26/10/17
374 Pte Carter, Stratten John
    K.I.A., Anzac, 25/4/15
1920 Pte Carter, William W.
3021 Pte Carter, Wm. Wilfred
    D.O.W., France, 24/8/18
59 Pte Cartledge, Benjamin
2614 L/Cpl Cartledge, Leonard
889 L/Cpl. Cartner, Alfred J.
    D.O.W., France, 9/8/16
698 Pte Cartwright, Arthur E.
6726 Pte Cartwright, George F.
525 Pte Cartwright, Thos. H.
5670 Pte Casbolt, Harold N.
4452 Pte Case, Geoffrey
4164 Pte Casey, Alfred (M.M.)
    D.O.W., France, 26/12/16
2603 Sgt. Casey, George H.
5669 Pte Casey, James
2593 L/Cpl. Casey, John Alfred
    K.I.A., France, 23/8/18
5665 L/Cpl Casey, William J.
1530 Pte Carnegie, Bert.
    Died after discharge
60656 Pte Carnie, Robert Young
6727 Pte Caro, Leslie
6737 Pte Carpenter, John
1731 Pte Carr, Robert
2875 Pte Carrick, Harold Ed.
2715 Pte Carroll, Edward
674 Pte Carroll, Herbert S.
1126 Pte Carroll, James
2119 Carroll, John Bernard
    D.O.W., France, 25/7/16
1323 Pte Carroll, John Charles
    K.I.A., Gall., 8/5/15
1122 Pte Cary, Claude
— Chaplain Cashman, W. P.
307 Pte Cass, Denis
4169 Pte Cass, Joseph
417 Pte Cass, Peter
6624 Pte Catley, Harold N.
2608 L/Cpl. Caton, Robert
2121 Pte Causon, Ernest A.
2596 Pte Causon, Wm. Henry
493 Pte Cavanagh, George C.
    D.O.W. at Sea, 26/4/15
55582 Pte Cavendish, William
66 Pte Cawley, Alfred
    K.I.A., Belgium, 4/10/17
740 Cpl. Cawthorn, R. O.
5359 Pte Cazaly, Albert Geo.
1520 Pte Ceirini, John
375 Pte Chadwick, John E.
55590 Pte Chaffey, John H.
2598 Chalmers, David Alex.
    K.I.A., France, 20/8/16
2590 Chalmers, Harry Wm.

5053 Chalmers, Frank
    K.I.A., France, 17/8/16
5054 Chalmers, John Peter
2599 Pte Chamberlain, R. P.
1521 Spr Chambers, Alfred E.
60660 Pte Chambers, Francis
648 Pte Chambers, H. H. H.
    D.O.W., Anzac, 28/4/15
2605 Chambers, Ll. Edwd.
55579 Pte Chambers, W. J.
55578 Pte Chandler, Arthur
2122 Dvr Chandler, Horace A.
2620 Pte Chanter, Arthur E.
    K.I.A., France, 25/7/16
— 2/Lt Chapman, Earl H. S.
    D.O.W. at Sea, 30/4/15
3544 Pte Chapman, Geo. S. S.
6731 Far Chapman, Henry C.
1074 Pte Chappell, S. J.
    K.I.A., Anzac, 11/9/15
2610 Cpl Charles, Andrew
55583 Pte Charles, Edward H.
1452 Pte Charles, Noah Willie
1318 Private Charles, Stanley
391 Pte Charlesworth, S. G.
    D.O.W. at Sea, 26/4/15
800 Pte Charlton, F. A.
    K.I.A., Anzac, 25/4/15
2601 Cpl Charlton, George V.
7215 Pte Charlton, James D.
2600 L/Cpl. Charlton, Thomas
    Died France, 4/3/17
1247 Pte Charouneau, A. W.
495 Pte Charters, Richard E.
2334 Sgt Charville, John ("D.C.M.")
6607 Pte Cheater, Ernest G.
    D.O.W., France, 9/8/18
5662 Pte Checkley, Arthur L.
2877 Pte Cheel, Fdk. Henry
7464 Pte Cheeseman, Alfred S.
60652 Pte Cheevers, James
6482 Pte Chenhall, Harold B.
    D.O.W., France, 12/8/18
2602 Pte Chenoweth, Edgar W.
    K.I.A., France, 27/6/16
1023 Pte Cherry, Stephen F.
2115 Pte Chesterfield, H. T.
4172 Pte Checkett, Herbert
4158 Pte Chibnall, Arthur L.
    K.I.A., France, 25/7/16
1123 Pte Child, Walter Owen
1112 Pte Childs, Earl Stanley
2619 Act/Cpl Chilton, John R.
    K.I.A., France, 17/8/16
1922 L/Cpl Chisholm, David
7465 Pte Chirnside, Russell M.
2612 Pte Christensen, Patrick
1316 Pte Christie, Alex
    Died after discharge
6474 Pte Christie, Clive John
    K.I:A., France, 9/8/18
3745 Pte Christie, Edwin

3271 Cpl Christie, George S.
3020 Pte Christie, Robert
    K.I.A., France, 19/8/16
6234 Pte Christmas, Robert
    K.I.A., Belgium, 26/10/17
6969 Cpl Christy, Henry
2591 Pte Chunder, Bervin Geo.
2595 Pte Church, Robert H.
    K.I.A., Belgium, 4/10/17
55592 Pte Church, Thomas E.
1727 Pte Clague, Thomas Wm.
2719 Pte Clancy, John L.
1308 Cpl Clapp, Arthur
5056 Pte Clark, Arthur
6245 Pte Clarke, Albert E.
7466 Pte Clarke, Alfred Ern.
320 Pte Clarke, Bert
4224
2613 Pte Clarke, Clarence A. J.
3289 Pte Clarke, Charles E.
3290 Pte Clarke, Charles Wm.
3278 Dvr Clark, David Wm.
524 L/Cpl Clark, Ernest
2611 Pte Clarke, Ernest C.
884 Pte Clarke, Francis A.
2260
    K.I.A., Anzac, 17/8/15
2847 Sgt Clark, Francis A.
6728 Pte Clarke, George S.
6736 L/Cpl. Clarke, Ivo Victor
2125 Pte Clark, Joseph
2622 Pte Clark, John
    K.I.A., France, 16/5/16
6236 Pte Clark, Joseph
6732 Pte Clarke, John Geo. L.
736 Pte Clarke, James Robt.
    K.I.A., France, 11/4/18
3011 Sgt Clark, Leslie J. G.
    K.I.A., France, 15/5/18
6730 Pte Clarke, Norman T.
    D.O.W., France, 17/4/18
1080 Pte Clarke, Oliver H.
2124 Pte Clark, Robert
2333 Pte Clarke, Rowland
55594 Pte Clark, Reuben
1325 Pte Clark, Stuart
6478 Pte Clark, Stanley
520 Pte Clark, Thomas
6396 Pte Clarke, William G.
3291 Pte Clarke, William H.
1522 Pte Clarkin, William
1725 Clarkson, Frederick
    D.O.W., Germany, 26/8/16
897 Er/S/Sgt Clarkson, H. A.
2870 Pte Claxton, Cecil Chas.
68 Sgt Cleeland, A. H. MacA.
890 Pte Cleland, Thos. A.
748 Pte Clements, Alfred
2617 Pte Clements, Cyril H.
60653 Pte Clencie, Wm. Albert
2572 Pte Clews, John Milton
    D.O.W., France, 19/8/16
26 Pte Clifford, Henry A.
894 Dvr Clifford, Wm. D.

2605A L/Cpl Clifton, Norman L.
55595 Er/2/Cpl Clinch, Leslie
2123 Pte Clinton, John
2230 Pte Clissold, Samuel E.
    D.O.W. Alexandria, 15/8/15
— Lieut Clowe, Clarence P.
5799 Pte Clowe, Robt. J. J.
    K.I.A., France, 20/2/17
588 Sgt Clutterbuck, Edwd. J.
7462 Er/2/Cpl. Clutterbuck,
    Henry Trevor
895 C.S.M. Clyne, Arthur D.
587 Pte Coall, James Michael
5819
23 Er/Cpl Coates, Albert E.
2623 Pte Coates, Lawrence
    K.I.A., France, 18/8/16
1121 Cpl Cobbledick, R. W.
4151 Pte Cochrane, Wm. A.
3272 Pte Cockayne, Robt. E.
1321 Pte Cockerall, Thomas
688   (stated to be
    Cockerall, Thomas L.)
1635 Pte Cockroft. A. J. B.
2247 Pte Coffey, Harry L.
    (enlisted as A. Smith)
35 Pte Cohen, Arthuh V.
211 S/Sgt Cohen, Cyril Wolf
1524 Gnr Cole, Albert Edward
55588 Pte Cole, Arthur Henry
3015 Sgt Cole, Frank
    (M.M.)
6973 Pte Cole, Harry Theodore
    D.O.W., France, 9/8/18
3273 Pte Coleman, Patrick
373 Pte Coles, Frederick S.
183 Cpl. Collier, John S. G.
    (Lieut Imperial Army)
320 Pte Collings, John
368 L/Sgt Collins, Alfred J.
    K.I.A., Anzac, 25/4/15
55591 Dvr Collins, Claude Wm.
324 Pte Collins, David D.
853 Pte Collins, George A.
5660 Sgt. Collins, Noel Tracy
1730 Pte Collins, Thomas
    (stated to be Manning, C.)
1454 Pte Collins, Thos. J.
5664 Cpl Collins, Walter A.
1160 Pte Collinson, Wm. R.
    K.I.A., Anzac, 7/8/15
4165 Pte Collis, David
3293 Pte Combe, Norman H.
891 Pte Comte, Albert E.
    K.I.A., Anzac, 25/4/15
5658 Pte Conboy, James Thos.
— Lieut Conder, Walter T.
2783 Dvr Condick, Ernest S.
1729 Pte Condon, Wm. Jos.
    K.I.A., Anzac, 8-9/8/15
2717 Pte Congdon, Charles
6479 Pte Coningsby, E. H.
    K.I.A., France, 23/8/18

1326 Pte Conlen, John
   K.I.A., Anzac, 9/8/15
2607 Cpl. Connell, James D.
— Mjr Connelly, Eric W.
   (D.S.O., M.I.D. 2)
   D.O.W., France, 9/9/18
2621 Sgt Connop, Edward Jos.
   D.O.W., France, 11/10/17
2598 Pte Connor, Edward E.
1734 Dvr Connors, John
668 Pte Conroy, Joseph
1924 Pte Conroy, Leo Joseph
2127 Pte Conway, Hubert
6480 Pte Cook, Arthur E. M.
2607 Pte Cooke, Charles
   K.I.A., France, 24/8/18
1322 Dvr Cook, Charles W.
2210 Pte Cook, James Leslie
1525 Pte Cook, John Thomas
2000
184 Dvr Cook, Philip E.
   (M.M.)
707 Pte Cook, Robert
   K.I.A., France, 27/5/16
6981 Pte Cook, Robert
   K.I.A., France, 13/8/18
2335 Pte Cooke, Robert Edwd.
2616 Pte Cooke, Ralph T.
   K.I.A., France, 29/6/16
4475 L/Cpl Cook, Thos. C.
   K.I.A., France, 9/8/18
3014 Pte Cook, William
   K.I.A., France, 23/3/17
60657 Pte Cook, Wm. A.
2126 Pte Cook, William H.
6398 Pte Cook, William John
3294 Pte Coombe, George
4174 Pte Coombes, George R.
4756 Pte Coombs, Alfred Baker
   D.O.W., France, 11/8/18
3275 Dvr Coombs, Harry L.
55585 Pte Cooper, Albert Edwin
6739 Pte Cooper, Charles E.
718 Pte Cooper, Frank E.
6239 Pte Cooper, H. I.
   K.I.A., France, 9/8/18
6621 Pte Cooper, Harold V.
813 Sgt Cooper, Leslie F.
3276 Dvr Cooper, John Hope
1732 Pte Cooper, Randolph
6481 Pte Cooper, Rupert C.
1925 Pte Cooper, Thomas J.
   K.I.A., Belgium, 7/10/17
2231 Cpl. Coppin, W. H. J.
   K.I.A., France, 16/8/16
657 Sgt Corbett, S. Elmo R.
   D.O.W., France, 4/7/18
1926 Pte Corcoran, Patrick
6734 Pte Cork, Sydney T.
4157 Pte Corkish, Oliver A.
90 Pte Cormack, James P.
   D.O.W. Alexandria, 14/6/15
— Lieut Cornell, John C.
996 Pte Cornford, Wm. J.

1927 Er/2/Cpl. Cornish, Lionel
   (M.M.)
1526 Pte Corrie, Wm. H.
   K.I.A., Anzac, 19/5/15
388 Gnr Corrigan, James
6978 Pte Costello, John
1528 Pte Costello, Kenneth
   K.I.A., Anzac, 17/12/15
2128 Pte Costello, Leon S.
55584 Gnr Costelloe, Bernard L.
1529 Pte Cottier, Philip
2932 Cpl Cottingham, Walter
6733 Pte Cotton, Robert
1523 Pte Coughlan, Talouchlan
   K.I.A., Anzac, 8-9/8/15
6475 Pte Coulter, John Robert
— Lieut Court, Adrian J.
55587 Pte Courtney, Charles W.
6611 Pte Courtney, George H.
1081 Er/W.O.(1) Cousin, Ron.
5667 Pte Cousins, Arthur R.
901 Cpl Coustley, Eli
   K.I.A., France, 26/8/16
55580 Pte. Couston, Kenneth F.
3012 Gnr Coutanche, C. S.
6977 Pte Coutts, Harold A.
7216 Pte Coutts, William P.
892 Pte Cowan, Albert W.
6982 Pte Cowan, Charles
   K.I.A., France, 9/8/18
— 2/Lt. Cowan, Charles D.
   K.I.A., France, 6/11/16
6238 Pte Cowell, Arthur G.
   K.I.A., Belgium, 4/10/17
540 Pte Cowell, John Wm.
   K.I.A., Gall., 8/5/15
568 Pte Cowell, Leslie
— M.O. Capt. Cowen, Stewart O.
360 Pte Cowham, Joseph
3019 Pte Cowl, Robert Henry
   K.I.A., France, 19/7/16
2835 Cpl. Cowles, Lincoln D.
2600 L/Sgt Cowley, Charles S.
2615 Pte Cowley, Harry
— Lieut Cox, Arthur J. G.
850 Pte Cox, Bertie
   D.O.W., 20/9/17
2211 Pte Cox, Edward Thos.
   K.I.A., France, 19/7/16
4152 Pte Cox, Percy
893 Pte Cox, Peter Gordon
1634 Dvr Cox, Wm. F. S.
6473 L/Cpl Cox, William Jas.
   (M.M.)
849 Pte Crabtree, C. H. L.
418 Pte Cracknell, James E.
5062 Pte Crammond Roy J.
2712 Pte Craven, G. McE.
4177 Sgt Crawford, George
   D.O.W., France, 9/8/18
530 Cpl Crawford, Leslie B.
1928 Pte Creighton, Alex.
   K.I.A., Anzac, 8/8/15

148

1737 L/Cpl Crewdson, Robert
2616 Pte Crichton, Eric C.
      Died England, 8/6/17
4176 Pte Crichton, Robert A.
2161 Pte Crichton, Walter
7467 Pte Cripps, Charles P.
  90 Pte Cripps, L. D. L.
896 Pte Crisfield, William H.
      D.O.W., Alexandria, 6/5/15
4156 Pte Cristofoletti, G.
346 Pte Crocker, John
2423 Pte Crockett, John Alfred
2120 Pte Croft, George
5991 Pte Croft, George John
      K.I.A., France, 9/8/18
701 Pte Croft, James Henry
      K.I.A., Anzac, 28/8/15
1664 Pte Cronin, Thomas
      D.O.W., at Sea, 9/9/15
2212 Pte Cronk, William
      K.I.A., Belgium, 20/9/17
1453 Pte Crook, William
6975 Pte Crosse, Edwin Geo.
7468 Sgt Crouch, Albert
5064 Pte Croughey, Nicholas
      K.I.A., France, 18/8/16
3277 Pte Crow, William F.
      K.I.A., France, 19/7/16
— Lieut Crowe, Maurice V.
6626 Pte Crowley, Joseph
1708 Cpl Crowther, Percy W.
      K.I.A., Anzac, 1/6/15
7855 Pte Croxford, James John
      K.I.A., Belgium, 8/10/17
7469 Pte Crundall, Frank H.
5659 Pte Crutchfield, Charles
      K.I.A., France, 24/2/17
— Capt Crooks, David R.
      (M.B.E., M.I.D.)
6625 Pte Crosbie, Wm. M. T.
6729 L/Cpl Croshaw, H. G.
      (M.M.)
2594 Cpl Cross, Ernest C.
      K.I.A., Belgium, 26/12/17
1726 Pte Cross, Ernest E.
4154 Pte Crute, William H.
2331 Pte Cullen, Thomas
7470 Pte Cumberland, J. F.
5367 Sgt Cumberland, J. W.
      (M.S.M.)
      D.O.W. France, 10/8/18
898 C.S.M. Cumming, A. T. G.
      D.O.W. at Sea, 10/8/15
6237 Pte Cumming, Wm. G.
2606 Mt Dvr Cummings, E. G.
2233 Pte Cummings, H. R.
5994 L/Cpl Cummins, B. A.
843 Pte Cummins, James W.
      (M.M.)
4163 Pte Cummins, Richard
      K.I.A. France, 18/8/16
5993 L/Cpl. Cummins, W. J.
      (M.M.)

5998 Cpl Cunning, Fred. A.
      (M.M.)
7471 Pte Cunningham, S. B.
— Lieut. Curdie, D. T.
      (D.C.M.)
2129 Pte Curram, Leslie R.
4175 Cpl Currie, A. A.
      K.I.A., France, 12/12/16
3298 Sgt Currie, Arthur W.
      K.I.A., France, 26/9/17
1125 Pte Currie, Chas. C.
      K.I.A., Anzac, 8-9/8/15
899 Dvr Currie, David H.
      (M.M.)
5997 Pte Curry, John
      K.I.A., France, 17/4/18
859 Pte Curry, James P.
      Died France, 5/12/18
2588 Far/Sgt Curtayne, Chas.
      (M.M.)
1929 Pte Curtis, Joseph J.
1063 Dvr Curtis, Wm. C.
6241 Pte Curwen, John A.
      K.I.A., Belgium, 4/10/17
3017 Pte Curwen, V. R. A.
      K.I.A., France, 19/7/16
3016 Pte Cuthbert, William
6242 Er/Arm/Cpl Cutler, S. G.
662 Pte Cutting, H. J.

D

70 Pte D'Altera, Stanley V.
— Capt D'Altera, W. R.
212 L/Cpl Daly, Ernest R.
      K.I.A., Gall., 25/4/15
4466 1/A.M. Daly, Fredk. C.
2234 Pte Daly, James H.
      K.I.A., Gall., 8-9/8/15
2635 Pte Daly, John Henry
2634 Sgt Daly, Matthew E.
3299 L/Cpl Dalzell, B. A.
      K.I.A. France, 19/7/16
2631 Pte Dack, John
6745 Pte Dale, Harold
      K.I.A., France, 17/4/18
3081 Pte Dale, William A.
  93 Pte Dale, William H.
      K.I.A., Belgium, 26/9/17
277 Pte Daley, Thomas E.
5082 Pte Dalgrin, Ernest
4764 Pte Dalgrin, R. H.
60667 Pte Dalitz, Ernest O.
1455 Cpl Dall, Edward R.
6250 L/Cpl. Dally, E. H.
287 Pte Damen, Charles
      K.I.A., Gall., 25/4/15
477 Pte Danaher, E. B.
      K.I.A., Gall., 25/4/15
498 Pte Dangerfield, C. J.
300 Sgt Daniel, James G.
      D.O.W., France, 28/2/17
2785 Cpl Daniel, Lionel H.

60665	Artfcr	Daniels, A. J.
213	Pte	Daniels, Thos. W.
2789	Spr	Dannock, C. C.
1743	Pte	Dannock, Leslie W.
1018	Pte	Darby, George
55604	L/Cpl	Darbyshire, Stan.
947	Dvr	Darcy, Ernest
3303	L/Cpl	Darcy, Joseph
1127	Pte	Dare, Adrian B.
2642	Pte	Dark, A. J. H.
2622	Pte	Darrah, Dawson
3300	Pte	Darvell, Wm. John
780	A/Sgt	Darwin, William
—	Lieut	Davey, C. B. T.
		D.O.W. at Sea, 27/4/15
6984	T/Cpl	Davey, S. W.
		(C. de G., Belgian)
2613	Gnr	Davey, Wm. R.
6246	1st A.M.	David, J. C.
2835	Pte	David, M. T. R. (M.M.)
589	Pte	Davidge, Alf. Wm.
1741	Pte	Davidge, Charles
2836	Pte	Davidson, George
6251	Pte	Davidson, Robert
		K.I.A., Belgium, 4/10/17
95	Pte	Davie, James McK.
		D.O.W., Malta, 16/5/15
778	Pte	Davies, David M.
		K.I.A., Gall., 25/4/15
2630	Pte	Davies, Ernest D.
2204	Dvr	Davies, Fredk. John
4381	Pte	Davies, Frank L.
715		
		D.O.W., France, 8/11/16
2786	Pte	Davies, Harold (M.M.)
2343	Cpl	Davies, Robert H.
902	Cpl	Davies, Richard O.
2574	Pte	Davies, Sydney D.
4765	H/Cpl	Davies, Wm. L.
55596	Pte	Davis, Alfred
60666	Pte	Davis, Archie
199	Pte	Davis, Arnold F.
		K.I.A., Anzac, 25/4/15
60113	Pte	Davis, A. G.
2618	Pte	Davis, Arch. H.
		K.I.A., France, 18/8/16
569	Pte	Davis, Edward C.
2625	Pte	Davis, Herbert A.
2623	L/Cpl	Davis, John M.
		K.I.A., France, 24/7/16
4182	Pte	Davis, James R.
94	Pte	Davis, Leonard N.
		D.O.W., France or Belgium, 23/9/17
187	Pte	Davis, Nassan W. J.
1930	Pte	Davis, Phillip
2624	Pte	Davis, Thos. John
6484	Pte	Davis, W. G. E.
4178	Pte	Dawes, Gladstone
		K.I.A., France, 17/6/18
1742	Pte	Dawkins, David G.
6254	Pte	Dawson, Cyril T.

4179	Sgt	Dawson, Sydney G.
732	Pte	Day, Ernest
		D.O.W. at Sea, 29/4/15
60668	Pte	Day, Frederick H.
1037	Pte	Day, Harold C.
6258	Pte	Day, John James
		K.I.A., France, 25/2/17
2705	Pte	Day, Walter C. (enlisted as Wilson, W.)
1652	Cpl	Deacon, C. M.
2627	R.S.M.	Deacon, G. L. W. (M.C.M., M.S.M.)
—	Lieut	Dean, Arthur
6252	Pte	Deane, George A.
1645	ER Sgt	Dean, R. C.
4766	Cpl	Deans, Harold J.
		D.O.W., Rouen, 6/10/1
4184	Pte	Dearling, Alex. C.
2619	L/Cpl	Dearnley, C. R. O.
6257	Pte	Deason, H. H.
105	Pte	Deboe, John
2620	Pte	Decker, A. W. C.
		K.I.A., France, 17/8/1
148	Pte	De Crespigny, H. V.
6493	L/Cpl	Deeley, Daniel
1327	Pte	De Fontenay, L. A.
		D.O.W., Belgium, 29/12/17
5671	Pte	Delaney, H. J.
		K.I.A., France, 21/4/17
6250	Pte	De La Rue, H. H.
		D.O.W., France, 17/5/18
6249	ER/2/Cpl	Delcasse, G.
2637	ER/2/Cpl	Dellar, O. L.
214	Pte	Deller, F. A. E.
2787	L/Sgt	Dench, Alf. Wm. (M.M.)
—	Lt-Col	Denehy, C. A. (D.S.O. & Bar, C. de G. Belgian, 3 M.I.D.)
—	Lieut	Denham, R. P.
1630	Pte	Denham, Wm. John
60663	Pte	Denison, James
737	Pte	Denkel, Henry R.
		D.O.W., B'logne, 15/8/18
2837	L/Cpl	Denman, Harold
1532	Pte	Dennis, Frank L.
94	Pte	Denston, Harold
		K.I.A., Anzac, 25/4/15
746	Sgt	Dent, Frederick
6487	Pte	Dent, Frank D.
5371	Pte	Dent, Guise B.
		Died after Discharge
—	Mjr	De Ravin, S. M. (M.I.D.)
6490	Pte	Devereaux, John
		K.I.A., Belgium, 4/10/17
2621	Pte	Devereaux, James C.
2132	Gnr	Dewsbury, Thomas
3027	Pte	Dewsnap, John Wm.
		K.I.A., France, 19/7/16
96	Pte	Dick, James
1274	Pte	Dickenson, Harry
1639	Pte	Dickinson, A. R.
		K.I.A. Belg., 21/9/17

— Lieut Dickinson, V. R.
2632 Pte Dickman, Ernest A.
      K.I.A., France, 23/7/16
2576 Pte Dickson, Henry G.
60670 Pte Dickson, Hebrun T.
7226 Pte Dickson, John Chas.
60669 Pte Dickson, N. G.
2622 Pte Didier, Geo. B.
      K.I.A., France, 29/6/16
6491 Pte Dihm, Dudley A. J.
6488 Pte Dihm, E. T. R.
7224 Pte Diment, Walter
2259 Pte Dimmick, Stanley
1151 L/Cpl Dineley, Edwd. B.
      D.O.W. Belgium, 21/9/17
55597 Gnr Dingfelder, L. T.
744 Pte Dingwall, Harry
682 Pte Dinneen, William
60661 Pte Disher, Arthur W.
2633 Pte Ditchburn, N. J.
      K.I.A. France, 18/8/16
1931 Pte Dixon, Albert J.
2575 L/Sgt Dixon, Frank A.
      K.I.A. France, 19/7/16
4185 L/Cpl Dixon, Robert Jas.
216 Pte Dixon, William G.
      K.I.A. Anzac, 25/4/15
— Lieut Dobbin, Chas. L.
2629 Pte Dobbs, Errol W.
      K.I.A. France, 23-27/7/16
904 Sgt Dobinson, Charles J.
55605 Pte Doble, Frank D.
5674 Pte Dobson, Frederick
2634 Pte Dobson, William W.
      K.I.A. Belgium, 4/10/17
2344 Pte Dodds, James
      K.I.A. France, 18/8/16
1275 Pte Dodgson, Roy H. W.
1646 Pte Dodson, Athol James
1629 L/Cpl Dodson, Horace C.
905 Pte Dodson, Walter L.
      (M.I.D.)
2628 Dvr Doherty, Owen S.
452 Pte Dolan, Albert G.
737 Pte Dolphin, Gordon H.
2633 Pte Donaldson, Herb. J.
2635 Pte Donaldson, Jack D.
7503 Cpl Donnelly, Frank
      K.I.A. France, 9/8/18
4180 Pte Donnelly, John
      K.I.A. France, 25/2/17
7125 L/Cpl Donnet, James
2639 Pte Donohue, John Wm.
— Lieut Donohue, Wm. C.
215 Pte Donovan, Joseph
      D.O.W. at Sea, 16/5/15
2788 Pte Donovan, Malachi
      K.I.A. Belgium, 20/9/17
862 L/Cpl Donavan, W. Ern.
      K.I.A. Belgium, 5/10/17
6744 Pte Doohan, Ernest
2625 Pte Doolan, Archie Jas.
      Died of Injuries (Acc.).
      Belgium, 23/10/16

1013 Pte Doran, Arthur J.
2637 Pte Dore, David
      K.I.A. France, 9/8/18
98 Pte Dorian, Edward
6483 L/Cpl Douglas, Alex. S.
1533 Pte Douglas, George
55603 Pte Douglas, John Roy
6627 Pte Douglas R. V. E.
6612 L/Cpl Dow, Leslie Wm.
      D.O.W. France, 9/8/18
2345 Bdr Dowdle, Norman C.
55598 Gnr Dowie, James W.
833 Dvr Dowling, Arthur
3307 Pte Downing, George A.
1266 Pte Doyle, A. Jas.
5673 Pte Doyle, James
906 Pte Doyle, Michael Jas.
6247 Pte Doyle, Thomas
1267 Pte Draffin, Isaac
11857 Pte Drake, Claude
3308 Pte Draper, Alex. M.
779 Pte Draper, Hubert Jas.
      K.I.A. Gallipoli, 8/5/15
4195 Pte Draper, John Arthur
1932 Pte Dridan, John Henry
465 Sgt/Cook Drinkwater,
      Harold Thomas
6489 Pte Driver, Robert Thos.
55717 Pte Dromey, Nicholas P.
1534 Pte Drummond, Arch. C.
2636 Sgt Dudley William H.
      K.I.A. France, 22/4/17
4079 Cpl Duffell, Stewart Jack
2160 Pte Duggan, Harold S.
535 Pte Duggan, John
1535 Pte Dummett, George L.
2167 Cpl. Dunbar, Alexander
313 Sgt Dunbar, Frederick
850 Pte Duncan, Robert T.
99 Pte Dunden, Richard
55601 Pte Dunkling, George
1029 Dvr Dunn, Alfred
100 Pte Dunn, David Henry
      K.I.A. Gallipoli, 8/5/15
1039 W.O.Cl.1 Dunn, Alf. G.
907 Pte Dunne, Edward F.
3309 L/Sgt Dunn, Herbert S.
6747 Pte Dunn, John E.
      K.I.A. Belgium, 4/10/17
3302 Pte Dunn, Leonard
      D.O.W. Etaples, 30/3/18
1744 L/Cpl Dunn, Leo John
1933 Pte Dunne, Michael L.
      D.O.W. France, 28/7/16
2207 Pte Dunn, Peter James
      D.O.W. Alexandria,
      17/8/15
1642 Pte Dunn, William McL.
7474 Pte Dunphy, Thomas
      K.I.A. France, 9/8/18
2131 Pte Dunphy, Thos. S. M.
      K.I.A. France, 17/8/16
758 Cpl Dunstan, Stanley O.
      K.I.A. Anzac, 25/4/15

534 Pte Dunstan, Stephen S.
    K.I.A. Belgium, 4/10/17
2130 A/Cpl Dunstan William
    (V.C., M.I.D.)
1536 Cpl Durman, Reginald
    (stated to be Reginald
    Durman Culley)
1838 Pte Dutton, Edwin Jas.
60662 Pte Dwyer, Arthur
1128 Sgt Dwyer, Daniel Leo
1739 Pte Dwyer, Herbert Jas.
1934 Pte Dwyer, Martin James
1935 Pte Dwyer, Michael Wm.
3310 Pte Dyall, Alfred
1132 Pte Dyer, Ralph Stanley
— Lieut Dyett, G. J. C.
67 Pte Dykes, George Irvine

E

6987 Pte Eacott, Charles A.
    K.I.A. Belgium, 20/9/17
102 C.S.M. Eades, Cecil T.
1129 Cpl Eadie, Allan Keith
    K.I.A. Gall., 8/5/15
5067 Pte Eames, Alfred E.
4773 Pte Earl, Charles O.
2351 Pte Earl, Frederick
— Mjr East-Almond, G. N.
2624 L/Cpl Eastick, Herbert V.
2347 Pte Eastman, Orell
719 Pte Easton, Clement
    K.I.A. France, 24/8/18
5804 Pte Eastwood, David
412 Cpl Eastwood, Roger
3311 Pte Eaton, Hugh Percy
7475 Mt Dvr Eaton, John
2577 Pte Eaton, Raymond
55607 Pte Eddy, Leslie David
5675 Pte Eddy, Samuel
6749 Pte Eden, George
    D.O.W. France, 15/8/18
6008 Pte Eden, James
1748 L/Cpl Edgar, John
    K.I.A. France, 18/8/16
433 Pte Edgcumbe, Jas. A.
    K.I.A. Gall., 25/4/15
— Lieut Edgoose, Percy L.
713 Pte Edmonds, Francis W.
60673 Pte Ednie, Andrew Jas.
2952 Pte Edwards, Albert L.
1539 Cpl Edwards, Benjamin J.
— 2/Lt Edwards, Ben. N.
    K.I.A. Kall., 8-9/8/15
— Capt. Edwards, David W.
    Died after Discharge.
    22/7/19
817 Pte Edwards, Frank
1332 Sgt Edwards, George
2205 Pte Edwards, Jack
    K.I.A. Gall., 8-9/8/15
1334 Pte Edwards, John A.
— 2/Lt Edwards, John A. P.
3319 Dvr Edwards, John Wm.

1648 L/Cpl Edwards, Percy L.
— Lieut Edwards, Richard
7476 Pte Edwards, Thos. M.
2477 Pte Edwards, Victor C.
910 Pte Edwards, Wm. A.
    K.I.A. Gall., 25/4/15
200 Pte Egan, Timothy M.
911 Pte Eggleston, Chas. R.
4480 Pte Elder, Frank Reg.
    K.I.A. France, 20/8/16
913 Pte Eliason, Victor
    (M.S.M.)
    K.I.A. France, 15/5/18
3029 Pte Ellaway, Henry
1331 Pte Ellefsen, Thos. E.
    K.I.A. Gall., 25/4/15
912 Pte Elliot, Arthur
    K.I.A., Gall., 27/4/15
4191 L/Cpl Elliott. Angus V.
— Capt Elliott, Charles
6628 Pte Elliott, Daniel R.
4481 Pte Elliott, Edward
7478 Pte Elliott, Harold B.
— Brig Gen Elliot, Harold E.
    (C.B.), (C.M.G.),
    (D.S.O.), (D.C.M.),
    (C.deG., French), (Order
    of St. Anne, Russian),
    (M.I.D. 7)
— Lieut Elliott, Henry Jas.
1130 Pte Elliott, John Wm.
    D.O.W. at Sea, 2/6/15
6947 Pte Elliott, Leslie Fredk.
782 Pte Elliott, S. H. R.
    K.I.A. Gall., 25/4/15
7277 Pte Elliott, William G.
422 Pte Elliott, Wm. W. H.
    *D.O.W. Dardanelles,
    26/4/15*
3032 Pte Ellis, Arthur
6986 Pte Ellis, Ernest G. J.
    D.O.W. France, 18/4/18
2628 Pte Ellis, Edward H.
168 Dvr Ellis, Henry A. M.
    K.I.A. France, 23/8/18
2629 L/Cpl Ellis, Harold G.
1745 Pte Ellis, Joseph F.
1937 Pte Ellis, Owen John
    K.I.A. Gall., 8-9/8/15
    (M.I.D.)
6407 Pte Ellis, Paul
2349 L/Cpl Ellis, Thomas H.
3033 Sgt Elson, Fredk. H.
2645 Cpl Eltringham, C. T.
2644 Pte Elvins, James H.
    K.I.A. Belgium, 20/9/17
4180 L/Cpl Elvins, John M.
702 L/Sgt Ely, Ernest H.
    K.I.A. France, 18/8/16
7479 L/Cpl Ely, Frederick C.
2348 Pte Embry, Bert
5676 L/Cpl Emery, Fredk. W.
    K.I.A., 9/8/18

4192 Pte Emery, Wilfred T.
    K.I.A. France, 18/8/16
1647 Pte Emmerson, Wm. G.
875 Pte Engledow Wm. R. B.
2625 Pte Enman, James F.
1747 Pte Ennis, Joseph
233 Pte Ennis, John Arch.
    K.I.A. Gall., 8-16/5/15
1749 Pte Erikson. John
    D.O.W. Alexandria, 13/8/15
5070 Pte Ermel, George H.
— Lieut Errington, Arnold R.
1330 L/Cpl Erwin, Sydney F.
    D.O.W. France, 25/4/18 (M.M.)
6750 Pte Esmond, Sydney E.
781 Pte Esposito, Mervyn H.
    Died Egypt, 7/8/15
425 Pte Evans, Abraham
    K.I.A., Gall., 25/4/15
2645 Pte Evans, Cecil
    K.I.A. France, 18/8/16
1746 Pte Evans, David Owen
218 Pte Evans, Ernest W.
2647 Pte Evans, George F.
169 Sgt Evans, Harold H.
705 Pte Evans, Hector Wm.
3028 Cpl Evans, Pyke
    K.I.A. Belgium, 21/9/17
2648 Pte Evans, Reginald Jas.
591 Pte Evans, Reginald R.
3030 Dvr Evans, Thos. M.
2478 Cpl Evans, William G.
2646 Pte Evans, William R.
    D.O.W. France, 23/9/17
914 Pte Everett, Augustus
1540 Sgt Every, George Edwd. (M.M.)
2016 Sgt Ewans, Robert G.
4344 Pte Ewart, Eric John
    K.I.A. France, 6/11/16
94 Pte Ewen, Alexander

F

364 Pte Fahey, Edward
2710 Pte Fairbank, Alfred E.
1456 Pte Fairbank, Henry
443 Cpl Fairnie, Leslie H.
2630 L/Cpl Fanning, John
    K.I.A. Belgium, 20/9/17
2634 Pte Faragher, Leslie V.
    K.I.A. France, 16/5/16
226 Dvr Farleigh, George H.
1139 Cpl Farley, William V.
2135 Pte Farquharson, John C.
5379 L/Sgt Farrands, John H.
55614 Gnr Farrant, Percy
2713 Cpl Farrell, Edward Jos.
    D.O.W. Belgium, 2/10/17
3547 Sgt Farrell, Hugh
3350 Pte Farrell, Robert Jas.
521 Pte Farrelly, Wm. Jas.

2136 Pte Farrer, Allen B.
    K.I.A. Anzac, 8-9/8/15
614 Pte Farrow, Alfred Geo.
4778 L/Cpl Faulkner, F. W. G. (M.M.)
3351 Cpl Fear, Stan. R. Wm.
    K.I.A. France, 23-26/7/16
325 Dvr Fearn, John
5677 L/Cpl Fearn, William
5680 Pte Featherston, Wm.
    D.O.W. France or Belgium, 21/9/17
219 Gnr Fedderson, Arch. E.
2648 Pte Feltman, Charles (M.M.)
2838 Sgt Fenton, Allan M.
27 Sgt Fenton, Cecil G.
2352 Pte Fenton, Harry (M.M.)
— Lieut Fenton, John W.
4050 Pte Ferguson, Alan
    K.I.A. France, 11/8/16
55610 Pte Ferguson, John D.
1750 Pte Ferguson, William
    K.I.A. France 19/7/16
2354 Pte Ferrari, Andrew M.
5252 Pte Ferrie, William G.
    D.O.D. Fremantle, 25/6/17
103 L/Cpl Ferry Joseph C.
859 L/Cpl Fevin, Reginald
615 L/Cpl Fiddian, Perc. D.
440 Pte Field, Colin Victor
784 Pte Field, Harold
2065 Pte Field, Hilton
6399 Pte Field, Henry Jos.
7480 Pte Field, William M.
    D.O.W. France, 9/8/18
3728 Pte Fielding, George V.
1545 Pte Findlay, David
2641 Cpl Fineran, George F.
    K.I.A. France, 25/7/16
— Capt Finlayson, Chris.
1638 Pte Firebrace, Arthur
3104 Pte Fischer, Arthur
60676 Pte Fish, Cyril
1135 Pte Fisher, Albert C.
783 Pte Fisher, Ernest S.
439 A/Cpl Fisher, John M.
    D.O.W. at Sea, 9/8/15
— 2/Lieut Fisher, Walter
3548 Pte Fitton, John Henry
6260 Pte Fitzclarence, Harry
750 Pte Fitzgerald, A. L.
1046
2632 Sgt Fitzgerald, Jas. C.
    K.I.A. Belgium, 20/9/17
22 L/Cpl Fitzgerald, Thomas
1462 Pte Fitzgerald, Thomas
6013 Pte Fitzpatrick, Joseph
    K.I.A. Belgium 20/9/17
2649 Pte Fitzpatrick, John P.
    K.I.A. France, 23-26/7/16
55611 Pte Fitzpatrick, Reg. C.

541 Pte Fitzpatrick, William
5074 Pte Fitzsimons, John
355 Sgt Fizelle, Herbert V.
3035 Pte Flack, Robert John
    K.I.A. France, 17/8/16
1676 Sgt Flanagan, James
60678 Pte Flanagan, William
1337 Pte Flanders, Alfred G.
5679 Pte Flanigan, Edwd. F.
2206 Pte Flannery, John M.
6263 Pte Fleer, Cyril A.
2652 Pte Fleet, Fredk. Jas.
2790 Dvr Flenley, Arthur E.
1751 Pte Fletcher, Archibald
1469 Pte Fletcher, A. J. McD.
2937 Pte Fletcher, John
2654 Pte Flecher, Jas. W. P.
1541 L/Cpl Flood, Mat. D.
331 Pte Florence, William P.
1752 Pte Floyd, Henry H.
    K.I.A. France, 9/8/18
2579 Pte Flynn, Lawrence
    Died after Discharge
— 2/Lieut Foers, Frank
    K.I.A. Belgium, 20/9/17
2650 Pte Fogarty, Daniel
    K.I.A. France, 17/4/17
60679 ER/Sgt Fogarty, Thos. B.
6752 Pte Foley, Bartholomew
592 Pte Foley, Thomas Edwd.
2652 Sgt Foley, William
    (M.M.)
6996 Pte Follett, Donald Milo
28 Pte Forbes, William
2839 L/Cpl Ford, Arthur R.
1754 Cpl Ford, Fredk. Jas.
2633 Pte Forrest, Richard
915 Spr Forrester, Alfred E.
1131 Sgt Forrester, Arthur E.
3546 Pte Forrester, John H.
55613 Pte Forsberg, Albin E.
2635 Pte Foster, Andrew R.
    K.I.A. France, 23/8/18
792 Pte Foster, Joseph
2791 Pte Foster, John (stated to be Zoch, Thos. H.).
2137 Pte Foster, Joseph Alfred
7481 Pte Foster, James H.
3312 L/Cpl Foster, William
6016 Pte Fowke, Alex. Wm.
— Hon Capt Fowler, John
    (M.C., M.I.D.2)
2134 Pte Fowler, John C.
2636 Pte Fowler, Thomas S.
319 Pte Fowles, Edward F.
    Died after Discharge
727 Pte Fox, Robert
1544 Pte Foxcroft, Arthur F.
    (Stated to be Hannabury, Michael Chas.).
6497 Pte Francis, William E.
72 C.Q.M.S. Franks, Andrew
459 Pte Fraser, Alexander

— Capt. Fraser, Alex.
    (M.C., M.I.D.)
    Died after Discharge
5783 ER/Sgt Fraser, Arthur B.
6268 Pte Fraser, Alex. S.
    K.I.A. France, 23/4/17
6264 Pte Fraser, Bruce
    K.I.A. France, 3/7/18
1339 Dvr Fraser, Finlay
2657 Sgt Fraser, Geo. A. E.
    (Stated to be Schmahl, Adolph Fredk. Anton).
2261 Sgt Fraser, Leslie
    K.I.A. Anzac, 8-9/8/15
2578 Sgt Fraser, Robert Thos.
    (M.M.)
5383 Pte Fraser, Verner W.
    K.I.A. France, 16/12/16
6014 Pte Frederickson, L. N.
5678 Pte Frederickson, V. F.
6267 Pte Freeman, George
916 Pte Freeman, George Air
2856 Pte Freeman, Thomas
    K.I.A. France, 23/8/18
2638 2/Cpl French, Arthur F.
2133 Cpl. French, William
2660 Pte Frencham, H. F.
1163 Pte Frewin, William H.
519 Dvr Friend, Jacob Joseph
6753 Pte Frith, Fredk. N.
2661 Pte Fritsch, Leslie
29 Dvr Froggitt, David H.
104
6993 Pte Fry, Frank
    K.I.A. Belgium, 20/9/17
6991 Pte Fry, Percy Gordon
    K.I.A. Belgium, 4/10/17
— Lieut Fryberg, Louis
    (M.M.)
2846 Cpl Fryer, Walt W.
917 Pte Fulford, S. W. J.
876 L/Sgt Fullagar, Josephus
    K.I.A. Gall., 25/4/15
2651 Pte Fuller, Furneaux
6994 Pte Fuller, Jarvis Bunting
    K.I.A. Belgium, 4/10/17
55609 Pte Furniss, Rupert
2792 Pte Futerieal, Ruben
2639 Sgt Fynmore, Harry L.
    K.I.A. France, 13/6/18
1340 Cpl Fryer, John Fredk.
    K.I.A. France, 18/8/16
1707 Sgt Fynch, Andrew Roy
    D.O.W. France, 4/7/18

G

3314 Pte Gaborit, Thos. L.
    K.I.A. France, 19/7/16
743 Pte Gaggin, Basil W.
2653 Pte Gailey, Frank
    K.I.A. France, 23-26/7/16
2653 Pte Gailey, Frank
    (M.I.D.)

882 Sgt Galbraith, John
903 Pte Gale, Walter John
7346 Pte Gallagher, Edwd. G.
446 T/Sgt Galland, A. G.
    K.I.A. Belgium, 4/10/17
1546 Pte Galvin, Thomas M.
— Lieut Gamble, W. M. F.
    (M.C.)
3645 Sgt Game, Edward A.
    D.O.W. France, 22/8/16
— Lieut Gandon, Philip Geo.
60680 Pte Gandy, K. A. J.
2664 Pte Gange, Gilbert
7002 Pte Gannon, James
7003 Pte Gannon, John
763 L/Cpl Garden, N. D.
    Died Malta, 23/10/15
2272 Pte Gardiner, Alfred John
    K.I.A. Gall., 8-9/8/15
593 Sgt Gardiner, R. J.
321 Pte Gardiner, Wm. A.
489 Pte Gardiner, Joseph R.
    K.I.A. Gall., 25/4-2/5/15
551 Pte Gardiner, Thomas
    Died after discharge
2651 Pte Garlick, Samuel
411 Sgt Garner, George
    D.O.W. at Sea, 14/7/15
60681 Pte Garner, George H.
60685 Pte Garrett, Henry R.
1755 Pte Garrett, James
    K.I.A. Anzac, 29/5/15
5966 Pte Gartly, John George
— Lt/Col Gartside, Robert
    (V.D.)
    K.I.A. Gall., 8/5/15
6754 Pte Garvan, Clement Jos.
    (M.M.)
2793 L/Cpl Gasson, Edwin W.
— Lieut Gaulton, Fredk. B.
2643 Pte Gawne, Thomas H.
7484 Pte Gay, Leslie (stated to be Ball, Edwin A. L.).
2860 Gnr Gaylard, John W.
    (M.M.)
918 Pte Geake, Alfred
4565 Pte Geary, Patrick Jas.
1547 Dvr Geddes, Robert H.
1090 Pte Gee, David
    K.I.A. Gall., 8/5/15
762 Cpl Gee, Frederick
868 Pte Gee, Harold
    K.I.A. Gall., 8/5/15
1357 Pte Geikie, John C.
1756 Pte Geisler, George
55720 Pte Gell, Allan Raymond
1942 Pte Gellie, Albert
785 Pte Gellon, P. J. G.
    K.I.A. Anzac, 5/7/15
55718 Pte Gemmell, Frederick
367 Pte Gemmill, John Thos.
2208 Pte George, Arch. H.

1549 Pte George, Edward J.
2794 Pte George, Ralph
7127 Pte Gerard, Thomas
55623 Gnr Geuer, Arthur Wm.
6501 Pte Gibbons, Arch. H.
    (M.M.)
4200 Pte Gibbs, David M.
5093 Pte Gibbs, N. E. I.
408 Sgt Gibbs, Richard R.
1943 Pte Gibney, James
    K.I.A. Anzac, 8-9/8/15
60682 Pte Gibson, James
2795 Pte Gibson, John Joseph
    (M.M.)
55625 L/Cpl Gibson, John Lenno
2669 Cpl Gibson, William
    K.I.A. France, 9/8/18
2804 Dvr Gibson, William F.
1665 Pte Giddins, Leonard
2356 Pte Gilbert, Charles N.
    D.O.W. France, 16/9/18
2581 Pte Gilbert, Edward
5685 Spr Gilbert, George F.
    D.O.W. Belgium, 13/10/17
4201 Pte Gilbert, Reuben N.
5683 Pte Gilbert, Sydney
2355 Pte Gilbert, Thos. H.
1134 Pte Gilbody, L. C. J.
416 Sgt Gilchrist, George A.
1550 Pte Gilder, Herbert S.
    D.O.W. France, 20/8/16
55616 Pte Gilding, George R.
1551 Cpl Gill, William Alex.
    K.I.A. France, 19/7/16
46 Pte Giles, Henry Claude
1030 Dvr Giles, James
42 Pte Gilham, Fredk. C.
7113 L/Cpl Gillard, James
5081 Pte Gillespie, Noel Jas.
    D.O.W. France, 6/10/17
2796 Pte Gillies, James
5386 Pte Gillin, Jas. F. Jos.
1057 Pte Gillison, Thomas A.
    K.I.A. Gall., 25/4/15
5687 Pte Gilmore, Edward
2649 Cpl Gilmour, Frederick
5387 Pte Girven, Thomas Jas.
    K.I.A. France, 9/8/18
2213 Pte Gittoes, Ernest C.
    K.I.A. France, 19/7/16
5758 Pte Gladstone, Robert J.
1758 Gnr Glascott, John
1642 Pte Glasspool, William H.
    (M.M.)
3549 Pte Gleeson, David. Jos.
    K.I.A. France, 19/7/16
7486 Pte Glover, Ernest
1671 Pte Goacher, George R.
4495 L/Cpl Gobbett, James
3038 Bdr Godden, George
5082 Pte Godden, Vivian V.
    K.I.A. France, 2/11/16
2655 Pte Godman, William M.

557	L/Cpl Godrich, A. S. A. *K.I.A. France, 9/8/18*	6629	Pte Grail, William
3550	Sgt Goldby, William *K.I.A. France, 19/7/16*	223	Pte Grange, Richard
1553	L/Cpl Goldie, Charles E. *K.I.A. France, 19/7/16*	2714	Pte Grange, Harold Wm.
6271	Pte Gonsal, Pierce L.	—	Lieut Granger, Wilfred B. *D.O.W. Anzac, 22/8/15*
919	Cpl Gooda, Thomas *D.O.W. London 7/9/15*	6503	L/Cpl Grant, Eric St. C.
7005	Pte Goodall, James S.	6998	Pte Grant, Gordon
2648	Pte Goodchild, P. F.	11	Sgt Grant, Leslie
2660	Pte Goodear, Ruben J.	55615	Pte Grant, Reginald A.
3313	2nd A.M. Goodes, Arthur	—	Lieut Grant, Thomas Roy *K.I.A. France, 11/8/18*
3315	Pte Goodes, Horace Geo.	7490	L/Cpl Grant, William
400	Pte Goodfellow, R. E.	2139	Pte Grasby, George Wm. (M.M.)
2644	Pte Goodger, Edwd. J.	1143	Pte Graves, Frederick *K.I.A. Gall., 8/5/15*
2670	Pte Goodingham, W. W. *K.I.A. Belgium, 20/9/17*	1847	Pte Gray, Alexander
4792	Pte Goodlet, A. T. J. *K.I.A. Belgium, 4/10/17*	5094	L/Cpl Gray, Arthur H. (M.M.)
5083	Pte Goodridge, Cape	1757	L/Sgt Gray, Andrew J. (M.M.) *K.I.A. France, 15/5/18*
657	Cpl Goodridge, F. H.	921	Pte Gray, Aubrey S.
1346	Dvr Goodwin, A. N.	1548	ER/2/Cpl Gray, Charles
5684	Pte Goodwin, John H.	2799	Pte Gray, John Millyard *K.I.A. France, 19/7/16*
2358	ER/Cpl Gook, Alfred J.	2800	Cpl. Gray, Leonard
2654	Pte Gordon, Ewen Jas. *K.I.A. France, 18/6/16*	—	Lieut. Gray, Leyton E.
222	T/R.S.M. Gordon, Harold Brunton G. (M.S.M.)	7236	Pte Gray, Robert John
6999	ER/Sgt Gordon, John F. (M.S.M.)	2661	Pte Gray, Verner James
		3359	Pte Gray, William Jas.
—	Lieut Gordon, J. H. G.	5682	Pte Greaves, William J. *D.O.W. Rouen, 11/5/17*
7487	Pte Gorman, Edward H.	7491	Pte Green, Augustus *K.I.A. France, 9/8/18*
60684	Pte Gorman, John E.	55617	Pte Green, Albert Victor
7354	Pte Gorman, John Thos.	55618	T/Bdr Green, Clifford C.
6847	Pte Gormly, James *Died France, 29/5/18*	6504	Pte Green, Ernest K. *D.O.W. Belgium, 24/9/17*
1073	Dvr Gosden, Frederick	2851	Pte Green, Gordon
4196	Pte Goslin, Clive H. W.	71	Pte Green, Gilbert Peter
1737	Pte Goudge, Alfred H. *Died after Discharge*	2676	Pte Green, Herbert Lucy *K.I.A. France, 18/8/16*
1698	Pte Gough, Harry	3360	Pte Green, Leslie
1554	Pte Gough, John	2654	L/Cpl Green, Ormand C.
29	S/Sgt Gould, Harold	3036	Cpl Green, S. F. W. H. *K.I.A. France, 19/7/16*
6757	T/Sgt Gould, Leslie W.	1347	Pte Greene, Francis E. *D.O.W. Alexandria 16/5/15.*
3316	ER/Cpl Goulder, J. R.		
47	Cpl Goulding, Stanley J. *D.O.W. Alex'dria, 1/5/15*	2801	Pte Greenaway, R. E. W.
2672	Sgt Gourlay, David D.	1133	T/Cpl Greenaway, W. G.
4202	Pte Gow, Robert McG. *D.O.W. France, 11/10/17*	572	T/Sgt Greengrass, C. M. *K.I.A. Belgium, 4/10/17*
2841	L/Sgt Gow, Walter	2652	Pte Greenham, Sidney L. *K.I.A. France, 18/8/16*
3044	Pte Goyne, Albert V.	3039	Pte Greenshields, Jos. T.
2798	Pte Grace, George H. *K.I.A. France, 19/7/16*	2657	Cpl Greenwell, Joseph B. *K.I.A. Belgium, 28/1/18*
1945	Pte Grace, William *K.I.A. Belgium, 20/9/17*	617	Pte Greenwood, E. R. E. *K.I.A. Gall., 25/4/15*
4091	Pte Graham, Alfred Jas.	—	Lieut Gregg, George Robt.
7001	Pte Graham, George S.	594	Pte Gregor, Robert S.
837	Pte Graham, Hugh B. *K.I.A. Anzac, 25/4/15*	571	Pte Gregory, Arthur R.
6507	Pte Graham, James Wm.		
—	Lieut Graham, Robert Jas. (M.C.)		

407 C.S.M. Greig, Geo. F.
    K.I.A. Gall., 8/5/15
— 2/Lieut Greig, Norman J.
    K.I.A. Gall., 12/7/15
5686 Pte Gretton, Herbert H.
3646 Pte Grew, William H.
787 Pte Grey, Edmund Jos.
2650 L/Cpl Grey, Henry
335 Pte Greyman, Frank Roy
2803 Pte Grierson, Henry
    K.I.A. France, 10/8/18
873 C.S.M. Griffin, Horace
    K.I.A. France, 18/8/16
3041 Sgt Griffin, Rex. V.
6848 Pte Griffith, Francis J.
450 Pte Griffith, Gerald R.
    D.O.W. Gall., 11/5/15
920 L/Cpl Griffiths, Arthur E.
1345 Pte Griffiths, Harold W.
428 Pte Griffiths, Rhys Emlyn
    K.I.A. Anzac, 25/4/15
7493 Pte Griffiths, Stanley A.
    K.I.A. France, 15/5/18
554 Pte Grigg, John William
— Lieut Grigsby, Joseph E.
— Mjr Grills, Shannon
    (M.I.D.)
2842 Cpl Grimble, Charles F.
    (M.M.)
224 Pte Grimmer, William
7494 Pte Grimshaw, Sam
3317 Pte Grogan, Patrick
4788 Pte Gronn, Claus V.
3042 Pte Groom, William C.
    D.O.W. France, 29/7/16
1657 Pte Grose, Arthur B.
55622 Pte Groves, Horace R.
2232 Pte Guilfoyle, W. M. J.
— Capt Guinn, F. A. S.
    (2 M.I.D.)
2646 ER/Cpl Gullick, G. H. D.
2647 Cpl Gullick, W. T. S.
1068 Pte Gulliver, William G.
    K.I.A. Anzac, 25/4/15
— Lieut Gunn, Frank Swan
6756 Pte Gunn, John Reid
3361 Sgt Gunther, Henry V.
    (M.M.)
2138 Pte Guppy, Edward Chas.
    D.O.W. at Sea, 10/8/15
2359 Sgt Guthridge, James F.
    (M.M.)
— Lt-Col Gutteridge, E. W.
    (Medical Officer).
6270 Pte Guy, William E.
1948 L/Cpl Guyatt, George
106 Pte Gwynne, Dennis
    (Stated to be Gwynne,
    Sackville W. N.).
    K.I.A. Gall., 8/5/15

H

1705 Pte Haar, Charles Henry
    K.I.A. Belgium, 4/10/17
5800 Pte Habel, Louis
5085 Pte Haddock, John Geo.
2683 Pte Hadler, William E.
    K.I.A. France, 18/5/18
2669 Pte Hague, Frdk. A. W.
    D.O.W. France, 19/8/16
1555 C.Q.M.S. Haines, A. J.
3343 Pte Haines, David Isaac
2805 Pte Haines, Stephen Jas.
2806 Sgt Halbert, Hubert Jas.
4203 Pte Haley, Patrick
    K.I.A. Belgium, 4/10/17
7252 Pte Hall, Arthur James
999 Pte Hall, Charles Vernon
    K.I.A. Anzac, 25/4/15
55629 Pte Hall, Daniel
55626 Gnr Hall, Frederick D.
7362 Pte Hall, Frank John
4509 Dvr Hall, George
1950 Pte Hall, George Wm.
    K.I.A. Anzac, 7/8/15
1949 Pte Hall, Henry Horace
4805 Pte Hall, James
7495 Sgt Hall, John Leslie
4210 Pte Hall, John Thomas
897 Pte Hall, Walter
    K.I.A. France, 4/3/17
2179 Pte Halliday, Clarence E.
7496 Pte Halliday, David
1556 Dvr Halliday, John M.
— Lieut. Halligan, John
    Killed France, 31/5/17
3324 Pte Halligan, William R.
    K.I.A. France, 24/7/16
3344 Pte Halpin, Patrick Jos.
5390 Pte Halpin, Thomas
191 Pte Halstead, Harold
— Lieut Hamblett, John H.
    K.I.A. France, 9/8/18
7015 L/Cpl Hambly, Percy E.
    (M.M.)
— Lieut Hambrook, H. R.
— Lieut Hambrook, M. B.
— Capt Hamilton, Arthur N.
107 L/Cpl Hamilton, Alf. W.
297 L/Cpl Hamilton, Oscar R.
2687 Pte Hamilton, Robert J.
5101 Pte Hamilton, R. J. S.
1358 Pte Hamilton, Thos. A.
2685 L/Sgt Hamilton, William
— Lieut Hamilton, Wm. E.
3325 Dvr Hammand, Chas. E.
    K.I.A. France, 30/5/18
1351 Pte Hammill, John L.
922 Pte Hammond, Alfred H.
    K.I.A. Gall., 8/5/15
6762 Pte Hammond, Chas. W.
    D.O.W. France, 9/8/18
1868 Pte Hammond, Richard
6763 Pte Hammond, Stanley
1769 Pte Hammond, Wm. Jas.
12 Dvr Hampton, Collin
2734 Dvr Hampton, Stanley G.

1350 Pte Handcock, Albert J.
    K.I.A. Anzac, 25/4/15
6119 Pte Hando, George H.
6033 L/Cpl Handson, John F.
    D.O.W. France, 6/6/18
3048 Pte Hanks, Edward Jas.
2807 Pte Hannah, George
939 Pte Hansen, Carl Roland
7497 Pte Hansen, Emanuel C.
    K.I.A. France, 16/4/18
55632 Pte Hansen, Griffith H.
— Lieut Hansen, Norman V.
2670 Pte Hansen, Stanley Hans
7498 Pte Hansen, Thomas W.
1740 Pte Hanslow, Thomas P.
    K.I.A. Belgium, 4/10/17
1903 L/Cpl Hanson, Clarence
    K.I.A. France, 19/4/18
— Lieut Hanson, Thos. B.
1902 T/Sgt Hanson, Vivian
24 L/Cpl Harbison, Eric F.
5088 Pte Harbour, Henry John
2672 L/Cpl Hardie, Alex. G.
    (D.C.M., M.M.)
1951 Pte Hardiman, Gerald
574 Pte Harding, Claude
    D.O.W. Gall., 26/4/15
5099 Pte Harding, Eric R.
7240 Pte Harding, Guieal
2499 Cpl Harding, Jas. W. M.
2659 Pte Harding, Walter E.
947 Pte Hardingham, James
6759 Pte Hardman, Hubert Jos.
1008 C.S.M. Hardner, F. A.
3326 L/Cpl Hardy, Edward T.
363 Pte Hardy, Nelson A.
    K.I.A. Gall., 23/8/15
1097 Pte Hargrave, Felix
2673 Pte Hargreaves, A. M.
2674 Pte Hargreaves, John A.
5802 Pte Harley, James G.
1557 Pte Harlow, Charles J.
543 Cpl Harmon, Charles
2693 Cpl Harney, John
    D.O.W. France, 9/8/18
1558 Sgt Harper, James
3327 L/Cpl Harrap, Ernest M.
    K.I.A. France, 26/9/17
3345 L/Cpl Harrap, James W.
    K.I.A. France, 26/9/17
7010 Pte Harries, Henry H.
2928 L/Cpl Harrington, L. F.
    (M.I.D.)
    Died France, 13/2/17
5803 Pte Harrington, Thomas
1952 Pte Harrington, Wm. S.
6511 Pte Harris, Alfred C.
2711 Pte Harris, Bertie John
    D.O.D., Eng., 22/1/19
2953 Pte Harris, Charles A.
    K.I.A. France, 25/2/17
53835 Pte Harris, Harry
2675 Pte Harris, Joseph A.

— Lieut Harris, Oliver J. E.
    (M.C.)
1570 C.Q.M.S. Harris, P. Jas.
— Lieut Harris, Thomas V.
    D.O.W. France, 9/8/18
2808 Cpl Harris, V. S. V.
— Lieut Harrison, A. B.
1137 Pte Harrison, Arthur F.
    K.I.A. Gall., 8/5/15
5801 Pte Harrison, Claude K.
6510 L/Cpl Harrison, Leslie H.
737 Pte. Harrison, Leslie R.
1559 Pte Harrison, Robert J.
2626 Pte Harrison, Sydney
1762 Pte Harrison, Thomas
839 Pte Harrison, William A.
7501 Pte Harrower, N. W.
1764 Pte Harry, Edgar Lewis
2597 Pte Hart, Arthur C.
— Mjr Hart, Arthur G. C.
5089 Pte Hart, Bertie R.
    K.I.A. France, 18/8/16
1561 Pte Hart, George
    K.I.A. France, 18/8/16
1354 L/Cpl Hart, Henry
    K.I.A. Gall., 18/5/15
1356 Pte Hart, Horatio
2691 Pte Hart, Henry Wm.
    K.I.A. France, 23/8/18
1562 Pte Hart, Jack (stated to
    be Daly, James)
    K.I.A. France, 27/9/17
6465 Pte Hart, John
    Died France, 20/4/19
3551 Pte Hart, John James
    K.I.A. France, 16/12/16
267 L/Cpl Hart, Leslie
    D.O.W. Gall., 4/5/15
6768 Pte Hart, Reginald Geo.
2811 Pte Hart, William H. G.
    K.I.A. France, 19/7/16
60698 Pte Hartwick, Herbert
449 Sgt Harty, Leo James
    (M.M.)
    K.I.A. France, 29/6/16
793 Pte Harvey, Henry P.
2844 Pte Harvey, John Alex.
1140 Pte Harvey, Peter
6275 Pte Harvey, Thomas J.
6518 Pte Harvey, Walter Thos.
618 Pte Harwood, Oliver Jas.
    (M.M.)
1953 Spr Haskell, George
2809 Pte Haslam, H. R. M.
9134 Pte Haslam, H. W. T.
    (M.M.)
    K.I.A. Belgium, 20/10/17
2810 Pte Haslam, Trevor Jas.
2585 Pte Haslem, Robert Henry
    K.I.A. France, 9/8/18
4209 Pte Hastings, Frank B.
    (M.M.)
— Lieut Hatfield, Percy T.

1853	Pte Hateley, Harry		60793	Pte Hegney, Patrick F.

1853 Pte Hateley, Harry
    D.O.W. France, 27/12/16
583 Pte Hatty, Leslie Thomas
3552
3514 Gnr Haverland, Lewis
3574 Pte Hawkins, Albert Roy
542 Pte Hawkins, David
    K.I.A. Gall., 25/4/15
496 Pte Hawkins, G. G. C.
    K.I.A. Gall., 25/4/15
2862 Cpl Hawkins, George H.
789 Pte Hawkins, Leonard
    D.O.W. at Sea, 27/4/15
575 Pte Hawthorne, George
2663 Pte Hawthorn, Henry R.
3362 L/Cpl Hay, James
1768 Pte Hayden, George
2145 Pte Hayden, Sydney T.
5101 Pte Hayes, Albert John
    K.I.A. Belgium, 4/10/17
447 L/Cpl Hayes, Allan M.
    K.I.A. Gall., 25/4/15
2812 Pte Hayes, Ernest
5102 Pte Hayes, James
1357 Pte Hayes, James L.
1473
    K.I.A. Gall., 5/6/15
410 Sgt Hayes, James M.
6025 Pte Hayes, John S.
2662 Pte Hayes, John Thomas
    K.I.A. France, 23-26/7/16
575 OR/Sgt Hayes, Wm. Jos.
5103 Cpl. Hayes, Wm. Jos.
— 2/Lieut Haynes, Albert
    Died Mesopot., 27/7/17
1759 Gnr Haynes, Clifford A.
2588 Sgt Haysey, Robert E.
    (C. de G. Belgian)
3363 Dvr Hayward, Alfred C.
3330 Pte Hayward, Harry
38 Cpl Head, Colin Wilfrid
    K.I.A. Anzac, 25/4/15
1563 Pte Head, Harold
65 Sgt Head, Wm. W. J.
    K.I.A. Anzac, 25/4/15
7007 Pte Heal, Frank A. J.
5106 Pte Healey, Harry
1197 L/Cpl Heap, William
    K.I.A. Belgium, 20/9/17
— Capt Chap Hearn, Joseph
    (M.C.)
2815 Pte Heather, Horace G.
    K.I.A. France, 19/7/16
55630 Pte Heather, William E.
5393 Pte Heatherington, Julian
— Lieut Heaton, George
    K.I.A. Belgium, 4/10/17
1044 Pte Hecker, Arthur H.
    D.O.W. France, 2/8/18
3346 Pte Heffernan, Fredk. C.
3540 Pte Heffernan, Harry Jas.
227 Pte Heffernan, William
3347 Dvr Heffernan, Wm. T.

60793 Pte Hegney, Patrick F.
— Lieut Heighway, A. R.
6614 Pte Hellyer, Joseph D.
    K.I.A. Belgium, 7/10/17
990 Pte Helsham, John G. D.
    K.I.A. Anzac, 25/4/15
1025 Sgt Hempel, Arthur E.
1136 Pte Hempel, John
    (M.M. and Bar)
— Lieut Henderson, Alan D.
    D.O.W. at Sea, 27-30/4/15
2677 Pte Henderson, David
3348 Pte Henderson, Fredk. A.
    K.I.A. France, 19/7/16
2140 Cpl Henderson, Henry
55627 Pte Henderson, Harold D.
3045 Pte Henderson, Henry R.
792 Cpl Henderson, Joseph J.
2669 L/Cpl Henderson, L. W.
— Capt Henderson, Rup. H.
    (M.I.D.)
    K.I.A. Gall., 8-12/5/15
2586 L/Cpl Henderson, Wm.
6514 Pte Hendy, Gilbert N.
55633 Pte Hendy, William F.
221 C.S.M. Henley, Albert E.
    K.I.A. Gall., 11/5/15
2814 Cpl Henley, Charles P.
1763 Pte Hennebery, Martin
466 Pte Hennessey, Joseph R.
6286 Sgt Hennessy, L. S.
    D.O.W. France, 26/2/17
2500 Sgt Henry, Donald
    K.I.A. France, 8/8/18
6766 Pte Henry, Ernest
1954 Cpl Henshall, Alfred
60697 Pte Henshaw, Joseph W.
924 S/Sgt Hepburn, John
6276 Pte Hepburn, James John
    K.I.A. Belgium, 4/10/17
6631 Pte Herd, Walter Victor
745 Pte Heritage, Francis P.
6508 Pte Herlihy, John Alex.
1770 Pte Herman, Eric
167 Pte Heron, Herbert John
2144 Pte Heron, William Chas.
— Capt Heron, Wilfrid L.
— Lt-Col Herrod, Ernest E.
    (C.M.G., D.S.O., 4
    M.I.D., White Eagle
    5th Class Serbian)
596 Pte Hetherton, Arthur
    K.I.A. Anzac, 25/4/15
925 Pte Heuston, John Hague
2679 Pte Hewat, Richard
1051 Pte Hewet, George F.
    K.I.A. Anzac, 8-9/8/15
— Mjr Hewitt, Frank R.
    (M.C.)
2661 L/Sgt Hewitt, Rupert M.
    D.O.W. France, 11/7/16
1760 Pte Hewitt, Walter
    K.I.A. Anzac, 8-9/8/15

177 Sgt Newland, Charles J. (M.I.D.)
2702 Pte Heyward, Alfred
1761 Pte Hiam, Walter Geo.
  K.I.A. France, 9/8/18
2850 Pte Hibbert, Cecil S. S.
  D.O.W. Belgium, 5/10/17
855 Pte Hibbert, Harry
6281 Pte Hickman, James
794 T/Sgt Hicks, Lisle
2816 Cpl Hicks, Sidney
2584 T/Sgt Hicks, Thomas H. (M.M. and Bar)
1659 Pte Hickson, Gordon
  Died Malta, 30/8/15
2678 Cpl Higgins, Bertram W. (M.S.M.)
2817 Pte Higgins, Stanley
3333 Pte Higgs, Samuel J.
3334 L/Cpl Higgs, William A.
5093 Pte Higman, Albert
926 Cpl Hill, Allan
  D.O.W. France, 21/9/17
6277 Pte Hill, Ernest Stanley
7502 Pte Hill, Edwin Thomas
  D.O.W. Wisgnes, 12/5/18
— Lieut Hill, Eric W. (M.I.D.)
570 Dvr Hill, George
6767 Pte Hill, George
  K.I.A. Belgium, 20/9/17
369 Sgt Hill, George Albert (M.M., M.I.D.)
1683 Pte Hill, George G.
6401 Pte Hill, Leslie Thomas
2681 Dvr Hill, Peter Victoria
6283 Pte Hill, Roland (M.M.)
6284 Pte Hill, Reginald S. (M.M.)
927 L/Cpl Hill, Sydney R.
3774 Pte Hill, Thomas V.
228 Pte Hill, William C.
  K.I.A. Gall., 25/4/15
6765 Pte Hilleard, Francis G.
— Mjr Hillard, Robert Irvine (M.C.)
280 Pte Hillman, Ernest
  K.I.A. France, 25/2/17
1097 L/Cpl Hillman, Joseph
229 Pte Hillman, Leslie Thos.
3349 Pte Hills, Charles
108 Sgt Hills, William
  K.I.A. Gall., 19/5/15
1955 Pte Hilsly, Cecil Ernest
  K.I.A. France, 3/5/17
3335 Pte Hinch, Edgar
5096 Pte Hind, Hector
790 L/Cpl Hindley, Francis G.
595 Pte Hine, Arthur W.
  Died at Sea, 22/5/15
60690 Pte Hinsley, Harold
7114 Pte Hinton, Fredk. H.

1565 Pte Hinsley, Joseph
  K.I.A. Anzac, 7-9/8/15
560 L/Cpl Hipworth, John A.
706 Pte Hird, Henry
  D.O.W. Anzac, 10/5/15
1666 Pte Hird, William B.
  K.I.A. Belgium, 12/10/17
2657 Cpl Hiskins, James N.
— Capt Hoad, F. J. S.
  D.O.W., 13/8/16
2576 Pte Hoare, Bertram
506 Cpl Hoare, Patrick
  D.O.W. Belgium, 5/10/17
3366 Cpl Hoath, Melville C.
— 2/Lieut Hoban Daniel J.
7011 ER/S/Sgt Hobbs, Fredk.
3367 Pte Hobbs, Geo. J. A.
  K.I.A. France, 18/8/16
60691 Pte Hobbs, William G.
  Died England, 1/11/18
6027 L/Cpl Hobson, Chas. B.
6413 Pte Hocking, Albert
1348 Pte Hocking, Arthur J.
4835 Pte Hocking, Edward
3336 Pte Hodge, Reginald H.
  Died England, 19/9/16
714 Pte Hodge, Wilfred
3337 Pte Hodgens, Herbert
2142 ER/Cpl Hodges, H. G.
4809 Pte Hodgetts, Walter C.
2705 Pte Hodgkinson, Arthur
  K.I.A. Belgium, 2/9/16
5693 Cpl Hodgson, Robert J. (M.M.)
— Lieut Hoffman, Clyde
1032 C.Q.M.S. Hoffman, W. J.
395 Pte Hoffman, Alfred F.
6773 Pte Hogan, John Edward
  D.O.W. Belgium, 20/9/17
2706 Pte Hogan, Matthew M.
1082 Pte Hogan, William
5097 Sgt Hogg, John Henry (D.C.M.)
1672 Pte Hogg, Leslie
55631 Pte Holbrook, William J.
5692 Pte Holder, Charles
2849 Pte Holland, Andrew
  K.I.A. France, 18/8/16
544 Sgt Holland Geo. W. F. (M.M.)
1664 Pte Holland, Lawrence A.
788 Pte Holland, Vernon
  K.I.A. Gall., 8/5/15
5695 Pte Holliday, John Wm.
2707 Pte Hollier, Edgar Chas.
  K.I.A. France, 17/8/16
2057 Sgt Hollings, Gerald
992 Pte Hollings, Kenneth B.
— Lieut Hollings, Alex. D.
7505 Pte Holman, Cecil George
1957 Pte Holman, Leonard S.
2666 Pte Holme, John
6632 Pte Holmes, Charles A.

6771 Pte Holmes, Reginald J.	497 Pte Howes, George S.
6760 Pte Holmes, William	377 Pte Howlett, Percy N.
K.I.A. Belgium, 20/9/17	2682 Pte Hoyne, Jeremiah P.
2819 Sgt Homden, Leslie G.	1961 Sgt Hubbard, Ernest A.
2665 Pte Honan, Edward Jos.	K.I.A. France, 16/10/17
K.I.A. France, 25/7/16	2714 Pte Huckle, Herbert C.
2582 Spr Honey, Alfred	1352 Pte Hudson, Henry H.
(M.M.)	60692 Pte Hudson, John Chas.
2667 Pte Honeybone, Alfred	533 Sgt Huf, Carl Wilhelm
— Mjr Honman, Andrew V.	D.O.W. at Sea, 13/5/15
(M.I.D.)	3781 Pte Hughes, Albert
K.I.A. France, 20/5/17	4347 Pte Hughes, Cyril
573 Pte Hook, Norman Atlee	K.I.A. France, 18/8/16
— Lieut Hooker, Francis H.	1962 Pte Hughes, Edward F.
378 Pte Hooper, Basil John	55639 Pte Hughes, Edward J.
K.I.A. Anzac, 25/4/15	55636 T/Sgt Hughes, Harry W.
1374 Pte Hooper, Francis H.	2658 Pte Hughes, Peter L. R.
K.I.A. Gall., 8/5/15	2668 Pte Hughes, Robert James
2851 Sgt Hooper, Thomas Jas.	5690 L/Cpl Hulett, Charles F.
Died France, 27/11/16	K.I.A. France, 9/8/18
60689 Artfcr Hopcroft, Herbert	1767 Sgt Hume, John Albert
1349 Pte Hopgood, Frank	2863 L/Cpl Hume, Francis
— 2/Lieut Hopkins, Ernest J.	262 Pte Hume, John Hamilton
— Mjr Hopkins, Joseph W.	3553 Pte Humphrey, Stanley G.
(M.C. and Bar)	1642 L/Cpl Humphreys, Herbt.
6613 Pte Hopkins, John Wm.	K.I.A. France, 19/7/16
— H/Capt Hopkinson, Albt.	5109 Pte Humphreys, L. J.
2820 Pte Horgan, Clarence	1963 Pte Humphries, Albert G.
— Capt Hornby, Leslie L.	1870 ER/2/Cpl Humphries, J.
K.I.A. France, 29/9/18	2660 Pte Hunt, Edmund
6761 Pte Hornby, William J.	6764 Pte Hunt, George
2366 Cpl Hornsey, Wm. A.	4348 Pte Hunt, Sydney Walter
2684 Pte Horton, Percy O.	2680 Pte Hunt, William James
2709 Pte Horwood, Edward G.	— Capt Hunter, Herbert H.
334 Pte Hoskin, Percy	K.I.A. Gall., 8-12/5/15
5397 Pte Hosking, Clarence L.	1765 Pte Hunter, Jackson B.
1141 Pte Hoskins, Peter	2664 Pte Hunter, James Dick
1959 L/Cpl Houghton, C. H.	K.I.A. France, 29/6/16
K.I.A. France, 9/8/18	4805 Spr Hunter, John O. S.
7504 Pte Houghton, Harold R.	619 Pte Hunter, William
170 Pte Houston, Fredk. F.	K.I.A. Anzac, 8-9/8/15
230 Pte Howard, Alfred	1568 Pte Huntingford, James
K.I.A. Gall., 8/5/15	6509 Pte Huntsman, Henry R.
584 Pte Howard, Charles L.	K.I.A. Belgium, 20/9/17
Died Malta, 12/5/15	3342 Pte Hurley, George
3338 Gnr Howard, Frank	(Std. to be Herlihy, G.)
D.O.W. France, 20/5/18	K.I.A. France, 11/4/18
6515 Pte Howard, George H.	1001 Pte Hurn, Arthur
2227 Pte Howard, John A.	1569 Pte Hurne, Albert Edwd.
1083 Pte Howard, Robert A.	D.O.W. Anzac, 10/5/15
1153	60696 Pte Hurrell, Leslie Roy
1353 Cpl Howat, Matthew	55635 Gnr Hurrell, William A.
K.I.A. France, 9/8/18	863 Pte Hurst, Herbert Edwd.
6280 Pte Howden, Allan G.	K.I.A. Gall., 8/5/15
2709 Sgt Howe, Leslie George	2670 L/Cpl Hussey, Bernard
(D.C.M.)	2665 MT/Dvr Hussey, Leonard
5107 Pte Howe, Norman Leslie	2666 Pte Hussey, Patrick
D.O.W. Belgium, 5/10/17	2824 Pte Hutcheson, David W.
164 Pte Howe, Robert	K.I.A. France, 19/7/16
55162 Pte Howell, Cecil M.	2370 Pte Hutchings, Richard A.
1567 Pte Howell, George	5111 Pte Hutchins, John
2711 Pte Howell, George	2922 Pte Hutchinson, Thos. A.
7243 Pte Howell, John	Died France, 11/12/17

545 Pte Hutchinson, Bert
 (Correct name Robert-
 shaw, Bartimas)
 K.I.A. Gall., 25/4/15
231 Pte Hutchison, Arch. Jas.
 K.I.A. Gall., 25/4/15
5110 Pte Hutson, Frederick
1357 L/Cpl Hutton, Cleveland
633 Cpl Hyde, Robert Jas.
6467 Pte Hyland, Francis W.
1766 Pte Hynes, Michael
1149 Pte Hyslop, James
3339 Pte Howard, T. W. H.

I

2720 Pte Ibbotson, Thomas E.
2825 T/C.S.M. Ilsley, Henry R.
1005 L/Cpl Incledon, Frank A.
1648 Pte Ingham, Charles E.
2827 Pte Ingram, Wilfred
6408 Pte Interman, Roy Ernest
 K.I.A. France, 11/3/18
1742 Pte Ireland, George Wm.
1743 Pte Ireland, Roy Maxwell
 K.I.A. Belgium, 21/9/17
3554 Pte Irvin, Alan Hedley
179 Pte Irwin, John A. T.
2828 ER/Sgt Isaacs, L. D.
4838 L/Cpl Isaacs, Samuel
5400 L/Cpl Isaacs, Sydney W.
6287 Pte Issell, Ernest A. C.
858 Pte Ivens, Charles Wm.
2672 Pte Izard, Laurence
 K.I.A. France, 20/8/16
1142 Pte Izzard, George

J

2088 Pte Jack, John Gormley
5697 Pte Jackman, Percival A.
— Lieut-Col Jackson, Alfred
 (O.B.E.)
2839 Cpl Jackson, Alfred Geo.
55643 Pte Jackson, Arthur H.
1360 Pte Jackson, George
1024 Pte Jackson, Maurice
1472 Pte Jackson, Percy
2683 Pte Jackson, Roy
7508 Pte Jackson, Robertson
1362 Cpl Jacobs, Albert
— Capt Jacobs, Hubert S.
1772 Pte Jacobs, Louis William
 D.O.W. Anzac, 3/12/15
48 Pte Jacobsohn, Julius R.
3786 Pte Jacques, George W.
87 Pte James, David Walter
1854 Pte James, Frederick
 K.I.A. Anzac, 8-9/8/15
409 Sgt James, George Edwin
2591 Pte James, George Edwd.
930 Pte James, George Thos.
1965 L/Cpl James, Laurie
 K.I.A. France, 25-26/8/18

2592 Pte James, Leslie Gordon
 K.I.A. France, 21/9/18
109 Pte James, Sydney (stated
 to be Seyfang, Syd. J.)
 Died France, 9/11/18
2677 ER/2/Cpl James, Wm. C.
— Lieut. James, William H.
4815 Pte James, William O.
1964 Pte Jamieson, Albert S.
3997 Pte Jamieson, William
1069 Pte Jamieson, James Y.
2473 *K.I.A. France, 19/7/16*
690 Sgt Jamieson, William
 K.I.A. Anzac, 12/8/15
1457 Pte Jamison, Hugh (stated
 to be Muir, H.)
 K.I.A. Gall., 8/5/15
— Lieut Jardine, Thomas A.
2829 Pte Jarrad, Frank Leach
— Lieut Jarvie, Kenneth R.
137 Dvr Jayne, Albert
7510 Pte Jeffcott, William J.
7019 Pte Jefferies, Ernest John
6778 Pte Jeffress, Arthur John
7254 Pte Jeffs, Thomas
2831 Cpl Jenkin, Thomas H.
 D.O.W. England, 9/1/17
— 2/Lieut Jenkin, William
 K.I.A. France, 19/8/16
6777 Pte Jenkins, Alexander
6292 Gnr Jenkins, Stanley
636 Pte Jenkins, William H.
 (M.M.)
3049 Pte Jenkins, William P.
2679 Cpl Jenkinson, Francis H.
 (M.M.)
430 Pte Jenkinson, Hubert H.
 K.I.A. France, 23/7/16
2675 Pte Jenner, James
2673 Pte Jenner, James Thomas
4584 Pte Jennings, Clarence G.
— Capt Jennings, Richard
6289 Pte Jensen, Anton
 D.O.W. France, 11/8/18
— Brig-Gen Jess, Carl H.
 (C.M.G., D.S.O.,
 M.I.D. (2). Order of
 White Eagle, 4th Class
 Serbian)
6363 T/Cpl Jewell, Arthur G.
2674 Pte Jewell, Gordon
2957 Pte Jewell, Herbert Jas.
 K.I.A. France, 19/7/16
2832 Pte Jiggins, Alexander J.
327 L/Cpl Jobling, Ernest
1571 Pte Jobson, Walter H.
2723 Pte Johannsen, Ernest
 K.I.A. Belgium, 20/9/17
60705 Pte Johnson, Alfred John
7511 Pte Johnson, Bernard
 K.I.A. France, 9/8/18
3371 Dvr Johnson, Charles
2833 Cpl Johnson, Charles F.

3790 Pte Johnson, Charles S.
655 Cpl Johnson, D'arcy F.
  K.I.A. France, 16/5/18
354 Pte Johnson, Francis
  D.O.W. at Sea, 11/8/15
2724 Pte Johnson, Frederick
997 Pte Johnson, Harry
932 Pte Johnson, Harold John
  D.O.W. Alexandria, 2/5/15
1144 Pte Johnson, John
385 Pte Johnson, James C.
  K.I.A. Gall., 8/5/15
52073 Pte Johnson, Joseph F.
3380 Pte Johnson, James Jos.
1677 Pte Johnson, Thomas
  K.I.A. Anzac, 8-9/8/15
55641 Gnr Johnson, Walter G.
55719 Pte Johnson, William J.
3524 Pte Johnston, Albert
  K.I.A. France, 19/7/16
3372 Pte Johnston, Andrew A.
  D.O.W. France, 20/7/16
245 Sgt Johnston, Arthur H.
234 Pte Johnston, Donald W.
  K.I.A. Gall., 8/5/15
— Lieut Johnston, Jas. A. K.
  D.O.W. Cairo, 19/5/15
1647 Pte Johnston, James P.
  D.O.W. Alex'dria, 15/5/15
3374 Pte Johnston, Mark M.
3381 Pte Johnston, Thomas V.
2682 Cpl Johnston, William E.
235 L/Cpl Johnston Wm. Jas.
4215 Pte Johnston, Wm. Thos.
1127 Pte Johnstone, George
2474 Pte Johnstone, Walter G.
— Lt-Col Jolley, Alan F.
  (C. de G. Belgian)
  (M.I.D.)
3375 Pte Jolly, Edwin Rupert
2681 Cpl Jonas, Edward
  D.O.W. France, 6/10/17
2837 L/Sgt Jonas, George M.
1020 Pte Jones, Aaron
1364 Pte Jones, Alex. Albert
2151 Pte Jones, Albert Bert
4974 Pte Jones, Alfred Charles
1054 A/Cpl Jones, Albert Ed.
1363 Pte Jones, Archibald H.
  (Stated to be Bidwell, Harold Henry)
2680 Pte Jones, Alfred Henry
504 Pte Jones, Charles Edwin
  K.I.A. Gallipoli,
  25/4/15—2/5/15
2235 Pte Jones, Edward
5248 L/Cpl Jones, Ernest Paul
  K.I.A. Belgium, 20/9/17
2834 Pte Jones, Frederick
  K.I.A. France, 21/8/16
757 Cpl Jones, George
  K.I.A. Gall., 8/5/15
236 S/Sgt Jones, Henry
6520 Pte Jones, Harold Edward

55640 VO/Sgt Jones, Harry P.
6461 Pte Jones, John
  (Enlisted as Brown, John)
  K.I.A. France, 13/6/18
3382 Pte Jones, James Dalling
2684 L/Cpl Jones, James Leo
  K.I.A. France, 23/7/16
2150 Pte Jones, John Wilson
  K.I.A. Anzac, 8-9/8/15
1949 Pte Jones, Leslie Albert
7512 Pte Jones, Lewis Alfred
2152 Pte Jones, Leslie Theo.
  K.I.A. Anzac, 8-9/8/15
2914 Pte Jones, Robert John
  (D.C.M.)
3523 Pte Jones, Rolf Stanley
  Died England, 15/2/17
1573 Pte Jones, Sidney Gerald
  K.I.A. France, 28/7/16
2835 Pte Jones, Thomas
  (Stated to be Ashe, Clive Langtree)
5403 Pte Jones, Thomas
  Died England, 2/11/18
13 Dvr Jones, Thomas T.
6035 Pte Jones, William Edwd.
6521 Pte Jones, William Edwd.
  K.I.A. France, 21/4/17
2726 Sgt Jones, William F.
  (M.M.)
  K.I.A. Belgium, 4/10/17
1966 Pte Jones, William John
387 Pte Jones, William Thos.
2836 Pte Jones, William Thos.
6780 Pte Jordan, Alfred James
  K.I.A. France, 11/4/18
1143 Pte Jordan, Joseph
7253 L/Cpl Jorgensen, Jas. C.
55721 Pte Jory, William Alfred
4213 Pte Jose, Clarence A. S. J.
2149 Pte Jose, Horace Stephen
6522 Pte Joseph, Sydney A.
  K.I.A. France, 9/8/18
845 Pte Joy, Walter Edward
3555 Pte Joyce, John
6633 Pte Joyce, Leslie Charles
1622 Pte Joyce, Robert
6779
1773 Pte Joyce, Thomas
2589 Pte Joyner, Benjamin B.
  (M.M.)
2590 Sgt Judd, Walter John V.
5114 Pte Judge, George E.
1361 Pte Julin, James Leopold
463 Pte Junier, Edward W.
  D.O.W. Gall., 25/4/15

K

— Interpreter Kaloustian, Z.
1967 Pte Kane, William Jas.
  K.I.A. Gall., 7-9/8/15
2840 L/Cpl Kaniers, William J.
  D.O.W., Eng., 30/8/18

7021 Pte Karmel, Ellis Morris
2841 Pte Kealy, Richard T. P.
481 Pte Keam, Herbert
    K.I.A., 25-30/4/15
919 Pte Keam, Richard Albert
237 Pte Kean, Thomas
    K.I.A. Gall., 25/4/15
2727 Pte Keane, Vincent
621 Pte Kearney, John N.
    K.I.A. Gall., 8/5/15
2689 Pte Kearney, Leo
1146 Pte Keating, Albert H.
    (M.M.)
— Lieut Keating, James Ed.
    (M.C., M.I.D.)
6294 Pte Keating, Thomas F.
    K.I.A. France, 23/8/18
351 Pte Keefe, William
55644 Pte Keen, Henry Richard
2728 Pte Keighley, Charles Jas.
3385 Cpl Keir, Wallace H.
6300 Pte Kelley, William H.
1776 Pte Kellow, John Henry
    (M.M.)
2154 Cpl Kellow, John W.
1671 Pte Kelly, Arthur
3556 Pte Kelly, Daniel
238 Pte Kelly, Henry Victor
— Capt Kelly, Lester H.
1968 Pte Kelly, Patrick
    K.I.A. Gall., 8-9/8/15
2688 Pte Kelly, Robert
2842 Cpl Kelly, Thomas
5810 Pte Kemeys, William R.
2729 Pte Kemp, Eric George
1775 ER/2/Cpl Kemp, Robert
111 Pte Kemp, Walter
6295 Pte Kempt, Arthur
    K.I.A. Belgium, 4/10/17
480 Pte Kennedy, Edward
797 Pte Kennedy, Ern. T. J.
    K.I.A. Gall., 8/5/15
642 Pte Kennedy, Francis
810 Cpl Kennedy, Harold V.
2153 T/Cpl Kennedy Leslie A.
2375 Sgt Kennedy, Leslie E.
1777 Pte Kennedy, Joseph
796 Pte Kennerley, Thomas F.
    K.I.A. Gall., 18/7/15
5702 Dvr Kennett, Albert F.
5699 Pte Kenny, Thomas Neil
2593 Dvr Kenshole, Louis L.
29 Pte Kent, Herbert
6296 Pte Kent, Hubert Clive
2376 Pte Kent, John Thomas
1145 Pte Kent, Robert
6297 L/Cpl Kent, S. J. J.
3386 Cpl Kent, William
— Mjr Kent Hughes, W. S.
    (M.C., M.I.D.4)
6526 Pte Kenyon, Ben. Ambery
1969 Sgt Keogh, William
115 Pte Kerby, N. V. G.
    K.I.A. Anzac, 25/4/15

4827 Pte Kerr, Arthur James
6037 Pte Kerr, Bert
    K.I.A. France, 28/1/17
661 Cpl Kerr, Martin Brown
2690 Sgt Kerr, William John
    (M.M.)
    D.O.W. France, 10/8/18
2686 Pte Kerr-Neison, Walter
    K.I.A. Belgium, 25-26/10/17
3798 Pte Kershaw, Edward
    K.I.A. Belgium, 4/10/17
1779 Pte Kett, Dennis
3388 Pte Kew, William Henry
113 Pte Keyes, Clifford E. T.
4218 Dvr Keys, Daniel John
3389 Pte Kidd, Herbert Chas.
    (M.M.)
112 Pte Kiely, Frank
    K.I.A. Anzac, 25/4/15
1000 Pte Kiely, John William
55645 Pte Killeen, Thomas Jos.
1147 Pte Kilpatrick, Wm. Jas.
7514 Pte Kimpton, Aug. Edwd.
3390 Pte Kimpton, Fredk. C.
3186 Dvr King, Arthur Cecil
1575 Pte King, Ernest Alfred
61889
114 Pte King, Frank
239 Pte King, Hainsworth
    K.I.A. Gall, 8-9/8/15
3531 Pte King, Henry Rupert
    (M.M.)
5701 L/Cpl King, Ira George
1855 Pte King, James
645 Sgt King, James Henry S.
    (M.M.)
1160 Pte King, James Silvester
921 Pte King, Thomas Joseph
1778 Sgt King, Thomas Leslie
1970 Pte King, Walter M.
    K.I.A. Gall., 27/8/15
2597 Cpl King, Walter Tasman
    K.I.A. France, 19/7/16
6298 MT/Dvr Kingsford, S. C.
799 Cpl Kingsley, Claude G.
4022 Pte Kingsley, Daniel
    (Correct name, Waters,
    William)
328 Pte Kingston, Herbert Jas
    K.I.A. Gall., 25/4/15
1971 Cpl Kingston, Wm. Jos.
    K.I.A. Gall., 8-9/8/15
1365 Pte Kinkaid, Andrew T.
3801 Pte Kinna, Reuben Victor
    K.I.A. France, 18/8/16
1673 Pte Kinnear, John
2687 L/Cpl Kinross, Thomas S.
    D.O.W. Belgium, 6/10/17
2844 Pte Kirkwood, Alfred J.
— T/Capt Kitchen, F. G.
    D.O.W. France, 10/8/18
116 L/Cpl Kitson, Arthur F.
    K.I.A. Gall., 8/5/15

2845 Pte Kitson, Percy Stewart
      D.O.W. Belgium, 3/9/16
7255 Pte Kneale, Patrick
2846 Pte Knell, Charles E.
 798 Pte Knight, Alexander R.
2594 Pte Knight, Bertie R.
      K.I.A. France, 27/6/16
1718 Pte Knight, Ernest Alfred
 933 Pte Knight, Edward L.
      K.I.A. Anzac, 25/4/15
2685 Pte Knight, Fredk. C.
      K.I.A. France, 18/8/16
2595 Pte Knight, Hugh Menoal
 117 Pte Knott, William E.
2847 Cpl Knowles, John V.
      D.O.W. France, 27/3/18
6299 Pte Kohn, Eric R. J.
  21 Sgt Kong-Meng, Herbert
  — 2/Lieut Kozminsky, M. E.
      D.O.W. France, 19/8/16
6781 L/Cpl Krantzcke, Robt. K.
2848 Cpl Krausgrill, Percy
  — Mjr Kuring, Herman Aug.
 356 Pte Kyffin, Arthur P.

L

 751 Pte Lachmund, Allan
2606 Pte Lafargues, Aaug. P.
1371 Pte Laidlaw, David
2696 Pte Laing, George
      Died England, 12/1/17
1576 Pte Laing, James Robert
2379 Sgt Laird, Fredk. A.
      (M.M.)
 240 ER/Cpl Lalor, Henry
2067 Pte Lamb, Charles H.
 586 Pte Lamb, George
2089 Pte Lambert, Jack Richd.
1577 Pte Lambert, Wm. Jos.
      K.I.A. Anzac, 8-9/8/15
6527 Pte Lamont, Kenneth E.
 118 Cpl Lamont, Leonard W.
1974 Pte Lampard, John
      D.O.W. at Sea, 12/8/15
1975 Pte Lampard, James Cyril
7515 Pte Lamplugh, C. F. X.
      Died France, 12-13/3/18
 241 L/Cpl Lancaster, T. C.
3557 Pte Lancefield, Daniel
3052 Gnr Landen, George A.
      K.I.A. Belgium, 26/9/17
2695 Pte Lander, Arthur G.
7029 Pte Lane, Arthur S.
1780 Pte Lane, Denis
      D.O.W. France, 11/4/18
60796 Pte Lane, Leslie John
  — Lieut. Lane, Walter E.
60716 Pte Lang, Robert Cecil
 171 Pte Langan, George L.
7258 Pte Lange, Albert Erwin
3050 Pte Langham, Joseph O.
 829 Pte Langhorn, Arnold E.

2697 Pte Langley, Chas. C.
      D.O.W. France, 2/8/16
5703 Cpl Lansdown, Robert J.
1782 Pte La-Peyre, Ernest
      D.O.W. Cairo, 29/4/17
5706 Pte Larkin, Thomas
2733 Pte Larkins, James
6529 Pte La Roche, Oscar Roy
6308 Pte Larsen, Albert H. S.
      (M.M.)
7261 L/Cpl Larsen, Daniel C.
 724 Pte Larter, Alfred Ernest
5642 Pte Larter, Fredk. C.
1784 Pte Lascelles, Sydney J.
2958 Pte Latham, Peter James
      K.I.A. France, 19/7/16
3805 Pte Lauder, Peter
60714 Pte Laurence, Roland C.
 665 Pte Laurenson, Sam. W.
1976 Pte Laurenson, W. A.
4228 Sgt Lavars, George A.
6138 Pte Lavers, Keith M.
6784 Pte Lawlis, John
2863 Pte Lawrence, Alfred H.
3391 Pte Lawrence, Frederick
4226 Pte Lawrence, Francis
7516 Pte Lawrence, Richard P.
4837 Pte Lawry, George R.
 717 Pte Lawry, Henry Arthur
 936 Sgt Lawry, Walter J. O.
2920 Pte Laws, Albert G. G.
 935 Pte Lawson, Robert
      D.O.W. at Sea, 20/8/15
3392 Pte Lawson, Thomas
1359 Pte Lawton, Leonard V.
1375
  — Capt Lay, Clarence W.
      (M.C.)
2729 Sgt Laycock, Raymond S.
      (M.M.)
      D.O.W. Belgium, 23/9/17
2605 L/Cpl Layfield, Alfred W.
      K.I.A. France, 25/2/17
  — Lieut-Col Layh, H. T. C.
      (C.M.G., D.S.O. and
      Bar, M.I.D.3)
1578 Pte Lazarus, Isaac
      K.I.A. Gall., 8/5/15
 838 Pte Lazarus, Louis
1579 Pte Lea, Frank
2236 Pte Leach, Leo
      D.O.W. Alex'dria, 13/8/15
1675 Pte Leahy, John Daniel
6383 Pte Leahy, John Patrick
1580 Pte Lear, Edwin Mervyn
      D.O.W. at Sea, 18/8/15
1283 Spr Leary, John Henry
2209
3393 Pte Le Brun, William M.
      K.I.A. France, 2/6/16
3401 L/Cpl Le Couilliard, F. G.
5712 L/Cpl Ledwidge, A. H.
1152 ER/2/Cpl Ledwidge, M. J.

1370 Pte Ledwidge, Walter S.
1581 Pte Lee, Alfred
1661 Pte Lee, Alfred George
   (M.M.)
2849 Pte Lee, Albert H.
383 Sgt Lee, Egbert H. A.
60708 Pte Lee, George G.
2602 L/Cpl Lee, John Edward
382 Cpl Lee, Rupert Acaster
60718 Pte Lee, Ronald E. B.
576 Pte Leech, Norman
5796 Pte Leech, Stanley R.
119 Pte Leeds, Harrie S. M.
362 Pte Leeming, Ralph
3396 Pte Lees, Wm. A. C.
   K.I.A. France, 26/7/16
4229 Pte Lehane, Jeremiah
   K.I.A. France, 22/12/16
4345 Pte Leigh, George R.
3809 Pte Leigh, Leslie Studdy
2600 Pte Leigh, Walter James
4223 Dvr Leighton, Percival J.
3397 Pte Leishman, Robert M.
546 Pte Lemon, Joseph R. S.
   Died Lemnos, 2/11/15
63 Pte Lempriere, Thos. C.
2694 Cpl Lench, Walter M.
1366 Pte Lennon, Richard
   K.I.A. Gall., 7-8/8/15
330 L/Cpl Lennon, William
1374 L/Cpl Leonard, Ernest
393 Pte Leonard, James Leslie
1372 Pte Leslie, Herbert
60715 Pte Leslie, John
55646 Pte Leslie, William C.
2693 Pte Letson, Charles A.
   Died 26/2/20
5812 T/Cpl Leworthy, S. H.
242 Pte Levens, George Hill
   K.I.A. Gall., 25/4/15
1582 Pte Leveridge, Thomas
2736 Pte Levings, Alex. E.
   K.I.A. France, 18/8/16
2737 Pte Levings, Norman Jas.
2850 L/Sgt Levoi, Ioris Philip
2851 Pte Levy, Harold Leopold
121 S/Sgt Levy, Reuben
311 Pte Lewis, Edwin James
2854 T/Sgt Lewis, Henry
4531 T/Sgt Lewis, Henry L.
1367 Cpl Lewis, John Arnold
2604 Cpl Lewis, Leonard
2855 Dvr Lewis, Ormond
7260 Pte Lewis, Sydney L.
2691 Pte Lewis, William
   K.I.A. France, 25/3/17
7125 Pte Lewis, William Enos
7093 ER/2/Cpl Leys, John
181 Cpl Leyshon, George A.
   D.O.W. Alex'dria, 7/5/15
— Capt Liddelow, Aubrey
   K.I.A. France, 19/7/16
745 Pte Liddiard, John Harold
   K.I.A. France, 6/11/16

6531 Pte Lidstone, Clifford A.
   K.I.A. Belgium, 4/10/17
1781 Pte Light, Albert George
1977 Pte Light, Edward Geo.
   D.O.W. France, 11/8/18
— Capt Lilford, A. G. R.
   (M.C.)
2738 Pte Lilley, Richard
   K.I.A. France, 11/4/17
2155 L/Cpl Limerock, John G.
   K.I.A. Anzac, 8-9/8/15
1148 Pte Lindsay, Allan
   K.I.A., Gall., 8/5/15
1583 Pte Lindsay, Albert
3153 Pte Lindsay, William J.
   K.I.A. Belgium, 4/10/17
874 Sgt Lindsay, David G.
2856 Pte Linton, Joseph Roy
60713 Pte Litchfield, Albert D.
1978 Pte Litchfield, William H.
3398 Pte Lithgow, Philip
598 Pte Little, John
2601 Cpl Littlemore, Thomas
   K.I.A. France, 3/11/16
2598 Dvr Livermore, C. R.
3316 Sgt Lloyd, Geo. R. P.
5710 Pte Loader, Arthur John
6306 Pte Lock, James Alfred
   Killed Acc. France, 5/9/18
5144 Pte Locke, George D.
6307 Pte Locke, Herbert W.
243 Pte Locker, Fredk. Thos.
   K.I.A. Anzac, 25-4/2/5/15
122 Pte Lockhart, James L.
765 Pte Lockyer, George W.
6782 L/Cpl Logan, David A.
60710 Pte Logan, Ernest
123 Pte Logan, Frank
5711 Pte Lomax, Albert
1153 Pte Long, Albert Charles
3154 Pte Long, Charles
3402 Pte Long, Charles Henry
469 Pte Long, Cuthbert Jones
   K.I.A. Anzac, 25/4/15
6783 Pte Long, Edward Chas.
3399 Pte Long, George Wm.
1783 T/Cpl Long, Joseph E. J.
4840 Pte Long, William H.
2157 ER/WO(1) Long, W. T.
802 Dvr Longbottom, Benj.
7258 Pte Longmuir, Geo. Alex.
   Died France, 28/11/18
3155 Cpl Loriman, John B.
7027 Pte Lorimer, William G.
3157 Cpl Loud, Fredk. Leslie
   D.O.W. France, 27/7/16
2857 Pte Loudon, James
2599 Pte Loughnan, G. R. McC.
3051 Pte Love, Arthur K.
— Chaplain Love, Francis S.
   (late No. 60717 G.S. Rfts.)
2156 Cpl Love, George F.
3320 Spr Love, James E. C.

1979 Pte Lovelace, James Thos.
4224 Pte Lovell, Douglas A.
6528 Pte Loveridge, Henry
        K.I.A. France, 3/7/18
60709 Pte Low, James Alex.
2845 Pte Lowe, Edward W. F.
937 Pte Lowe, Thomas G. R.
7517 Pte Lowell, John A.
1369 Pte Lowrie, James Wm.
938 Pte Loxton, Percival
       K.I.A. Gall., 25/4/15
5127 Pte Loy, Samuel A. J.
769 Pte Lubke, William J.
       Died Egypt, 27/1/15
1161 Pte Lucas, Charles E.
1980 Dvr Lucas, Edmund J.
1163 Pte Lucas, Fredk. N.
2869 Pte Lucas, John
764 Pte Ludemann, Herman
7519 Pte Lugg, Robert G.
577 Pte Lukey, Percy
— Capt Lukin, Francis T.
2858 Pte Lundquist, A. B.
60711 Pte Lusic, Nicholas T.
5701 Pte Lutherborrow, A. J.
308 Pte Luxford, Percy A.
547 Dvr Lyle, Charles L.
— Lieut Lyle, John Munro
2859 Pte Lynch, John
6629 Pte Lynch, John
       (D.C.M.)
1981 Cpl Lynch, James P.
2860 Pte Lynch, Michael A.
3158 Pte Lynch, Walter John
2861 Pte Lyons, John
       K.I.A. France, 18/8/16
7520 Pte Lyons, James Henry
       K.I.A. France, 9/8/18
2862 Pte Lyons, Noel
124 L/Cpl Lyons, Stanley
       K.I.A. Gall., 21/5/15
1167 Pte Lythgo, Francis W.
       (M.M.)
472 Pte Lyttle, Harold
— M.O. Capt Lyttle, S. P.
125 Pte Lyttleton, Benjamin

M

5152 Pte Maag, Thomas Henry
       K.I.A. Belgium, 20/9/17
3064 Pte Mabbett, F. W. J.
3086 Pte Maddams, George
1385 Pte Madden, Charles F.
       K.I.A. Anzac, 25/4/15
3060 Pte Madden, Gerald T.
270 Pte Madden, James
1983 Pte Madden, John
3404 Pte Madden, John Victor
3082 Pte Madden, Sidney
461 Sgt Maddern, William
5713 L/Cpl Maddison, Fredk.
2384 Pte Magnus, George H.
       D.O.W. Belgium, 26/10/17

2930 Pte Maguire, William
       K.I.A. France, 9/8/18
3159 Pte Maher, Denis S.
3410 Pte Maher, Frank
2746 Pte Maher, Hugh
       K.I.A. France, 9/8/18
7522 Pte Maher, James A. T.
       K.I.A. France, 9/8/18
2921 Pte Maher, Thomas
2917 Pte Maher, William
2927 Pte Maher, William J.
1984 Pte Mahoney, Patrick
2398 Pte Mahoney, William
       D.O.W. France, 31/7/16
2747 Pte Main, John
4232 Pte Maine, Henry Allan
2165 Pte Mair, Charles Peter
2698 Pte Maitland, Leslie G.
       D.O.W. France, 19/8/16
3413 Pte Major, George H.
       K.I.A. France, 17/8/16
55663 L/Cpl Major, Herbert H.
132 Pte Major, Herbert S.
135 C.Q.M.S. Makeham, John
4230 Pte Makepeace, Ernest A.
2628 Sgt Makepeace, E. W.
       (M.M.)
3074 Cpl Makin, John R.
5146 Pte Malan, Henry D.
693 Pte Malcolm, John A.
       K.I.A. Gall., 25/4/15
2699 Pte Male, Samuel H.
— Lieut Mallett, Arthur W.
279 Pte Mallinson, Alexander
6792 Pte Mallinson, James E.
       K.I.A. Belgium, 4/10/17
3160 L/Cpl Mallows, H. C.
3160 Cpl, Maloney, Charles E.
       (M.M. and Bar)
       D.O.W. France, 23/9/17
709 Pte Maloney, F. E.
1796 Pte Maloney, Richard
       D.O.W. Belgium, 4/10/17
1383 Pte Manallack, William
       K.I.A. France, 26/9/17
131 Pte Mancell, Herbert J.
3067 Dvr Mankey, Albert
       (M.M.)
55650 Pte Manley, Robert L.
3072 Pte Mann, Alex. P.
6649 Pte Mann, Fredk. Wm.
— Lieut Manners, Henry F.
830 Pte Manning, Alfred
4535 Pte Mansbridge, George
       K.I.A. France, 19/8/16
5718 Dvr Mansell, W. C. S.
4256 Pte Mansfield, Percy D.
       K.I.A. France, 19/8/16
1388 Pte Manuell, W. L. C.
       D.O.W. France, 24/8/18
55668 Pte Marchant, Charles T.
6785 Pte Marchant, John C.
       K.I.A. Belgium, 4/10/17

2866	Pte Marfleet, Wilfred		3084	Pte Mathieson, C. G.
4843	Pte Mark, Arthur			*K.I.A. France, 19/7/16*
—	Lieut Marks, Fredk. B.		3085	Sgt Mathieson, Fred W.
3083	Pte Marks, Reuben		3541	Gnr Matthew, Ernest M.
2748	Cpl Marlow, George T.		1641	Pte Matthew, William J.
	D.O.W. Belgium, 21/9/17			*D.O.W. at Sea, 11/8/15*
55655	Pte Marriott, William E.		49	L/Cpl Matthews, Francis
942	L/Cpl Marsh, Robert		50	T/Sgt Matthews, James R.
1827			3165	Pte Matthews, M. W.
	K.I.A. France, 1/3/17		5142	Pte Matthews, Wm. H.
244	Pte Marshall, Albert			*K.I.A. France, 16/8/16*
3414	Dvr Marshall, Alfred Eric		4350	Pte Mattson, George H.
6793	Pte Marshall, Harrie F.		3066	Pte Maule, Alexander J.
	D.O.W. France, 9/10/17			*K.I.A. France, 19/7/16*
55722	Gnr Marshall, H. R. G.		1985	T/Sgt Maund, F. J. E.
2617	Pte Marshall, John S.		5811	Pte Maunder, Raymond
55671	Gnr Marshall, M. R.		5714	Pte Maunder, V. J. R.
600	Pte Marshall, Reuben E.		985	Pte May, Ernest
	Died France, 24/11/18			*D.O.W. at Sea, 28/4/15*
4257	L/Cpl Marshall, Robert R.		1585	Pte May, Joseph
	Died France, 12/1/17			*D.O.D. at Sea, 4/9/15*
3162	Pte Marshall, Robert W.		4251	Pte Mayall, Harold Roy
	K.I.A. France, 9/8/18			*K.I.A. Belgium, 30/9/16*
730	Pte Martin, Charles C.		4250	L/Cpl Mayall, Sidney E.
	K.I.A. Anzac, 29/5/15		3053	Pte Maye, Robert
3070	Pte Martin, Edgar (M.M.)		1033	Cpl Mears, William L.
			729	Pte Mead, Trevor B.
6786	L/Cpl Martin, Godfrey F.		2862	Pte Meads, Edwin
3837	Cpl Martin, Herbert S.		3087	Cpl Mears, William L.
	K.I.A. Belgium, 20/9/17		1033	Pte Meatchem, Thos. H.
1376	Pte Martin, Kenneth		6319	L/Cpl Meehan, Patrick
6787	Pte Martin, Leonard			*D.O.W. France, 15/4/18*
—	Lieut Martin, Leslie Jas.		1986	Pte Meehan, Richard J.
5144	Pte Martin, Percy Ward		841	Pte Meintjes, Cyril
622	Pte Martin, Robert		3071	S/Smith Meldrum, J. D.
	Killed (Accident), Cairo, 26/2/15		3167	Cpl Melotte, Melville
			249	Pte Melville, John R.
4249	Pte Martin, Robert A.			*K.I.A., 25/4/15*
2164	Pte Martin, Tom		743	L/Cpl Menadue, William
	K.I.A. Gall., 8-9/8/15			*D.O.W. at Sea, 11/8/15*
803	Pte Martland, Ernest Jas.		728	Pte Menz, Wm. A. R. (M.M.)
	D.O.W. Alex'dria, 15/5/15			
3415	Pte Marwick, Samuel J.		596	Pte Mepham, George C.
807	Cpl Mason, Albert			*K.I.A. Belgium, 4/10/17*
—	Lieut-Col Mason, Chas. C. (D.S.O., M.I.D.)		2618	Gnr Mercer, Alfred W.
			4234	Pte Mercer, William
3055	Pte Mason, Frederick C. (M.M.)		2864	Pte Meredith, Thomas
				K.I.A., France, 19/8/16
1795	Pte Mason, Frank Henry		2716	Pte Merlin, Cecil Thos.
	K.I.A. Gall., 8-9/8/15		6542	L/Cpl Merlin, John Thos.
2749	Pte Mason, Leslie V.		250	Pte Merriman, Lewis G.
1164	Cpl Mason, William		4235	S/Sgt Metcalfe, Albert E.
	K.I.A. Gall., 12/7/15		399	Pte Metcalfe, Fredk. B.
2768	Pte Massey, Alfred			*K.I.A. Gall., 3/5/15*
485	Pte Mather, Harold		7126	Pte Methven, Alexander
5728	Pte Mathews, F. L. R.		—	2/Lieut Mettan, Albert F.
442	Pte Mathews, George			*K.I.A., 15/5/18*
5410	Pte Mathews, Thomas M. (Correct name Dwyer, T. M.)		—	Lieut Meyer, A. P. F.
				K.I.A. France, 16/4/18
	K.I.A. France, 19/8/16		6317	Pte Meyer, Herbert J.
2714	Pte Mathews, Walter		1996	Pte Miche, Arthur
3164	Pte Mathieson, Archibald		836	Pte Michelly, Percy
			577	Pte Middlemiss, Harold

457 L/Cpl Middlemiss, James
656 Pte Middleton, A. W.
    (M.M.)
53 Pte Middleton, Clifton H.
180 Cpl Middleton, George I.
    K.I.A. Anzac, 25/4/15
1997 Pte Middleton, Wm. R.
6537 Pte Midgley, Edwin L.
    D.O.W. France, 10/8/18
7030 Pte Miles, Alan Adrian
— Lieut Miles, George H.
55651 Pte Miles, William J.
944 Pte Milgate, Fredk. J.
    K.I.A. Anzac, 25/4/15
934 Sgt Milgate, Fredk. M.
    (M.M., French; M.I.D.)
    K.I.A. France, 9/8/18
2386 Pte Milgate, James Wm.
1789 Pte Millar, Percy E. W.
    K.I.A. Anzac, 8-9/8/15
3073 Cpl Millard, Arthur R.
3062 Pte Miller, Alfred
1381 Dvr Miller, Charles S.
747 Pte Miller, George E.
6789 Pte Miller, James
— 2/Lieut Miller, Randolph
    D.O.W. at Sea, 19/5/15
60721 Pte Miller, William H.
6794 Pte Miller, William J.
3170 Pte Miller, William R.
1586 Pte Milliard, Thomas
60723 Pte Millichip, Richard
1587 Pte Millington, Amos
2402 Cpl Millington, Frank G.
1387 Pte Milloy, Edward John
    D.O.W. Gall., 10/5/15
634 Arm/S/Sgt Mills, A. W.
2700 L/Cpl Mills, James Edwin
3851 L/Cpl Mills, Jonathan L.
    K.I.A. Belgium, 4/10/17
4236 Pte Mills, Patrick J.
    D.O.W. France, 29/8/16
2619 Pte Mills, William
386 Sgt Mills, William A.
2191 L/Cpl Millward, Harry
2621 L/Cpl Milne, Arch. F.
    K.I.A. France, 9/8/18
30 Pte Milne, James Gordon
339 Sgt Milroy, James
4237 Pte Minns, John
3171 Cpl Minogue, Jercy Jos.
5720 Pte Mintern, George E.
6320 Pte Mitchell, Alan Keith
    K.I.A. France, 24/8/18
721 Pte Mitchell, Arch. L.
578 ER/Cpl Mitchell, D. S.
1998 Pte Mitchell, F. C. P.
2931 Pte Mitchell, George H.
6540 Pte Mitchell, Harry A.
133 Pte Mitchell, Harold W.
3559 ER/2/Cpl Mitchell, John
6538 Pte Mitchell, James Alex.
945 Pte Mitchell, Thomas

806 Pte Mitchell, James G.
    K.I.A. France, 19/5/16
1573 L/Sgt Mitchell, Thos. W.
    (M.M.)
2702 Pte Mitchell, William
1786 Pte Mitchell, William J.
7033 Pte Mock, Thomas
2238 Pte Mole, Stanley George
2715 L/Cpl Molloy, Michael
3057 Pte Moloney, Michael
734 Pte Monaghan, Bernard
733 Sgt Monaghan, Edward
4555 Pte Monaghan, Francis
7039 Pte Monaghan, James
    K.I.A. France, 9/8/18
943 Cpl Monar, William John
    K.I.A. France, 18/8/16
6046 Pte Moncrieff, John
    K.I.A. France, 27/4/17
— Lieut Moncur, William A.
3173 Pte Mongan, John Thos.
7525 Pte Monger, Alfred H.
4851 Pte Monk, Herbert F.
3069 Pte Montague, Philip
936 Pte Monteith, Walter
    K.I.A. Belgium, 4/10/17
2872 Pte Montgomery, Wm.
2217 Pte Montgomery, W. H.
    K.I.A. France, 19/7/16
4238 Pte Moog, Ernest Val
7526 Pte Mooney, Chas. J. J.
    (Stated to be Mooney,
J. C. J.)
    K.I.A. France, 9/8/18
7527 Pte Mooney, Thomas H.
1797 Pte Moore, Alexander
    K.I.A. Anzac, 29/5/15
5717 Pte Moore, Armond C.
3174 Pte Moore, Alexander G.
3324 Pte Moore, Frank A.
3175 Pte Moore, George E.
2634 Pte Moore, George M.
1798 T/Cpl Moore, John L.
    (M.S.M.)
3176 Pte Moore, Ralph E.
3177 L/Cpl Moore, William
60722 Pte Moore, William J.
55652 Pte Moorfield, Horace P.
2214 Pte Moran, Daniel W.
    K.I.A. Anzac, 8-9/8/15
3431 Sgt Moran, Edward D.
    K.I.A. France, 11/5/17
3178 Pte Moreland, James B.
1588 L/Cpl Moreland, John F.
3179 Pte Morgan, Albert J.
370 Pte Morgan, Arch. Thos.
453 Pte Morgan, Cecil H.
6544 Pte Morgan, Ernest R.
6313 Pte Morgan, Francis A.
3180 Pte Morgan, George F.
    (M.M.)
55670 Pte Morgan, Thomas F.
7506 Pte Moriarty, William M.

1204 Pte Morgan, William T.
    K.I.A. Anzac, 25/4/15
2632 Pte Morison, Lochlan
2627 Pte Morison, R. J. McK.
6536 Pte Morison, William
    K.I.A. Belgium, 4/10/17
7528 Pte Morland, Arthur H.
55653 Pte Morley, John Alex.
3081 Pte Morran, Percy J.
1388 L/Sgt Morrell, Ernest W.
1096
    Died after Discharge
4239 Pte Morrel, Joseph L.
    K.I.A. France, 25/7/16
692 Pte Morris, George H.
    K.I.A. Gall., 8/5/15
2387 Sgt Morris, John
6318 Pte Morris, Wm. H. V.
1792 Pte Morrisby, Henry
6547 Pte Morrison, John Knox
    K.I.A. Belgium, 4/10/17
502 Pte Morrison, Robert
    K.I.A. Anzac, 25/4/15
55654 Pte Morrison, Robert E.
3558 L/Cpl Morrison, William
4140 Pte Morrison, William
    D.O.W. France, 17/9/18
— Lieut Morrow, A. D.
    D.O.W. France, 21/7/16
5722 Pte Morrow, John Thos.
2847 Pte Morse, Percival N.
7272 Pte Morton, Leslie
    (Stated to be Simm, W.E.)
    D.O.W. Belgium, 8/11/17
3059 Pte Morton, Vincent E.
    K.I.A. France, 19/7/16
1589 Pte Moseley, Harry
1377 Pte Moss, Arthur James
2392 Pte Moss, Thomas Wm.
3181 Pte Mott, Arthur
1379 Pte Mottarelli, Ferdinando
    K.I.A. Gall., 8/5/15
7530 Pte Mounsey, Edwin T.
1681 Pte Mounsey, Fisher
    Died after Discharge
1358 L/Cpl Mounsey, Geo. R.
    D.O.W. at Sea, 9/5/15
3186 Pte Mounsey, Robert
    K.I.A. France, 9/8/18
4255 Pte Mountjoy, Reginald
    D.O.W. Belgium, 25/10/17
60727 Pte Mousley, Leslie J.
3063 Pte Mowbray, Arthur C.
    D.O.W. England, 31/7/16
1093 Arm/S/Sgt Mowbray, B.
7037 Pte Mowbray, Fredk. E.
    K.I.A. France, 9/8/18
3342 Pte Moxon, Albert
2750 Pte Moyle, Albert John
2400 Dvr Moyle, Charles
60724 Pte Muir, James Keith
2263 Bmbdr Muirhead, J. L.
    Died after Discharge

— Capt Muirson, Kenneth
    (M.C. and Bar, M.I.D.)
66 Dvr Mulcahy, James
2288 Pte Mulder, Harold L.
301 Sgt Muhlhan, Edwin C.
482 Pte Mulkearns, Jos. L.
    D.O.W. Alex'dria, 1/6/15
946 Pte Mulligan, Ernest J.
55656 Pte Mullin, Reginald I.
2163 Pte Mullin, Vernon I.
350 Pte Mullins, William P.
3428 Pte Munday, Benjamin J.
3429 L/Sgt Mundelein, F. C.
    K.I.A. France, 9/8/18
3183 Pte Munro, Alexander
1389 Pte Munro, David
    K.I.A. Belgium, 4/10/17
1378 Pte Munro, George D.
3184 Pte Munro, Herbert
377 Pte Munro, James
    K.I.A. Gall., 25/4/15—2/5/15
598 Pte Munro, Neil Gilbert
597 Pte Munro, Robert Alex.
7042 Pte Murch, Edward A.
3825 Pte Murch, James Thos.
2701 Pte Murchell, Robert J.
    (Stated to be Mercer. A.J.)
    K.I.A. France, 25/7/16
2612 Pte Murcutt, Bruce H. S.
2772 Pte Murdin, Arthur
552 Pte Murdoch, Alexander
    D.O.W. Alex'dria, 30/4/15
3185 Pte Murdoch, Victor
3186 Pte Murphy, Arthur A.
4543 Pte Murphy, Ernest H.
67 Pte Murphy, James
    K.I.A. Gall., 8/5/15
— Capt/Chap Murphy, J. D.
579 Pte Murphy, Peter
494 L/Cpl Murphy, Peter J.
    D.O.W. Gall., 10/5/15
2613 Pte Murphy, Thomas H.
6314 Pte Murray, Frank
    K.I.A. France, 27/4/18
2775 Pte Murray, James
3187 L/Cpl Murray, W. P.
6315 Pte Murrells, Sidney
1675 Pte Murtagh, Henry
    K.I.A. Anzac, 8-9/8/15
3061 Dvr Mustard, Andrew P.
3430 Sgt Myers, Thomas J.
2744 Pte Macaree, Charles H.
251 L/Cpl Macaulay, A. M.
    K.I.A. Anzac, 25/4/15
4263 Pte MacDonald, E. A.
    K.I.A. France, 25/7/16
6550 Pte MacFarlane, Alex.
3818 Pte MacInnes, Neil
1982 Pte Mack, John
1668 L/Cpl Mack, Robert E.
7521 Pte Mackay, George M.
55669 Pte Mackay, Kenneth D.

1687 Pte Mackay, Roderick
    D.O.W. France, 18/4/18
523 Pte MacKechnie, Donald
    (V.C.)
    Died after Discharge
1793 L/Cpl MacKenzie, George
2405 T/Cpl Mackereth, Alfred
    (M.M.)
2162 Gnr Mackey, Albert
— Lieut Mackinnon, D. C.
2745 L/Sgt Mackwell, Jas. R.
872 C.S.M. MacLaren, W. J.
    K.I.A. Gall., 8/5/16
7043 Pte MacLaurin, Ronald
518 Pte MacNab, Hamish
    K.I.A. Anzac, 25-30/4/15
2389 Pte MacPherson, Duncan
5424 ER/2/Cpl MacVean, A. P.
1639 Pte McAree, Michael J.
    Died after Discharge
1392 Pte McArthur, Archibald
475 Pte McArthur, Alex. J.
    K.I.A. Anzac, 25/4/15
3188 Pte McArthur, A. W.
2630 L/Cpl McAsey, Walter
2218 Pte McAskill, John Monk
    D.O.W. at Sea, 10/8/15
358 T/Cpl McAuley, Norman
664 Cpl McAuliffe, J. J.
816 Pte McAuliffe, Michael
426 Pte McAuly, Norman
1987 Dvr McCaig, James
2615 Pte McCallum, Donald C.
2713 L/Cpl McCallum, E. W.
    K.I.A. France, 9/8/18
2399 C.Q.M.S. McCallum, Roy
    (M.M.)
2194 L/Cpl McCalman, Angus
6548 Pte McCann, Richard J.
5416 Pte McCann, William
— 2/Lieut McCardel, C. E.
60728 Pte McCarthy, Wm. R.
3189 Pte McCartin, B. A.
677 L/Cpl McCasker, E. C.
    K.I.A. Anzac, 8/8/15
52 L/Cpl/Dvr McCasker, F.
678 Pte McCasker, William J.
3560 L/Cpl McChrystal, D.
741 Pte McCleary, Thos. S.
2633 L/Cpl McClelland, R. H.
3088 Pte McClure, Norman
298 Pte McColl, Alfred
    K.I.A. Anzac, 25/4/15
4260 Pte McColl, J. A. D.
    K.I.A. France, 18/8/15
3820 Pte McComish, George H.
2711 L/Cpl McConnell, A. R.
    K.I.A. Belgium, 20/9/17
744 Dvr McConnell, James
5155 Pte McConnell, James P.
1825 Sig McConnell, L. S.
549 Pte McConnochie, Leslie J.
7277 ER/2/Cpl McCormack, F.

4856 Pte McCormack, D. D.
    K.I.A. France, 17/8/16
1395 Pte McCormack, W. P.
1396 Sgt McCormick, David
    (M.M.)
3418 Pte McCormick, David E.
55658 Pte McCoy, Daniel J.
7531 Pte McCracken, C. R.
— Mjr McCrae, Geoffrey G.
    (M.I.D.)
    K.I.A. France, 19/7/16
2863 Pte McCullough, W. F.
3419 Pte McCurdy, Frank
1391 Pte McDevitt, Hugh
    D.O.W. France, 22/5/18
2403 Pte McDonagh, Frank
    Died after Discharge
2751 Pte McDonald, Albert
    D.O.W. France, 21/8/16
60732 Pte McDonald, Alan C.
2391 A/Sgt McDonald, A. H.
    (M.M.)
345 Pte McDonald, Albert R.
    (C. de G., Belgian)
940 C.S.M. McDonald, Frank
    (D.C.M., M.I.D.)
2394 Pte McDonald, Frank
127 Pte McDonald, Fenley J.
    K.I.A. Gall., 25/4/15
5420 Pte McDonald, G. C. G.
15 Dvr McDonald, Henry
    K.I.A. Gall., 24/6/15
1791 Pte McDonald, James E.
6551 Pte McDonald, James L.
    (Stated to be McDonald,
    James William)
2850 Cpl McDonald, James W.
    (D.C.M.)
— Capt McDonald, Keith G.
    (M.C.)
500 Pte McDonald, L. G.
    K.I.A. Gall., 25/4/15
2710 Pte McDonald, Lachlan L.
    K.I.A. Belgium, 4/10/17
1678 Pte McDonald, Ronald
    K.I.A. France, 19/7/16
4261 Pte McDonald, Robert J.
1154 Pte McDonald, William
    K.I.A. Gall., 25/4/15
6796 Pte McDonald, William
5148 Pte McDonald, Wm. A.
1692 Pte McDonald, William J.
3192 Pte McDonald, Wm. M.
    D.O.W. Cairo, 8/5/17
3193 Pte McDonnell, John E.
835 Pte McDonough, P. M.
    K.I.A. Gall., 5/7/15
126 L/Cpl McDougall, A. K.
    K.I.A. Gall., 13/7/15
1393 Pte McDowell, Patrick
3420 Pte McDuff, Ernest E.
867 Pte McElroy, James C.
1682 Pte McEntee, John

5149 Pte McEvoy, John J.	— Lieut McKee, James
246 Pte McEwan, James	941 Pte McKee, Ralph W.
7036 Pte McEwan, James	— Capt McKenna, Edwd. A.
1041 Cpl McEwan, James R.	*K.I.A. Gall., 25/4/15*
2614 Pte McEwan, Ted E.	2616 Gnr McKenzie, Alexander
55660 Pte McFadzean, Fredk. L.	5421 Pte McKenzie, Andrew
663 Pte McFall, Frank	5716 Pte MacKenzie, C. R.
1988 Cpl McFarlane, Francis J.	2159 Pte McKenzie, Edward
3406 Cpl McFarlane, Robert J.	— Lieut McKenzie, H. W. (M.C.)
7275 Pte McFaull, Henry P.	
3343 Pte McFee, Leonard C.	2849 Cpl McKenzie, John A.
6553 Pte McFerran, N. L.	— Lieut McKenzie, K. J. D.
7276 Pte McGee, Charles S.	3054 Dvr McKenzie, Leo Colin
K.I.A. France, 2/7/18	55662 Pte McKenzie, Leslie C.
4247 T/Cpl McGee, Vivian	1679 Pte McKenzie, Lionel F.
346 L/Cpl McGennisken, C. L.	3197 Pte McKenzie, Leslie M.
1158 Pte McGillivray, Angus	2160 Spr McKenzie, Peter
247 Pte McGillivray, James	2631 Pte MacKenzie, R. H.
K.I.A. Anzac, 25/4/15	*K.I.A. France, 19/7/16*
7045 L/Cpl McGinnis, L. F.	749 Pte McKenzie, William
6800 Pte McGough, Robert	804 Cpl McKeogh, Joseph P.
4242 Pte McGowan, Thomas	*K.I.A. France, 13/4/18*
1155 Pte McGowan, Walter T.	3397 Pte McKeown, John
1989 L/Cpl McGowran, Joseph	— Lieut McKeown, J. A. H.
K.I.A. Anzac, 8-9/8/15	*K.I.A. France, 14/10/18*
3195 OR/Sgt McGrath, F. L.	128 Pte McKeown, Leslie H.
517 Pte McGrath, James W.	3827 Pte McKeown, Wm. G.
2216 Pte McGrath, Matthew	6054 Pte McKindley, Samuel E.
1722 Pte McGregor, C. E.	720 Pte McKinnon, B. D.
— Lieut McGregor, C. H. L.	2383 Sgt McKinnon, Ralph H. (M.M.)
1723 T/Sgt McGregor, Eric O. (enlisted as Teale, Roy)	
	129 Pte McKinstry, C. M.
444 Cpl McGregor, L. C. (Stated to be McGregor, Frederick Roy)	*Died after discharge*
	1788 Pte McKneil, Cedric
	5153 Pte McKnight, William
K.I.A. Belgium, 7/9/16	1990 Pte McKone, Ernest
1390 Pte McGregor, Roy S.	*K.I.A. France, 9/8/18*
1794 Pte McGuire, William	2624 Pte McLarty, Peter
4265 Pte McHugh Thomas W.	4266 Pte McLaughlin, A. D.
6554 Pte McIlwraith, D. I.	3199 Sgt McLean, Duncan
K.I.A. France, 20/9/18	*K.I.A. France, 25/7/16*
3407 Pte McInnes, Norman J.	2635 L/Cpl McLean, Ronald
7040 Pte McIntyre, C. F. St.C.	12 L/Cpl McLean, Roy Wm.
5726 Pte McIntyre, John A.	3200 Pte McLean, Thomas S.
D.O.W. Belgium, 5/10/17	*K.I.A. France, 23-26/7/16*
3421 Pte McIntyre, John L.	2395 Pte McLennan, Colin
3591	2875 Pte McLennan, G. G. B.
5725 H/C.S.M. McIntyre, N. A. (M.M.)	1709 Pte McLeod, Alex. J.
	K.I.A. Anzac, 16/8/15
1394 Sgt McIver, Peter	6402 Pte McLeod, Hector N.
2422	1787 Pte McLeod, James
7533 Pte McKacknie, James W.	2196 Pte McLeod, John
D.O.W. France, 13/6/18	*D.O.W. France, 18/4/18*
291 Sgt McKaige, Eric C.	3089 Pte McLeod, Laverick H.
1157 Pte McKay, Charles	1591 Gnr McLeod, Thomas H.
D.O.W. Alex'dria, 7/6/15	1991 Sgt McLeod, William J.
618 Pte McKay, Charles A.	808 Pte McLoughlin, John P.
2707 Pte McKay, George	248 Pte McMahon, Ernest J.
K.I.A. France, 18/8/16	1100 Pte McMahon, Herbert
939 Pte McKay, Herbert	3202 Pte McMahon, James
4246 Pte McKay, John A.	*K.I.A. France, 24/7/16*
7489 Pte McKay, Robert G.	3203 Pte McMahon, John
994 Pte McKee, Arthur S.	*K.I.A. France, 24-25/4/18*

6316 L/Cpl McMahon, James	2725 Pte Neale, Edward M.
6556 Pte McMahon, Reuben C.	*K.I.A. France, 25/7/16*
1156 Pte McMillan, Charles	— Capt Neale, Stanley W.
6549 Pte McMillan, Francis E.	(M.C.)
1992 Pte McMillan, Percy	*D.O.W. France, 29/9/18*
3056 Pte McMillan, Stanley	2721 Pte Nealy, Mathew C.
796 Pte McNally, Clyde J.	6801 Pte Neary, Francis M.
55657 Pte McNamara, John F.	6802 Pte Neary, John Miles
55666 Pte McNamarra, W. A.	4270 Pte Neck, Reginald
5422 L/Cpl McNamara, W. T.	3532 Pte Needham, Donald E.
K.I.A. Belgium, 4/10/17	*K.I.A. France, 11/8/18*
2396 L/Cpl McNeil, George J.	1593 Pte Neely, John
(M.M.)	*K.I.A. Gall., 8-9/8/15*
3204 Cpl McNeilly, George A.	2406 L/Cpl Neil, L. J. J.
D.O.W. Belgium, 23/9/17	*K.I.A. France, 19/7/16*
— Brig-Gen McNicoll, W. R.	7361 Pte Neil, Alfred
(C.B., C.M.G., D.S.O.,	3206 Pte Neilson, Kenneth J.
C. de G., Belgian,	6322 Pte Nelken, F. A.
M.I.D, 5)	2761 2/Cpl Nelms, Victor L.
742 Pte McPartian, Wm. J.	948 Pte Nelson, Alexander G.
130 Pte McPhee, Allan	5731 Pte Nelson, Alfred John
K.I.A. Gall., 8/5/15	60734 Pte Nelson, Charles L.
6797 Pte McPhee, Hugh	2762 Pte Nelson, Olaf
1993 Pte McPherson, Andrew	(Stated to be Neilson, O.)
460 Pte McPherson, A. G.	5734 Pte Nethercote, Ernest H.
K.I.A. Anzac, 25/4-2/5/15	6805 Pte Nettleton, Edward J.
2705 L/Cpl McPherson, A. S.	1856 Pte Nettleton, George
2706 Pte McPherson, A. W.	1859 Pte Nettleton, James
2622 Sgt McQueen, M. W.	1857 Pte Nettleton, William
(C. de G., Belgian)	1858 L/Cpl Nettleton, Thomas
2158 Pte McKuie, Alick C. H.	*K.I.A. France, 9/8/18*
K.I.A. Anzac, 8-9/8/15	4554 L/Cpl Neve, Cyril A.
5417 Pte McRae, Donald	4555 L/Cpl Newbery, Frank
1994 L/Cpl McRae, Ernest W.	*K.I.A. Belgium, 4/10/17*
(M.M.)	3432 Pte Newborn, H. J. R.
7535 Pte McRae, John A.	949 Pte Newbound, George
1660 Pte McRae, William	14 Pte Newey, Thomas
1995 Pte McShanag, Henry S.	2724 Pte Newman, Edward G.
623 Pte McShane, Arthur	1703 Pte Newson, James
5723 Pte McSweeney, C. F.	2719 Cpl Newstead, Stephen C.
5721 Pte McSweeny, James J.	*K.I.A. Belgium, 26/12/17*
1463 Pte McTaggart, Herbert	624 Pte Newton, Tom
K.I.A. Anzac, 28/7/15	4267 Dvr Nice, Charles Royal
6557 Pte McVitty, Alex. E.	4268 L/Cpl Nicholas, Cecil
7536 Pte McWaters, F. B.	5733 Pte Nicholas, Sydney
548 Pte McWatt, Ronald	6056 Pte Nicholas, Wm. B.
60729 Pte McWigan, Walter G.	60737 Pte Nicholls, George A.
	252 Pte Nicholls, Harold
N	5427 Pte Nicholls, Percival T.
	3854 Pte Nicholls, Sydney S.
3342 Spr Nagle, Alfred Thos.	— Capt Nicholson, B. B.
55673 Pte Naismith, P. C.	986 Pte Nicholson, Donald
1001 Dvr Namana, Kiwa	322 Pte Nicholson, M. B.
5156 T/Cpl Nancarrow, Albert	670 C.S.M. Nicholson, R. H.
5157 Pte Nancarrow, H. R.	417 Cpl Nicholson, Walter
458 Pte Nankervis, H. H. T.	685 Pte Nicol, James Walter
374 S/Sgt Narik, Andre J.	580 Pte Nicol, Stanley H.
1860 Sgt Nash, Charles H.	3562 Pte Nicolls, John F.
K.I.A. France, 1/11/16	3392 Pte Nicolson, Peter
2677 L/Cpl Nash, Ilton E. R.	1398 Pte Nightingill, Chas. P.
1799 Pte Nash, Henry	809 Cpl Ninnis, George
1160 Pte Neal, Arthur F.	669 Pte Nisbett, Hugh F.
3563 Sgt Neal, Keith	5730 Pte Nixon, George B.
642 Pte Neal, Rex Raymond	

— Lieut Nixon, Herbert	3515 Pte O'Connor, John R.
2935 Pte Noble, Edward E.	*K.I.A. France, 15/7/16*
2409 Pte Nogren, Charles	3208 Pte O'Connor, John R. A.
5807 Pte Noonan, Edward	*K.I.A. France, 18/8/16*
K.I.A. France, 25/2/17	2501 Sgt O'Connor, Leonard J.
2765 Pte Noonan, Martin P.	*D.O.W. France, 22/12/16*
2722 Pte Norman, Edmund J.	2412 Pte O'Connor, Matthew
7281 L/Cpl Norman, Wm. D.	2001 Pte O'Connor, M. W.
2726 Pte Norris, Herbert	2954 L/Cpl O'Connor, Roy S.
K.I.A. France, 18/8/16	— Capt O'Connor, Thos. P.
3158 Pte Norrish, Alfred	413 Cpl Odgers, Cecil V.
3157 Dvr Norrish, George H.	3094 Pte Odgers, James
3159 Dvr Norrish, John L.	5161 L/Cpl Odlum, Leslie G.
666 Pte North, James	3443 Pte O'Donahoo, Alan K.
Died after Discharge	955 Pte O'Donnell, Neil A.
1397 Pte Northcott, Fredk. H.	2002 Pte O'Donnell, Thos. P.
253 Pte Norton, Alfred J.	1594 Pte O'Dwyer, Francis
K.I.A. Anzac, 25/4/15	3444 L/Cpl Oelmann, Geo. M.
7539 Pte Nugent, Percy H.	2003 Pte Officer, Geoffrey T.
K.I.A. France, 17/4/18	*K.I.A. France, 11/4/17*
2766 Pte Nunan, George P.	3098 Pte Ogilvie, David G.
60735 Pte Nunn, Norman S.	*K.I.A. France, 23-27/7/16*
1698 Pte Nunn, Philip	19709 T/Cpl Ogilvie, George C.
6803 Pte Nunn, William Albert	2185 Pte Ogilvie, William M.
60739 Pte Nuthall, William F.	7050 Pte O'Grady, Andrew J.
1999 Pte Nuttall, William R.	600 Pte O'Halloran, Arthur H.
D.O.W. France, 17/6/18	*K.I.A. Gall., 8/5/15*
3435 Pte Nylander, Alexander	6058 Pte O'Halloran, John P.
	844 Pte O'Heare, Chris. V.
O	2727 Pte O'Keefe, Clifford R.
	K.I.A. France, 29/6/16
3868 Pte Oakland, Philip E.	852 Pte O'Keefe, Hurtle W.
(Stated to be Wright, P. E.)	2732 Pte O'Keefe, John
Died after Discharge	2728 Pte O'Keefe, Peter T.
62 R.S.M. Oakley, Alfred J.	1056 Dvr Olden, Thomas H.
1173 Sgt Oakley, George C.	1162 Cpl Oldham, Ernest
— Capt Oates, Augustus (D.S.O., M.I.D.)	*K.I.A. France, 27/6/18*
396 R.Q.M.S. Oates, F. A. (M.S.M.)	3344 Pte Oldham, John
	6059 Pte Oldroyd, Wilfred A.
3105 Sgt O'Brien, Denis	*D.O.W. England, 9/10/18*
5428 L/Cpl O'Brien, George C.	343 Pte O'Leary, Daniel J.
3092 Pte O'Brien, Hubert	*K.I.A. Gall., 25/4/15*
2000 Pte O'Brien, John	2851 Pte O'Leary, Edmund A.
3102 Pte O'Brien, John	*K.I.A. France, 20/8/16*
376 Pte O'Brien, Joseph N. 1898	1801 Pte O'Leary, James
365 Pte O'Brien, John Wm.	581 Pte O'Leary, Thomas
1003 Pte O'Brien, Thomas A.	*D.O.W. Gall., 25/4/15*
37 Pte O'Brien, William	2730 Pte Oliver, David
K.I.A. Anzac, 25/4/15	2004 Pte Oliver, Joseph
853 Sgt O'Bryan, Claude	627 Dvr Oliver, Thomas
— Lieut O'Connor, Austin J.	2005 Pte Oliver, Thomas
D.O.W. Belgium, 24/9/17	357 Pte Olley, Allan Robert
2929 Pte O'Connor, Cornelius	*D.O.W. Gall., 25/4/15*
1661 Pte O'Connor, Edward	6326 Pte O'Loughlin, Albert J.
K.I.A. Anzac, 8-9/8/15	*Acc. Killed, France, 13/4/19*
3860 Pte O'Connor, Gabriel A.	6324 Pte O'Loughlin, Michael
3442 Pte O'Connor, John	*K.I.A. France, 31/8/18*
Died (S.I.W.) Egypt, 7/3/16	6325 Pte O'Loughlin, Wm. L.
60740 Pte O'Connor, James	4271 Pte Olsen, Herbert T.
Died France, 8/2/19	1161 L/Sgt Olsen, James A.
	486 Pte O'Malley, Jack
	638 C.S.M. O'Meara, John A.

6808	Pte O'Neil, Fitzgerald	60746	Pte Palmer, Albert H.
	K.I.A. Belgium, 20/9/17	2008	Pte Palmer, Charles J.
—	Lieut O'Neill, Henry F.	—	Lieut Palmer, Reg. W.
3093	Pte O'Neill, John Alban		*Killed France, 2/4/18*
3210	Pte O'Neill, James Percy (M.M.)		*2/4/18*
		3439	Pte Palmer, Thomas
6849	Pte O'Neill, Pervis Wm.		*Died after Discharge*
	K.I.A. Belgium, 4/10/17	1404	L/Cpl Palmer, William E.
317	Pte Onley, William H.		*K.I.A. France, 19/7/16*
	K.I.A. Gall., 8/5/15	3877	Pte Pannam, Arthur G.
799	Pte Opie, George	3121	Sgt/Mech Panwels, L. M.
—	Lieut Opie, Lyndsay G.	2747	Pte Parish, Frederick G.
7051	Pte Opper, John Henry		*D.O.W. Belgium, 20/9/17*
7052	Pte Orchard, Henry C.	139	Pte Parish, Montague
1007	L/Cpl Orde, Thomas		*D.O.W. Anzac, 11/5/15*
3100	Pte Oriel, William H.	420	Cpl Park, Ernest R.
	K.I.A. France, 19/7/16	5165	Pte Parker, Cecil
4877	Pte O'Rourke, Alex. D.	991	Pte Parker, Fredk. S. M.
2731	Pte O'Rourke, Thomas G.	950	L/Cpl Parker, George F.
	D.O.W. France, 23/9/17		*K.I.A. France, 25/7/16*
182	Sgt Orr, Ernest James	2867	Pte Parker, Hutchinson
	D.O.W. England, 14/11/15	1363	Pte Parker, Harry F.
2264	Cpl Orr, James		*D.O.W. at Sea, 9/8/15*
	K.I.A. France, 25/4/18	1638	L/Cpl Parker, James
2411	Sgt Osborn, James	3110	Gnr Parker, James
2167	Pte Osborne, Ernest A.	951	L/Cpl Parker, Thomas P.
2733	Pte Osborne, James P.	3127	Pte Parkes, Arthur E.
	K.I.A. France, 19/8/16		*K.I.A. France, 9/8/18*
4335	Pte Osborne, William	—	Mjr Parkes, Frederick
137	Pte O'Shea, Michael P.	7540	Pte Parkhill, Alan G.
2636	Pte Ostler, James	6814	Pte Parkhill, Robert
1399	Pte Ostler, Percy H.	2738	Pte Parkinson, Clarance G.
4560	Sgt O'Sullivan, Vivian P.		*K.I.A. France, 25/7/16*
5736	Pte O'Toole, Daniel T.	625	Sgt Parkinson, James
	D.O.W. France, 2/3/17	—	2/Lieut Parr, Alfred John (D.C.M.)
3104	Dvr Owens, Alfred Henry		
1800	Pte Owens, Edward		*D.O.W. France, 1/10/18*
	D.O.W. Alex'dria, 25/8/15	2168	Cpl Parrott, C. L. A.
3099	Pte Owens, George E.	7541	Pte Parry, Robert
1209	Pte Owen, Percy Thomas	6810	Pte Parsonage, Leslie R.
	K.I.A. Gallipoli, 8/5/15	2419	Pte Parsons, Albert D.
2064	Pte Oxley, Charles	2868	Pte Parsons, George
3095	Pte Ozanne, Claude	3213	Pte Parsons, Raymond S.
6807	Pte Ozanne, Ernest	2848	Sgt Partridge, Bert
			K.I.A. France, 9/8/18

P

		6331	Pte Pasley, Leslie Gibson
1595	C.Q.M.S. Pace, Charles	2169	Pte Patching, Henry S.
3109	Dvr Pagan, Leslie G.	2779	Pte Paterson, Daniel E.
7111	Pte Page, Albert C.	2174	Gnr Paterson, Ernest A.
2640	Pte Page, Ernest Edwin		*D.O.W. (S.I.W.),*
60747	Pte Page, Roy James		*England, 8/5/18*
2006	Pte Page, Charles E.	1802	Pte Paterson, Gordon S.
	K.I.A. Anzac, 8-9/8/15	2415	Pte Patience, Leslie G.
3981	Pte Paice, William E. (M.M.)	2010	Pte Paton, William C.
		2746	Pte Patterson, Charles H.
766	Pte Paine, Arthur		*K.I.A. France, 25/7/16*
6561	ER/Cpl Paine, Robert	1597	Sgt Patterson, George (M.I.D.)
6860	Pte Palethorpe, John C.		
5742	Pte Palliser, Wilfrid (M.M.)	1651	Pte Patterson, Hugh
		3118	Pte Patton, James R.
4398	Pte Palm, Harry L.	323	C.S.M. Patton, Thomas
6812	Pte Palmer, Alexander E.		*D.O.W. Malta, 9/8/15*
	K.I.A. Belgium, 4/10/17	232	Pte Paul, Bert

1598 Pte Paul, Claude
    K.I.A. Gall., 8-9/8/15
1806 Pte Paul, Ernest Clifton
    D.O.W. at Sea, 31/5/15
6061 Pte Paul, Frederick W.
527 Sgt Paul, William E. G.
431 Pte Paull, William S.
961 Pte Pavich, Antonio A.
    K.I.A. France, 11/8/18
963 Pte Pavich, Nicholas John
441 L/Cpl Pawley, Arthur J.
    D.O.W. Gallipoli, 20/6/15
689 Sgt Pawley, William T.
138 Cpl Pawsey, Norman
5166 Pte Paxton, George T.
2173 Pte Payne, Arthur Wm.
6330 Pte Payne, Bertie Albert
254 Pte Payne, Charles Tobias
2011 L/Sgt Payne, Harold A.
6334 Pte Payne, Peter
9599 Pte Payne, Percival J. G.
    (M.M.)
1400 Sgt Payne, Sylvester
3112 Pte Payne, William
4272 Sgt Peach, William E.
    (M.M.)
2012 Pte Peacock, Sylvester
1165 Pte Pearce, Alfred
418 Cpl Pearce, Arthur M.
    K.I.A. Gall., 25/4/15
2013 Pte Pearce, John Alex.
1192 Pte Pearce, James E.
3122 Pte Pearce, Norman A.
    K.I.A. France, 10/8/16
2869 Pte Pearce, Raymond
2870 Sgt Pearse, Samuel G.
    (V.C., M.M.)
    K.I.A., 29/8/19, with Russian Relief Force
869 Pte Pearson, Fredk. F.
    K.I.A. Anzac, 25/4/15
2872 Pte Peart, Roy Carlan
    K.I.A. France, 19/7/16
3124 Pte Peat, James Henry
1173 Sgt Peatey, George
1164
    (M.M., Medal Militaire, French)
2780 Cpl Peel, Frank
6333 Pte Peers, Edgar W.
— Lieut Pegler, Arthur R.
    (M.C.)
643 C.Q.M.S. Pegler, A. W.
2734 Pte Pegler, Edwin H.
752 Pte Pegler, Henry
    D.O.W. Anzac, 16/5/15
6566 Pte Peillon, Frank L.
3123 L/Cpl Pell, Horace W.
719 Pte Pellas, Percival
55676 Pte Pemberton, Thos. A.
4872 Pte Pemell, Percival E.
6329 L/Cpl Pender, J. P. A.
953 Sgt Pennefather, L. H.

1599 Pte Pennington, A. W.
3885 Pte Penny, Fred
1016 Pte Pennycook, Ronald
    (Stated to be Pennicuik, Ronald)
6371 Pte Penrose, Cecil B.
140 Cpl Penrose, Reginald A.
    K.I.A. Anzac, 25/4-2/5/15
1183 Pte Pepper, Alfred W.
1401 Pte Pepper, Ernest C.
2744 L/Cpl Pepper, Henry H.
    K.I.A. France, 9/8/18
60751 T/Dvr Percival, Stanley J.
2014 Pte Perkins, Colin Ernest
    K.I.A. France, 19/7/16
3114 Pte Perkins, George W.
    D.O.W. France, 30/7/16
255 Pte Perkins, Robert R.
    K.I.A. Gall., 8/5/15
842 Pte Perkins, Richard W.
2873 Pte Perkins, Stanley O.
12627 Dvr Perks, William D.
    D.O.D. France, 4/12/18
— Capt Permezel, Cedric H.
    D.O.W. Anzac, 14/7/15
— Capt Permezel, E. G. de T.
    (M.C.)
2015 Pte Perrett, Stanley C.
    K.I.A. France, 19/7/16
2220 Sgt Perrin, Joseph
3440 Pte Perry, Arthur James
    K.I.A. France, 19/7/16
7289 Pte Perry, Charles A. R.
3447 L/Sgt Perry, George A.
5739 Pte Perry, James Ivo
    D.O.W. England, 4/7/18
3448 Pte Perry, Robert F.
    K.I.A. France, 19/7/16
4901 Pte Perry, William H.
    K.I.A. France, 11/4/18
1458 Pte Perry, William
    (Stated to be Perryman, William)
60743 Pte Pert, James Austin
2875 Pte Pescott, Cecil Edward
2347 Pte Peters, Absalom
    K.I.A. Belgium, 20/9/17
4273 Pte Peters, Cyril V. H.
256 Pte Peters, Clyde Wm.
1600 Pte Peters, George Henry
3215 Pte Peterson, Carl
2876 Pte Peterson, Edward
811 Sgt Pethard, William H.
188 L/Cpl Pethebridge, J. A.
55679 Pte Petherbridge, Thos. R.
60750 T/Cpl Pettrie, James R.
316 Sgt Pettigrew, John McC.
55677 Gnr Pettigrew, Stuart C.
505 Pte Pettigrew, Trafford C.
    K.I.A. Anzac, 25/4/15
1168 Pte Pettis, Alfred James
    K.I.A. Anzac, 25/4-2/5/15
2739 Dvr Pettit, Jarvis E.

2416	Pte Pettis, Thomas		4875	Pte Pollard, Lawrence
	K.I.A. France, 26/7/16			D.O.W. France, 27/8/18
403	Dvr Pezet, William John		856	ER/S/Sgt Pollard, S. R.
2481	Cpl Phelan, Cecil		3216	L/Cpl Pollock, David
3119	Pte Phelan, Gerald John		—	Lieut Pollock, William G.
	K.I.A. France, 23/8/18			K.I.A. Belgium, 3/10/17
800	Pte Phelps, Francis W. E.		271	Dvr Ponting, Ernest E.
2877	L/Cpl Phelps, William T.			D.O.W. Belgium, 23/9/17
	K.I.A. France, 19/7/16		987	Pte Pool, Francis M.
1804	Pte Phillips, Alfred E.		3113	Pte Poole, Albert Robert
	K.I.A. France, 19/7/16			K.I.A. France, 25/4/18
—	Capt Phillips, Arthur F.		64	C.S.M. Poole, Leslie J.
6063	Pte Phillips, Alex. J.			K.I.A. Gall., 8/5/15
	K.I.A. France, 16/12/16		2417	L/Cpl Poole, Samuel A.
—	Lieut Phillips, Douglas G. (M.C.)		7542	Pte Poole, Walter F.
			—	Lieut. Poole, William J.
				K.I.A. France, 9/8/18
2638	Pte Phillips, Eric W.		1166	Cpl Pople, William
2171	Pte Phillips, Frederick R.			D.O.W. Gall., 15/7/15
6563	ER/Cpl Phillips, H. B.		58	W.O. Porteous, John E.
7053	Pte Phillips, H. G. M.		2783	Pte Porter, Arthur V.
4275	Pte Phillips, James Thos.		6335	Pte Porter, Claude
3111	Pte Phillips, Lawrence		3217	Pte Porter, George R.
7296	Pte Phillips, L. A. M.		5433	Dvr Porter, Hugh
195	Pte Phillips, M. V. St. J.		6811	Pte Porter, John
4276	Pte Phillips, Owen			K.I.A. Belgium, 4/10/17
	K.I.A. Belgium, 4/10/17		1808	Cpl Porter, Oscar P.
3888	L/Cpl Phillips, Robert			D.O.W. Belgium, 13/10/17
282	Pte Phillips, William		2175	L/Cpl Postgate, Matthew
1702	W.O.(1) Pickett, A. W.		6562	Pte Potts, Jabez Jagger
—	Capt Piercey, Roy L. (M.C.)		2878	Cpl Poulter, Reginald E. (M.M., Russian Medal of St. George, 4th Class)
318	Pte Piggott, John			
	K.I.A. Gall., 8/5/15			
1805	Pte Pike, Edward			K.I.A. France, 12/5/17
60749	Pte Pilcher, William A.		812	Cpl Powell, Albert C.
993	Sgt Pilmer, Frank		601	Sgt Powell, Frank
2222	L/Cpl Pinder, Arthur E.		1604	Pte Powell, Frederick
390	L/Sgt Pinder, Edward W. (D.C.M.)		3125	Pte Powell, George H.
			445	Pte Powell, Leo Thomas (M.M.)
16	Pte Pinder, Peter			
831	Pte Pinder, Thomas W.		5170	Pte Powell, Thomas E.
	K.I.A. Gall., 25/4/15-2/5/15		710	Pte Power, Kilian Patrick
2740	Pte Pine, Horace Colvin			K.I.A. France, 14/5/18
2172	Pte Pinney, Arthur James		347	Pte Powley, Charles
2879	Dvr Pitcher, E. W. J.			K.I.A. Gall., 25/4/15
2741	Pte Pizaro, Charles J.		348	Pte Powley, John Hall
—	Lieut Plant, John B.		3218	Pte Pratt, Charles E.
2017	Pte Platt, William H.			K.I.A. France, 25/7/18
4566	L/Cpl Plim, Joseph		2176	Pte Pratt, George James
	K.I.A. France, 18/8/16			K.I.A. Gall., 6/8/15
2639	Pte Pluck, Henry		3896	Pte Pratt, Lancelot Wm.
6332	L/Cpl Plummer, C. E.		3120	Pte Pratt, Thomas C.
4274	Pte Plunkett, Fredk. W.		1059	Pte Preston, William
	K.I.A. France, 9/8/18			D.O.W. Gall., 18/7/15
5167	Pte Pocock, Robert F.		7543	Pte Preston, William R.
6560	Pte Podmore, William G.		1167	Cpl Prew, Sydney
626	Pte Pohl, Thomas		2062	Pte Price, George
2018	Pte Polden, Bernard		1405	Pte Price, Herbert John
	K.I.A. France, 3/11/16		2926	Sgt Price, Moses Samuel
2418	Sgt Pole, Thomas F.			K.I.A. France, 17/8/16
	K.I.A. France, 23/8/18		2177	Dvr Price, Reginald A. (M.M.)
1809	Pte Pollard, James			
7054	Pte Pollard, Joshua			

4568 Pte Price, William N.
60744 Pte Pridgeon, Ewart W.
151 L/Cpl Priest, William
2200 Pte Priestley, Arthur
    D.O.W. Belgium, 6/1/18
55678 Pte Priestley, Leslie W.
3219 Pte Pringle, William J.
7299 Pte Prior, George J.
5741 Pte Prior, John Joseph
    K.I.A. Belgium, 4/10/17
3115 Pte Pritchard, Horace R.
    K.I.A. France, 19/7/16
3116 Dvr Pritchard, Herb. W.
2420 Sgt Pritchard, W. G. F.
    (M.M.)
1803 Pte Prouse, John
5808 Pte Prowd, Hugh James
    K.I.A. Belgium, 4/10/17
424 ER/S/Sgt Prunty, H. C.
966 Pte Pugh, Arthur John
2880 Pte Pugh Llewellyn D.
6809 Pte Pullen, Robert W.
705 Pte Pumpa, Ewald
602 Pte Punshon, Roy
— Lieut Purbrick, K. M.
— Lieut Purbrick, Rupert B.
    K.I.A. France, 9/8/18
1807 Dvr Purcell, Laurence
2170 Pte Purcell, Ronald
6062 Pte Purcell, William H.
3117 Pte Pye, Edward
7109 Pte Pyne, James

Q

4279 Pte Queripel, Harold
    D.O.W. France, 27/9/17
1861 Pte Quick, Robert Vernon
801 Pte Quigley, J. H. B.
4282 Gnr Quill, Sydney, John
2178
4278 L/Cpl Quinlan, John H.
3453 Pte Quinlan, Matthew F.
6568 L/Cpl Quinlivan, Richard
2750 Pte Quinn, Edward
4871 Pte Quinn, John William
6567 Pte Quinn, Joseph Wm.
55680 Pte Quinn, Joseph Wm.
    (Stated to be Nugent, J. W.)
4277 Cpl Quirk, Valentine

R

3454 Dvr Rabach, Carl W.
    D.O.W. France, 2/10/18
284 ER/2/Cpl Radcliffe, A. E.
3455 Pte Radcliffe, Arthur F.
3456 Sgt Radcliffe, James B.
    D.O.W. France, 10/8/18
5256 Pte Radonich, Albert G.
2645 Pte Rae, George Henry
1173 Pte Rae, Herbert
1364 Pte Rae, John William
    K.I.A. Anzac, 26/4/15

7299 Pte Rafferty, Arthur P.
711 Pte Rainbow, Edward G.
7306 Pte Ramsay, David A.
6573 Pte Ramsay, Herbert B.
6819 Pte Ramsay, John
7545 Sgt Ramus, Harold R.
    D.O.W. France, 18/4/18
191 Pte Rand, James G. W.
    (M.M.)
314 Dvr Randall, Orville
2423 Dvr Rankin, Alexander S.
536 L/Sgt Ransom, Roland K.
3457 Pte Ranton, Thomas
7300 Pte Raper, Keith R.
1644 Pte Raphael, Phillip M.
1643 Spr Rasmussen, Ernest C.
6342 A/Sgt Ratcliffe, Jesm E.
7059 Pte Ratten, Rupert A.
189 Pte Ratten, Walter G.
5435 Pte Rattue, Edward
192 Pte Raven, Alfred
3527 L/Sgt Raw, Walter W.
    K.I.A. France, 19/7/16
5436 L/Cpl Rawlings, James
60753 T/Cpl Rawlins, E. A. J.
3478 Sgt Rawlinson, Francis R.
55685 Pte Ray, Albert Nicholas
1605 Pte Ray, Herbert
    K.I.A. France, 20/8/16
3470 Pte Ray, Walter George
    (Stated to be Page, Walter George)
3567 Pte Rayner, Charles F.
3143 Sgt Rayson, Clem
    K.I.A. France, 29/9/18
7369 Pte Rea, George Lyell
341 Pte Rea, William Hanna
190 Pte Read, Charles Edward
1009 Pte Read, Richard J. R.
    K.I.A. Anzac, 25/4/15
5174 L/Cpl Reade, Graham P.
    (M.M.)
    K.I.A. France, 13/6/18
6570 Pte Reardon, G. R. J.
6571 Pte Reddick, Alexander J.
2881 Pte Reddie, William J.
954 Pte Reed, Clair William
    K.I.A. Anzac, 25/4/15
60754 Pte Reed, Edgar
2183 Pte Reed, Reginald G.
1656 Pte Reed, William
3471 Pte Reed, Walter
3135 Pte Reedman, Sydney W.
1459 Pte Rees, Thomas Walter
1098
3458 Pte Reeves, Alfred
    K.I.A. France, 19/7/15
7788 Pte Reeves, Arthur
4670 Pte Reeves, David Geo.
7546 Pte Reeves, Henry Leslie
1811 Sgt Reeves, Robert E.
    K.I.A. France, 19/7/16
6339 Pte Reeves, William

3221 Pte Reeves, William L.	2023 Pte Ricketts, Charles A.
K.I.A. France, 24/7/16	D.O.W. Belgium, 3/10/17
6815 Pte Regan, Leo William	2 Q.M.S. Ricketts, George
352 Pte Regan, William	6113 Pte Ridal, John E.
7547 Pte Regester, L. C. D.	7550 Pte Ridd, Arthur
1813 L/Cpl Reid, Arthur	3459 Pte Ridding, Ernest R.
7061 Pte Reid, Alexander J.	K.I.A. France, 30/5/16
K.I.A. Belgium, 4/10/17	— Lieut Ridgway, N. F.
989 Pte Reid, Cyril Lindsay	1061 Pte Ridley, Roderick
K.I.A. Gall., 25/4/15	3136 Cpl Rigby, James
708 C.Q.M.S. Reid, David	60756 Pte Ring, Michael John
1655 Pte Reid, John Clifford	1812 Pte Ritchie, Clarence C.
3222 L/Cpl Reid, Norman S.	4349 Pte Riva, Jack Eugene
(M.M.)	Died Prior to Discharge.
6575 Pte Reid, William E.	Victoria, 27/5/19
2022 Pte Reiffel, Leslie C.	7551 Pte Rivett, Cecil James
55684 Pte Reiffel, Roy	3565 Pte Roach, Edward
5748 Pte Reilly, James	K.I.A. France, 19/7/16
K.I.A. Belgium, 5/10/17	353 Sgt Roach John Henry
4881 Pte Renehan, M. J. P.	60758 Pte Roach, James H.
6850 Pte Renfree, Wm. G.	— Lieut Robb, Ernest G.
K.I.A. France, 14/5/18	(M.I.D.)
3140 Pte Renfrew, Alex.	531 ER/Sgt Roberts, Arthur
(M.M.)	955 Cpl Roberts, David W.
2752 Sgt Renfrey, Walter J.	Died after Discharge
2206 L/Cpl Rennick, John L.	60757 Pte Roberts, Edgar Eli
D.O.W. France, 21/9/18	6857 Pte Roberts, Francis H.
97 Pte Rennie, David M.	7064 L/Cpl Roberts, George
1814 Pte Resuggan, Jack	(M.M.)
K.I.A. Belgium, 26/10/17	K.I.A. France, 9/8/18
136 L/Cpl Rettner, Charles	2652 Spr Roberts, George E.
7307	5185 Pte Roberts, George H.
258 Pte Reynolds, Arthur T.	3461 Pte Roberts, Robert G.
3134 Pte Reynolds, George W.	2650 Spr Roberts, Thomas M.
K.I.A. France, 19/7/16	K.I.A. France, 17/11/16
3224 Pte Reynolds, James A.	545 Pte Robertshaw, Bartimas
5175 Pte Reynolds, James J.	(Stated to be Hutchinson, Bert)
— Lieut Reynolds, O. G.	K.I.A. Anzac, 25/4/15
(M.C.)	1171 Pte Robertson, Alexander
197 Pte Rialland, James Peter	2882 Pte Robertson, Arch. F.
1710 Pte Rice, Herbert G.	K.I.A. France, 20/7/16
K.I.A. Belgium, 5/10/17	3147 Pte Robertson, A. F. J.
4280 Pte Rice, John (M.I.D.)	490 Pte Robertson, Colin E.
D.O.W. France, 19/12/16	K.I.A. Anzac, 25/4/15
4281 Pte Rich, William F. W.	2266 Pte Robertson, David G.
259 L/Sgt Richards, Harry	2422 Pte Robertson, E. G. H.
3566 Pte Richards, Harold C.	1383 Pte Robertson, Fredk. C.
K.I.A. Belgium, 20/9/17	603 Pte Robertson, George
814 Cpl Richards, Joseph Roy	6572 L/Cpl Robertson, G. G.
D.O.W. France, 20/8/16	(M.M.)
5468 Pte Richards, James T.	4576 Pte Robertson, John
4282 Pte Richards, Roderick D.	(Stated to be Robinson, Thomas) (M.I.D.)
628 Pte Richardson, Allan	K.I.A. France, 15/10/17
3528 L/Sgt Richardson A. H.	260 Pte Robertson, Leonard L.
Died at Sea, 8/7/17	6403 Pte Robertson, Paul McP.
7549 Pte Richardson, G. L. C.	2242 Pte Robertson, Robert
604 Pte Richardson, Roy E.	6820 Pte Robertson, R. G. V.
K.I.A. Gall., 25/4/15	K.I.A. France, 9/8/18
5744 Pte Richardson, Wm. J.	2651 Pte Robertson, William H.
3227 Pte Richardson, W. S.	6817 Pte Robertson, William J.
2265 Pte Richens, Enoch W.	
K.I.A. Belgium, 20/9/17	
2788 Pte Richie, William C.	

658 L/Sgt Robertson, W. O.
    K.I.A. Gall., 8/5/15
2180 Cpl Robin, Arthur M.
    K.I.A. France, 29/6/16
4893 Pte Robins, Frederick
    (M.M.)
6336 Pte Robins, Stanley A.
141 Cpl Robinson, Archibald
2653 Pte Robinson, Arthur
    (M.M. and Bar)
6578 Pte Robinson, Albert G.
2883 Pte Robinson, Albert H.
    K.I.A. France, 24/7/16
5438 Pte Robinson, Arthur L.
7065 Pte Robinson, Charles S.
1606 C.Q.M.S. Robinson, E.
    D.O.W. France, 2/9/18
2024 Pte Robinson, E. F.
5747 Pte Robinson, George
    Died England, 31/10/18
7552 Pte Robinson, George H.
1177 Pte Robinson, Gordon S.
2184 Pte Robinson, Harold F.
    K.I.A. Anzac, 8-9/8/15
7303 Pte Robinson, Jack
359 Pte Robinson, James John
629 C.S.M. Robinson, Roy
    (D.C.M.)
— Lieut Robinson, Rupert C.
    (M.M.)
1412 Pte Robinson, Thomas
6818 A/Cpl Robinson, Thomas
4283 Pte Robinson, T. J. L.
5500 Pte Robson, Charles E.
    D.O.W. France, 22/12/16
1169 L/Cpl Robson, George C.
7302 Pte Robson, Matthew C.
726 Pte Robson, Percy
    K.I.A. Anzac, 28/4/15
297 L/Sgt Robson, William H.
142 Pte Roche, James Leo
877 Sgt Rochester, Alfred W.
    K.I.A. Gall., 8/5/15
5 S/Sgt Rochstein, Fritz S.
261 Pte Rocke, Cecil Harry
    K.I.A. Anzac, 25/4/15
2884 Pte Rodger, Claude H.
— Lieut Rodriguez, Paul C.
2025 Pte Rogan, Wilfred J.
419 Pte Rogers, Arthur E.
    D.O.W. at Sea, 26/4/15
818 Sgt Rogers, Frederick
— Lieut Rogers, Frank O.
3131 Pte Rogers, Henry
— 2/Lieut, Rogers, John
    K.I.A. France, 1/11/16
3467 Pte Rogers, Walter M.
    (M.M.)
5187 L/Cpl Rogers, William S.
428 Sgt Rogerson, A. A. P.
    K.I.A. France, 23-26/7/16
2649 Pte Rohner, Raymond S.
3141 Pte Rollason, Arthur

5790 Cpl Rolls, Richard T.
3233 Pte Rolls, William G.
    (M.M.)
4346 Pte Ronaldson, Adam L.
5186 Pte Ronaldson, David
143 Pte Ronke, Fredk. H.
7308 ER/Sgt Rooke, Andrew T.
5189 Pte Rooney, James
3468 Pte Roper, Frank
1174 Cpl Roper, Frederick C.
1137 Pte Rose, John
60760 Gnr Rose, Sidney F.
    Died France, 6/2/19
2885 Pte Ross, Allan Hector
    K.I.A. France, 29/6/18
5743 L/Cpl Ross, Allan Munro
— Capt Ross, David Bain
647 Pte Ross, Herbert Leslie
196 Cpl Ross, John
    D.O.W. France, 10/8/18
1608 Pte Ross, John
    D.O.W. at Sea, 21/5/15
1378 Pte Ross, James John
1414
582 Pte Ross, Robert J.
5249 T/Sgt Ross, Robert P.
— Lieut Ross, Thomas John
    K.I.A. France, 9/8/18
4284 Pte Ross, William Leslie
    D.O.W. France, 24/7/16
1622 Pte Rosser, Alexander
2702 Pte Rothery, Ernest R.
    D.O.W. Belgium, 29/10/17
5481 Pte Roughsedge, Wm. H.
60759 Pte Rouse, George M.
5749 Pte Rowan, Andrew G.
    K.I.A. Belgium, 4/10/17
2753 Pte Rowarth, John
    K.I.A. France, 22/12/16
4585 Pte Rowbottom, Leslie J.
558 Sgt Rowe, Albert
1406 Pte Rowe, Edward
— 2/Lieut Rowe, Ernest H.
262 Pte Rowland, Herbert
    K.I.A. Anzac, 25/4/15
4660 Pte Rowlands, James
    K.I.A. Belgium, 4/1:
3235 Pte Roy, Robert Walter
2647 Pte Royle, Robert
    K.I.A. France, 3/11/16
2424 Pte Rudge, Alfred Geo.
263 Pte Ruffin, Charles
3138 Pte Ruggles, Henry J.
815 Pte Rule, Albert
819 Pte Rushton, Charles W.
    K.I.A. Anzac, 12/7/15
2026 L/Cpl Russell, Carlyle
    K.I.A. France, 17/4/18
53838 Pte Russell, Charles F.
3133 L/Cpl Russell, Ernest M.
— Lieut. Russell, George B.
60755 Pte Russell, John Joseph
145 C.Q.M.S. Russell, L. S.

6 Sgt Rutherford Joseph M. (M.I.D.)	— Lieut Sara, Russell Eric *K.I.A. Belgium, 21/9/17*
144 Pte Rutherford, Robert J.	1425 Pte Sargent, Henry
2179 Pte Ruwoldt, Louis *Died 3/11/18*	4288 Pte Saul, Henry William *D.O.D. England, 8/1/17*
1464 Pte Ryan, Alfred (Stated to be Law, Alfred)	7554 Pte Saultry, Richard H.
	147 Pte Saunders, Albert B.
	5482 Pte Saunders, Charles D.
3465 Cpl Ryan, Austin J. *D.O.W. France, 31/8/18*	3238 Pte Saunders, Edward C. (M.M.)
3464 Pte Ryan, Duncan Ewart	4308 Pte Saunders, George C.
2182 Pte Ryan, Edward H.	761 Sgt Saunders, William G. *D.O.W. Gallipoli, 11/5/15*
146 Pte Ryan, James *K.I.A. Anzac, 25/4/15*	2029 Pte Savill, Albert
3137 Pte Ryan, James *K.I.A. France, 25/12/16*	7314 L/Cpl Saville, Edward
	694 Pte Saxon, William F.
6341 Pte Ryan, James	1426 Pte Saxon, Reuben Oliver *K.I.A., Gallipoli, 8/5/15*
2017 Pte Ryan, James Francis	
4897 Pte Ryan, John Fredk. *K.I.A. Belgium, 4/10/17*	754 C.Q.M.S. Sayers, Wm. J. *K.I.A. Gallipoli, 25/4/15*
2028 Pte Ryan, Michael *Died after Discharge 7/12/17*	6581 Pte Sayers, Walter John *K.I.A. Belgium, 14/10/17*
	— Lt-Col Scanlan, John J. (D.S.O. and Bar, 3 M.I.D.)
3139 Pte Ryan, Patrick	
4287 Pte Ryan, Stanley C.	406 C.Q.M.S. Scharness, C. *K.I.A. Gallipoli, 25/4/15*
54 Pte Ryan, Vernon C. M.	
264 Pte Ryan, Walter Thomas	6616 Pte Schlyder, E. R. A.
— Lieut Ryder, M. S. H.	4314 Pte Scholes, Frank
1410 Pte Ryder, Robert	— Hon Capt Scholes, John E. *D.O.D. France, 10/10/17*
1851 Pte Ryding, Bramwell	
4482	7358 Pte Schroder, George
7309 Pte Ryland, George *D.O.W. France, 11/8/18*	31 Cpl Schuldt, Harold
	4323 L/Cpl Schumann, John D. (M.M.)
3236 Pte Rymer, Ernest *D.O.W. France, 21/8/16*	
	970 C.S.M. Schwarer, J. W. *D.O.W. France*
S	
	285 Pte Scott, Andrew (M.M.)
820 Pte Saffron, Albert J.	
7068 Pte Salmon, Harold M.	957 Pte Scott, Alexander
2186 Pte Saloway, Charles H. *K.I.A. Gall., 8-9/8/15*	154 T/Sgt Scott, Alfred B.
	6580 Pte Scott, Bertram *Died at Sea, 1/2/19*
620 Sgt Salter, Frank S.	
2187 Pte Salter, George	2655 Pte Scott, Charles F.
5220 L/Cpl Salter, Herbert *K.I.A. Belgium, 5/10/17*	6354 Pte Scott, Edgar *K.I.A. France, 9/8/18*
2795 Sgt Salter, John Edward *K.I.A. France, 13/8/18*	2926 Pte Scott, George Arthur
	6345 Pte Scott, George Perry *K.I.A. Belgium, 20/9/17*
— Lieut Salthouse, Alfred L.	
17 Pte Samers, Cyril Roy	606 Pte Scott, John
265 Pte Sampson, Fredk. T.	958 L/Cpl Scott, James
1465 Pte Samson, Ernest	5763 Pte Scott, Leslie T. J.
1418 Pte Sandall, R. S. M.	767 Sgt Scott, Robert
4906 Pte Sandells, Rupert S.	1431 Pte Scott, Roy Clarence
1185 Pte Sanders, Frederick *K.I.A. Gallipoli, 25/4/15*	4593 Pte Scott, Robert Grant
	1183 Pte Scott, Walter
3237 Pte Sanderson, Chas. W.	— Lieut Scott, Walter Eric *K.I.A. France, 9/8/18*
476 Pte Sandford, A. H. (Alias Simpson, Arthur)	
	2654 Pte Scowcroft, R. J. *K.I.A. France, 19/7/16*
3810 Sgt Sands, Allan G.	
1609 Sgt Sands, Stephen J.	1185 L/Cpl Scown, Herbert G.
2432 Pte Sanger, John Henry	6948 Pte Scrivens, Martin H.
1467 Pte Sapple, Edward	1824 Pte Scuntaro, Louis A.
2887 Pte Sapwell, Albert H.	

— Capt Scurry, William C. (M.C., D.C.M., M.I.D.)
1817 Pte Seadon, Thomas
— Lieut Seager, John E. B.
4310 Pte Seamons, Alex. R.
4311 Pte Seamons, Charles J.
K.I.A. France, 17/8/16
4313 Cpl Seamons, Charles L.
4312 Pte Seamons, George W.
2026 Sgt Secomb, William E.
2888 Pte Sectrine, Herbert G.
1635 L/Cpl Sedunary, Edward
1193 Pte Seeger, John Alfred
1085
K.I.A. Anzac, 25/4/15
2189 Pte Seeley, Albert
K.I.A. Belgium, 27/9/17
4321 Pte Seeley, Albert
305 Pte Seeley, James L.
K.I.A. Anzac, 6/7/15
2708 Pte Sefton, William G.
366 Pte Seibert, Morris John
1823 Cpl Self, William (M.M.)
2435 Sgt Selkrig, Reginald W.
55687 Pte Selmon, Donald
5759 Cpl Senini, Joe
1188 Pte Sephton, Herbert
1186 Pte Seteridge, Charles (Stated to be Setterich, Charles C.)
D.O.W. Gallipoli, 10/5/15
2934 Pte Seymour, Hubert J.
K.I.A. France, 18/8/16
6856 Pte Seymour, Joseph
1422 L/Cpl Seymour, James A.
3240 Pte Seymour, James H.
3239 Pte Seymour, Reginald F.
719 Pte Shacklock, Leonard J.
649 Pte Shadbolt, Leslie J.
3241 L/Cpl Shallue, William
3484 Artificer (Sdlr) Shanahan, Cornelius Patrick G.
3242 Sgt Shanahan, William
D.O.W. France, 27/4/18
1459 Pte Shannahan, Arthur
959 L/Cpl Shannahan, John J.
1819 L/Cpl Shannon, Leslie J.
5223 Pte Shannon, Martin
6826 Pte Shannon, Richard
6579 Pte Shannon, William
198 Pte Sharp, Henry Wm.
3919 Pte Sharp, Joseph
D.O.W. France, 28/7/16
7308 Pte Shaw, Alfred C.
1184 L/Cpl Shaw, Charles E.
D.O.W. at Sea, 23/8/15
3920 Cpl Shaw, Charles P.
K.I.A. Belgium, 20/9/17
2444 Pte Shaw, Edward
5752 Pte Shaw, Neil
659 L/Cpl Shaw, Herbert V.
D.O.W. France, 14/3/17

2657 Pte Shaw, John Sydney (Stated to be Mortensen, Waldemar H.)
K.I.A. France, 27/7/16
5201 Pte Shearwood, Harold P.
3244 Pte Sheedy, Charles
4975 Pte Sheedy, Leonard B.
3150 Pte Sheffield, Edmund
K.I.A. France, 25/7/16
446 Pte Shelton, Richard
— Lieut Shepherdson, J. L.
534 Cpl Sheppard, George H.
K.I.A. Anzac, 25/4/15
7555 T/Cpl Sheppard, Wm. H.
2649 Pte Sheridan, Albert G.
2673 Dvr Sheridan, Donald L.
3479 Pte Sheridan, John
1430 Pte Sheridan, Peter L.
1468 Pte Sheriff, William H.
3571 Pte Sherlock, Albert
K.I.A. France, 20/8/18
2801 Pte Sherlock, George
1611 Pte Shevlin, Edward
681 Pte Shields, Robert
7556 Pte Shiel, Louis Andrew
2245 Pte Shiels, John Patrick
2799 Cpl Shilling, Bernard
266 Pte Shore, Edward James
189 Pte Shore, Felix W.
1612 Pte Short, William
4596 Cpl Shugg, Alexander
K.I.A. Belgium, 4/10/17
2915 Cpl Shutler, Richard C.
K.I.A. France, 25/7/16
— Lieut Shuttleworth, C. G.
5446 Pte Sibly, William Libby
1044 L/Cpl Silver, George W.
5447 Pte Sim, Donald F.
5448 Dvr Simmonds, James G.
3480 Pte Simmons, C. E.
1086 Pte Simmons, Norman H.
6828 Pte Simon, Thomas E.
5751 Pte Simons, Samuel
1419 Pte Simonsen, Martin
1827 Pte Simper, John W.
32 Pte Simpkins, Edward S.
1828 Pte Simpson, Albert
1460 Pte Simpson, Charles S.
K.I.A. Anzac, 29/5/15
2647 Pte Simpson, David
39 Pte Simpson, Eric Iona
2658 Pte Simpson, Fredk. A.
2660 L/Cpl Simpson, Jack
K.I.A. Belgium, 21/9/17
625 Pte Earle-Simpson, J. P.
1189 Pte Simpson, Thomas
671 Dvr Simpson, Victor
4292 Pte Sims, Albert E.
3151 Pte Sims, John T. E.
735 Pte Sinclair, George (Stated to be Worrall, G.)
3245 Pte Sinclair, Henry J.

508 L/Cpl Sinden, Leslie H.	3249 Pte Smith, Charles
1172 Pte Singleton, James	*K.I.A. Belgium, 4/10/17*
1138	4294 L/Cpl Smith, Clarence S.
K.I.A. France, 9/8/18	2246 Pte Smith, Clarence W.
2030 Pte Sinnott, George P.	1427 Pte Smith, David
K.I.A. France, 18/8/16	*K.I.A. Anzac, 8-9/8/15*
646 Pte Sissons, Harold	3250 Pte Smith, David Henry
407 Pte Skeggs, Richard H.	5453 Pte Smith, Edward
1360 Pte Skehan, Patrick R.	177 Sgt Smith, Ernest A.
1424	*K.I.A. Anzac, 25/4/15*
(M.M.)	1099 L/Cpl Smith, Ernest E.
1182 Pte Skeyhill, Thomas John	1420
157 Dvr Skidmore, Clifton	962 L/Cpl Smith, Ellis Henry
Killed France, 24/6/18	*K.I.A. Gallipoli, 8/5/15*
3925 Pte Skinner, William L.	963 Cpl Smith, Eric Lyndon
2800 Pte Skipper, Norman B.	*K.I.A. Gallipoli, 8/5/15*
2149 Pte Skurrie, A. S.	988 Pte Smith, Frank
2244 Pte Slater, Thomas Henry	1820 Pte Smith, Frank
D.O.W. at Sea, 10/8/15	3251 Sgt Smith, Francis
1179 Pte Slattery, James	1712 Pte Smith, Francis G.
1055 Pte Sleep, Harold Vincent	*D.O.W. France, 10/8/18*
2889 Pte Sloan, William	3930 Pte Smith, Fred James
7074 Pte Sloane, Robert D.	3252 Pte Smith, Frank S.
186 Pte Slocombe, Walter H.	2063 Pte Smith, George
K.I.A. Gallipoli, 25/4/15	*Died Cairo, 18/6/16*
3485 Pte Slockwitch, Anthony	*18/6/16*
K.I.A. France, 19/7/16	2950 Pte Smith, G. H. V.
960 Pte Slow, George Edward	*K.I.A. Belgium, 4/10/17*
1038 Pte Smart, Charles	3253 Pte Smith, George Leslie
336 Pte Smart, James Leslie	3254 Pte Smith, George Percy
344 Pte Smart, William H.	2502 Pte Smith, George Robert
6086 L/Cpl Smedley, Charles	5757 Pte Smith, George Thos.
— Lieut Smedley, Francis J.	739 Sgt Smith, Harry
(M.C.)	2267 Pte Smith, Hugh Maurice
D.O.W. England, 20/8/18	288 Pte Smith, John
1026 Pte Smith, Albert	1190 Cpl Smith, John
2247 Pte Smith, Alexander	2185 Pte Smith, John
(Correct name Coffey,	5755 L/Cpl Smith, John
Harry Lindsay)	840 Pte Smith, Joseph Elijah
2890 Sgt Smith, Andrew	3465 Pte Smith, John Edward
(M.M.)	6353 L/Cpl Smith, Joseph H.
6355 Pte Smith, Alfred	(M.M.)
7072 Pte Smith, Albert	*D.O.W. France, 23/8/18*
7320 Pte Smith, Alexander	2662 Pte Smith, John Patrick
60769 L/Cpl Smith, Archibald	1178 Pte Smith, Jonah R.
6349 Pte Smith, Aubrey A.	1613 Pte Smith, John William
586 Pte Smith, Allan Bryant	*K.I.A. Gallipoli, 14/7/15*
1014	6822 Pte Smith, Lot
286 L/Sgt Smith, Arnott C.	*K.I.A. Belgium, 20/9/17*
3248 Pte Smith, Albert F.	149 C.S.M. Smith, Leslie John
1821 Pte Smith, Allan George	*D.O.W. Belgium, 4/10/17*
7192	60762 Pte Smith, Maurice F.
4900 Pte Smith, Albert J. E.	1818 Pte Smith, Norman
821 L/Cpl Smith, Angus McI.	55726 T/Sgt Smith, Oliphant H.
4293 Pte Smith, Albert R.	3481 Pte Smith, Patrick C.
D.O.W. England, 29/8/16	*Killed France, 4/5/16*
6854 VO/OR/Sgt Smith, A. V.	147 S/Sgt Smith, Percy S.
55693 Pte Smith, Arthur Victor	691 Pte Smith, Reginald T.
1070 Pte Smith, Charles	663 Pte Smith, Sydney C.
349	*K.I.A. Belgium, 20/9/17*
(Stated to be Lock, J.	2807 Pte Smith, Sydney J. R.
C. W.)	5765 Pte Smith, Stephen Mark
60770 ER/Sgt Smith, C J. A.	*K.I.A. Belgium, 20/9/17*

2666	Pte Smith, Spencer S. *K.I.A. Belgium, 4/10/17*	5756	Pte Spark, D. L. G. *K.I.A. Belgium, 20/9/17*
337	Pte Smith, Thomas *K.I.A. Gallipoli, 8/5/15*	2893	ER/SSM Spedding, H.
3318	Pte Smith, Tom	843	Pte Spelling, Patrick
6404	Pte Smith, Thomas Arthur	4297	Pte Spence, Frank T.
185	L/Cpl Smith, Thomas G.	1815	Pte Spencer, Alfred F.
1416	Pte Smith, Vendor	1614	Pte Spencer, Henry G.
6350	Pte Smith, Vivian Victor	7563	Pte Spencer, Leslie D.
—	Lieut Smith, William C.	6821	Pte Spencer, Percival
2891	Pte Smith, Walter George *K.I.A. Belgium, 30/9/17*	3939	Pte Spicer, Frederick
		3262	Pte Spiers, Charles R. *K.I.A. France, 17/8/16*
2892	Pte Smith, William G. (Correct name Parfitt, Willie Walton)	4317	Pte Spinks, Charles H. *K.I.A. France, 9/8/18*
—	Lieut Smith, W. H. G. (M.C.) *D.O.D. England, 30/10/18*	6885	Pte Spivey, George (Stated to be Spivey, James John)
2032	Pte Smith, W. J. P.	4673	Pte Spivey, Harry
2808	Pte Smith, William L.	538	Dvr Spivey, William
3486	Pte Smith, Walter Leslie *D.O.W. France, 31/7/18*	3263	Pte Spokes, Robert H.
		55691	ER/2/Cpl Spokes, N. A.
60765	Pte Smith, W. R. L.	2663	Pte Spooner, Edward M. *D.O.W. England, 31/7/18*
766	Sgt Smith, William S.		
1829	Pte Smith, William Thos. *Killed France, 31/10/17*	2894	Dvr Spooner, William
		3483	Pte Sporle, James Henry
7560	Pte Smither, Barnard John	55689	Pte Spottiswood, H. A.
3256	Pte Smyth, George A. *K.I.A. France, 17/4/18*	4601	L/Sgt Spreadborough, G. (M.M.)
683	L/Sgt Smyth, Henry B. *K.I.A. France, 19/7/16*	2033	Pte Spriggs, Thomas
		427	Pte Sproston, Leonard G. *D.O.W. at Sea, 27/4/15*
3257	Pte Smythe, Walter E. *K.I.A. France, 25/7/16*	2438	Pte Squires, John
		55692	Pte Stacey, Alexander G.
3258	Pte Smythe, Walter E.	4298	Pte Stacey, Ernest Wm. *K.I.A. Belgium, 5/10/17*
4296	Pte Snaith, Leeman *D.O.W. France, 4/10/17*		
		6078	Pte Stacey, Walter C.
1181	Pte Snell, George M.	309	C.Q.M.S. Stafford, Thos.
1616	Pte Snelling, John W.	2257	Pte Stagall, Thomas E. (Stated to be Stagoll, Thomas Ernest) *K.I.A. France, 18/8/16*
754	Pte Snook, William		
60767	T/Cpl Snow, Abraham		
1822	Pte Snowdon, Alfred		
150	Sgt Soanes, Henry D. *D.O.W. at Sea, 13/7/15*	—	Lieut Stagg, Henry T. (D.C.M., M.I.D.)
5456	Pte Somer, John A. D.	965	Pte Stagg, Joseph Henry
969	Cpl Somerset, Percy C. *D.O.W. England, 2/8/16*	470	Pte Stagg, John Leslie *K.I.A. Anzac, 8-9/8/15*
3487	Dvr Somerville, Oliver	153	L/Cpl Staley, Henry S.
3488	Dvr Somerville, Walter	4299	Pte Staley, Robert P. *K.I.A. France, 15/4/18*
528	Sgt Sommerville, G. D. *K.I.A. Gallipoli, 8/5/15*		
		760	L/Sgt Stanford, John T.
3259	Pte Sommerville, William	3264	Pte Staniland, Percy W.
3936	Pte Sommerville, William	4300	Pte Stanley, Percival C.
7561	Pte Sorenson, Cyril J.	3265	C.S.M. Stanton, James (D.C.M.)
3260	Pte Souter, Robert Elliott		
3261	Pte Southgate, A. F.	2895	Sgt Stark, Ernest Peace (M.I.D.)
—	Capt Southwell, B. C. S.		
6824	Pte Southwell, Fred P.	1356	Pte Stead, Alfred
6351	Pte Spall, Albert R. (M.M.)	4371	L/Cpl Dvr Steel, E. A.
		6825	Pte Steele, Herbert L.
4290	Pte Spark, Harry *D.O.W. France, 19/12/16*	2896	Pte Steele, Thomas H.
		455	Pte Steeth, Walter Joseph *K.I.A. Anzac, 25/4/15*
7562	Pte Spark, William S.		
7360	Pte Spear, William	967	Cpl Stein, William C.

7564	Pte Stembel, George	1816	Pte Stores, Walter (Stated to be Cahill, William)
2035	Pte Stenning, William G.		
605	Sgt Stephen, Charles P.		
2897	Pte Stephen, Norman F.	4303	Pte Storey, Alfred K. *D.O.W. France, 19/12/16*
732	Pte Stephens, Francis D. *K.I.A. France, 14/4/18*	4016	Pte Storey, Edward J.
6343	Pte Stephens, Findley W. *D.O.W. France, 17/5/18*	1633	Pte Story, C. R.
		7322	Pte Stott, Frank Henry
2661	Cpl Stephens, Henry T.	2034	Pte Strafford, James T.
2810	Pte Stephens, Jonathan *K.I.A. France, 25/7/16*	7075	L/Cpl Stratton, F. G.
		304	Pte Straughair, T. D.
3948	Pte Stephens, John *K.I.A. Belgium, 30/12/17*	2190	Pte Straughen, G. F.
		70	Pte Streater, James
2898	T/Sgt Stephens, John G.	51715	
966	Pte Stephenson, A. J.	5210	Pte Street, John Halley *K.I.A. Belgium, 29/10/17*
6811	*K.I.A. France, 4/5/17*		
		699	Pte Stringer, George *D.O.W. Malta, 4/8/15*
2899	Gnr Stephenson, J. H.		
192	Pte Stephenson, Niels G.	4309	Pte Stubley, Robert W.
7903	A/Sgt Sternberg, S. H.	2436	Cpl Stuckey, Benjamin *K.I.A. France, 9/8/18*
6088	Pte Steven, Alexander J.		
5766	Pte Stevens, Andrew W. *Died England, 19/11/17*	3490	Pte Sturmer, E. B. S.
		2185	Pte Styles, Charles E.
834	Pte Stevens, Charles E. *Died England, 26/6/17*	451	S/Sgt Styring, Pierce J. (M.S.M.)
2900	Pte Stevens, John	1180	Dvr Suhan, Joseph (M.M.)
2439	Pte Stevens, Leslie		
846	Pte Stevens, Richard H. *K.I.A. Anzac, 25/4/15*	2659	Pte Sullivan, Daniel J.
		5795	Pte Sullivan, David J.
2440	Pte Stevens, Roy Joseph	1428	L/Cpl Sullivan, E. A. *K.I.A. Gallipoli, 8/5/15*
6582	Pte Stevens, William G.		
60763	Pte Stevenson, T. A.	1680	Pte Sullivan, Edward M.
3268	Cpl Stevenson, W. R. (M.M.)	2814	L/Cpl Sullivan, F. A.
		4305	Cpl Sullivan, Frank J. *K.I.A. France, 15/4/18*
1117	MT/Dvr Steward, M. N. (Stated to be Cosier, M.N.)	268	Pte Sullivan, Raymond *K.I.A. Gallipoli, 25/4/15*
4322	Pte Stewart, Albert A.	4306	Pte Sullivan, Richard D.
2155	Pte Stewart, Donald M.	822	Pte Sullivan, William
2901	Dvr Stewart, Ernest	3149	Pte Sullivan, William
2188	Pte Stewart, Leslie S. *D.O.W. at Sea, 9/8/15*	5796	Pte Sullivan, William D.
		269	Pte Summers, Albert W.
1679	Pte Stewart, Martin G.	—	2/Lieut Summers, Eli C. *K.I.A. France, 11/8/18*
—	Capt Stewart, R. Mc.G. F.		
862	Pte Stewart, Russell W. *K.I.A. Anzac, 25/4/15*	5758	Pte Summers, Stephen S. *D.O.W. France, 10/8/18*
178	Sgt Stewart, St. Clair M.	1645	Pte Sutcliffe, Robert
1420	Pte Stewart, Thomas	1066	Pte Suter, T. R. A.
4301	T/Cpl Stewart, W. C.	3569	Pte Sutherland, A. G.
3432	Pte Still, Henry W.	—	2/Lieut Sutherland, H. A.
3269	Pte Stillman, Arthur R. *K.I.A. Belgium, 20/9/17*	3271	Cpl Sutherland, Leslie J.
		1417	Pte Sutherland, John *K.I.A. Gallipoli, 8/5/15*
3270	Pte Stillman, William E.		
1423	L/Cpl Stirling, Reginald (M.M.)	2037	Pte Sutherland, Richard L.
		55688	Pte Sutherland, R. R.
968	Cpl Stockdale, Irving D.	609	Pte Sutherland, William *K.I.A. Anzac, 25/4/15*
879	Pte Stokes, Albert		
5762	Pte Stokes, John W.	152	Pte Sutton, Claude *D.O.W. Alex'dria, 17/5/15*
1826	Pte Stokes, Patrick J. *Died Cairo, 23/8/15*		
		6414	Pte Sutton, Fred
435	Pte Stone, Roy Frank *K.I.A. Anzac, 25/4/15*	7071	Pte Sutton, George H.
		4307	Pte Sutton, Hugh Roy
437	Pte Stones, Ellis Andrew	3272	Dvr Sutton, John

7567 Pte Sutton, Robert
2922 L/Cpl Swallow, R. C. H.
— Lieut Swallow, Robin W.
1421 A/Cpl Swayn, Leslie
6829 Pte Sweeny, Abraham
— Lieut Swift, Arthur G.
2038 Cpl Swift, Charles
— Mjr Swift, Claude Hibbert
(M.I.D.)
3493 Pte Swift, Henry G.
4886 T/Sgt Swift, Leslie C.
6346 Pte Swindells, Herbert
1182 Sgt Swindells, Ronald
(M.M.)
6827 Pte Swindells, William
236 Pte Syder, Frank William
Died England, 15/11/18
2430 Spr Sykes, Archibald
3659 Pte Sykes, Thomas
1001 Pte Symes, Arthur E.
D.O.W. at Sea, 4/9/15
5750 Pte Symington, W. H.
— Lieut Symonds, L. C.
— Capt Symons, William J.
(V.C.)

T

1193 Pte Tabbut, Fremont L.
K.I.A. Gallipoli, 25/4/15
7568 Pte Tainton, Percy W.
K.I.A. France. 16/9/18
7325 Pte Tampliton, Thos. H.
392 Pte Tanian, John David
971 Pte Tankard, Oswald Jas.
K.I.A. Gallipoli, 25/4/15
1834 Pte Tardif. William
6587 Pte Tatlock, Rolland
3273 Pte Tatti, Henry Martin
(M.M.)
— Lieut Taverner, N. G.
1835 Pte Taylor. Edward E.
722 L/Cpl Taylor, Edgar G.
K.I.A. Belgium, 20/9/17
55697 Pte Taylor, George E.
D.O.D. France, 4/2/19
3953 Pte Taylor, George J.
1725 Pte Taylor, George H.
823 Sgt Taylor, John Reed
60773 Pte Taylor, L. N. D.
1621 Pte Taylor, Norman A.
3274 Pte Taylor, Percy Wm.
312 Pte Taylor, Robert
1617 Pte Taylor, Victor
777 R.S.M. Teague, V. E.
— Lieut Teare, Athol Muir
(M.C.)
7569 Pte Teasdale, Albert
557 Pte Teasdale, Robert H.
7106 Pte Teggerth, Charles B.
1198 Sgt Telford, James C.
K.I.A. Gallipoli, 25/4/15
3495 Cpl Terry, Cecil Frank
1087 Sgt Tevendale, Charles

1196
K.I.A. Gallipoli, 25/4/15
1710 Pte Tew, Albert E.
803 Pte Thom, Reston Nish
3275 T/Sgt Thomas, Athol E.
3348 Pte Thomas, Albert John
4326 Pte Thomas, Albert Jas.
K.I.A. France, 25/2/17
3497 Pte Thomas, Albert R.
2671 Pte Thomas, Albert Wm.
556 Sgt Thomas, Herbert W.
1197 Pte Thomas, James Adner
6356 Pte Thomas, Joseph A.
K.I.A. France, 1/8/18
3498 Pte Thomas, John Chas.
2191 Cpl. Thomas, John Leslie
2446 L/Cpl Thomas, Leslie L.
K.I.A. Belgium, 25/9/17
2672 Pte Thomas, Michael
555 L/Cpl Thomas, Stanley G.
K.I.A. Gallipoli, 25/4/15
704 Cpl Thomas, Samuel R.
(D.C.M.)
2040 Pte Thompson, Alex.
D.O.W. Alex'dria, 13/8/15
6362 Pte Thompson, Andrew J.
4315 Pte Thompson, Charles A.
607 Pte Thompson, Charles H.
1618 Pte Thompson, George A.
972 Pte Thompson, Geo. W.
6361
1011 Pte Thompson, H. D.
759 Cpl Thompson, John
K.I.A. Anzac, 25/4/15
3277 Bdr Thompson, John H.
1831 Pte Thompson, John T.
2195 C.Q.M.S. Thompson, K. P.
973 Cpl Thompson, Reginald
(Stated to be Thompson, William Douglas)
757 L/Cpl Thompson, Stephen
484 Pte Thompson, Stanley D.
756 Pte Thompson, Sydney R.
1438 Pte Thompson, W. H. L.
1380 Pte Thompson, Will J.
1434
7078 L/Sgt Thomsett, P. T.
1988 Pte Thompson, Gordon
2039 Pte Thomson, Hugh H.
5458 L/Cpl Thorburn, Owen
1318 Pte Thorn, Alfred Wm.
6364 Pte Thorne, Harold Cyril
3278 Pte Thornley, P. W.
6861 Pte Thornton, Charles R.
2249 Whlr Thorp, George R.
5459 Cpl Thorpe, Harry
(M.M.)
D.O.W. France, 9/8/18
735 Pte Thouliss, George H.
7570 Pte Threadgold, William
1619 Sgt Tierney, Leslie H.
(D.C.M.)
55701 Pte Tiley, Ernest Leslie

1620 Pte Tiley, Henry Allen
7571 Pte Tiller, Allan Thomas
    (M.M.)
513 A/Cpl Tilley, Jack
1621 Pte Tingay, Louis James
2817 Cpl Tinkler, William M.
585 Pte Tinsley, Arthur
2670 Pte Tognola, G. (Jack)
5216 Pte Toll, George William
60776 Pte Tomasini, Maurice
55700 Dvr Tomlin, Albert Jas.
371 Dvr Tomlinson, William
    K.I.A. Anzac, 25/4/15
55696 Pte Toner, Patrick James
3572 Pte Toner, W. P. B.
3955 L/Cpl Tonkin, Allan T.
    D.O.W. Belgium, 24/9/17
1623 Pte Tonks, Albert
2192 Pte Tonsing, Frank
4613 Pte Tonsing, Fredk. W.
    K.I.A. France, 9/8/18
1435 Pte Toogood, Edward
    K.I.A. Gallipoli, 8/5/15
3279 L/Cpl Toogood, John
2226 Pte Toogood, Thomas
— Lieut Toohey, Daniel G.
    (M.C., M.I.D.)
667 Pte Topham, Francis J.
1624 Pte Tory, Arnold C.
148 Pte Towner, F. A. A.
    K.I.A. Anzac, 25/4/15
2193 Pte Townsend, Albert E.
    K.I.A. Anzac, 8-9/8/15
753 Pte Townsend, Roy Wm.
640 C.S.M. Townsend, T. H.
4330 Pte Tracey, Charles
155 Pte Tracey, George
2718 L/Cpl Tracey, Walter
    (D.C.M.)
1194 Pte Tracy, William H.
    K.I.A. Anzac, 8-9/8/15
1830 Pte Tracy, William S.
60775 Pte Trafford, Thomas H.
2819 Pte Trahair, Henry
    D.O.W. France, 7/5/17
1088 Pte Tranter, Albert M.
55235 Pte Travers, George
6830 Pte Travis, Harry Thos.
    K.I.A. Belgium, 4/10/17
— Lieut Trawin, Louis E.
    Died after Discharge
487 Pte Treacy, Thomas A.
2041 Pte Traynor, Albert
    D.O.W. France, 8/11/16
5218 Pte Tregonning, Alfred T.
35 Pte Treloar, Ernest
6585 Pte Treloar, Thomas W.
554 ER/WO (1) Trethewey,
    Harold (M.S.M.)
    Died after Discharge
1439 Sgt Trevan, Sydney R.
4325 Pte Trewin, Joseph W.
1436 Pte Trezise, John George

3281 Pte Trezise, Percy James
696 Pte Trickey, Frank
    K.I.A. Gallipoli, 25/4/15
6832 Pte Trimble, Joseph
2196 Pte Trinder, A. L. T.
2042 Pte Trompf, Eric E. R.
3439 Pte Tronfaroli, John
    D.O.W. France, 5/7/18
— 2/Lieut Trotman, G. L. S.
    D.O.W. France, 17/4/18
676 Pte Trowbridge, Alec R.
824 C.Q.M.S. Truesdale, John
— Mjr Tubb, Frederick H.
    (V.C.)
    D.O.W., 20/9/17
— Capt Tubb, Frank Reid
    (M.C.)
3282 Cpl Tucker, Arthur Cyril
    K.I.A. France, 18/8/16
4329 Pte Tucker, Stanley L.
— Lieut Tucker, Wilfred L.
    (D.C.M.)
    D.O.W. France, 25/7/18
156 Pte Tucker, William J.
3283 L/Cpl Tuckett, Charles E.
6358 Pte Tuff, Ringrose, B.
130 Pte Tulloch, William A.
6360 Pte Tuohy, Michael J.
975 Pte Turnbull, J. C. R.
2043 L/Cpl Turner, Charles A.
    K.I.A. France, 2/5/18
7077 Pte Turner, Charles S.
1672 Pte Turner, Esmond
7572 Pte Turner, Francis P.
1681 Pte Turner, John R.
    D.O.W. Alexandria, 18/8/15
2956 Pte Turner, William L.
— Lieut Turnour, John E.
    D.O.W. France, 28/9/17
1432 Pte Turp, Ambrose
6833 Pte Tutty, Frederick J.
278 Pte Twiner, Horace H.
483 Pte Twining, John James
    K.I.A. Gallipoli, 25/4/15
6586 Spr Tyers, Wilfred A.
7575 Pte Tyrrell, Charles T.
73 Pte Tyrrell, Joseph
    Died after Discharge, 10/1/17
2194 Pte Tyler, George Thos.
    K.I.A. Gallipoli, 8-9/8/15

U

2675 Pte Ukena, Fred
3573 Sgt Underwood, M. G.
2452 Pte Underwood, T. K.,
5770 Pte Unwin, C. W. J.
5462 L/Cpl Upton, John S.
2674 Sgt Usher, Forrest Wm.
82 Lieut Ussher, Athelstan N.
    K.I.A. Anzac, 25/4/15

V

1461 L/Cpl Vail, M. W. K.
3153 Pte Vallance, Roy

1626 Pte Valli, Joseph James
    D.O.W. Germany, 24/8/16
2823 Dvr Vansittart, Jesse
2677 R.Q.M.S. Vanstan, F. J.
    (M.S.M.)
 559 Pte Varty, John
    K.I.A. Gallipoli, 8/5/15
2456 Cpl Vass, Gerald White
    (M.M.)
2044 L/Sgt Vass, James J.
    D.O.W. France, 25/7/16
2454 Pte Vaughan, John D.
2060 Pte Vaughan, Joseph R.
2826 Cpl Vaughan, J. T. M.
60777 Pte Veilgaard, Geo. A.
 157 Pte Veitch, Arthur W.
    K.I.A. Anzac, 25/4/15
 158 Pte Veitch, Donald
    K.I.A. Anzac, 25/4/15
2455 Pte Vial, Roy Browning
1836 Pte Vincent, Leslie
7332 Pte Vinicombe, Keith R.
4931 Dvr Vistarini, R. J.
3286 Cpl Voigt, John Edward
2676 Pte Von Ende, D. A.
2825 Pte Vyner, Louis
    K.I.A. France, 15/8/16

W

2466 Pte Wade, Thomas
    K.I.A. France, 11/4/17
— Lieut Wadeson, John H.
    (M.C., M.I.D.2)
6593 L/Cpl Wadsworth, R. N.
1630 Pte Wagstaff, F. H.
    K.I.A. France, 24/7/16
2681 Pte Wain, William John
5779 Pte Wait, Alfred Gerald
4337 Pte Wakefield, John F.
5809 ER/Sgt Wakenshaw, G.
6598 Pte Waldon, William
7576 Pte Waldren, Chas. M.
2827 Pte Waldron, Alfred G.
 292 Sgt Waldron, Alfred L.
— 2/Lieut Wale, Philip G.
    D.O.W. Gallipoli, 8/5/15
4336 Pte Walkden, Henry
1708 Pte Walker, Albert C.
2829 Pte Walker, Arthur H.
    K.I.A. France, 25/7/16
 712 Pte Walker, Archibald J.
 56 R.Q.M.S. Walker, Frank
    (D.C.M.)
2830 Pte Walker, Frank
 681 Pte Walker, F. J. D.
 379 Pte Walker, George
 18 Dvr Walker, James
    D.O.W. France, 12/4/18
 731 Pte Walker, John
2046 L/Cpl Walker, John L.
    K.I.A. France, 9/8/18
5463 Pte Walker, Percy H.
— 2/Lieut Walker, K L.
    D.O.W. at Sea, 12/7/15

 827 Pte Walker, Percy S.
6372 Pte Walker, Sydney
1379 Pte Walker, William
— Lieut Walker, Wm. Jas.
2692 Pte Walker, William W.
    D.O.W. France, 16/4/18
1705 Pte Wallace, George
    K.I.A. France, 9/8/18
 561 Pte Wallace, James
6840 Gnr Wallace, John Wm.
 331 Pte Wallace, William I.
60786 Pte Waller, Edward John
1307 Pte Waller, John Henry
    K.I.A. Anzac, 27/4/15
2833 Pte Wallis, Claude F.
3287 Pte Walls, Albert Ernest
4618 Pte Walmsley, R. E.
    K.I.A. France, 17/8/16
 378 Pte Walsh, Gerald J.
3504 Pte Walsh, James P.
1181 Pte Walsh, John Thomas
    D.O.W. at Sea, 4/5/15
6406 Pte Walsh, Lawrence Jos.
 826 Pte Walsh, William A.
2678 ER/Sgt Walshe, D. L.
1196 Sgt Walshe, William E.
3506 Pte Walter, Alfred A.
3507 Pte Walters, Charles
    D.O.W. France, 31/5/16
1028 Pte Walters, Ernest Venn
1446 Pte Walters, Frederick C.
    K.I.A. France, 19/7/16
7577 Pte Walters, Francis C.
4619 Sgt Walters, John F.
    (D.C.M.)
 590 Pte Walters, William
5774 Spr Walton, A. J. E.
2045 Pte Walton, Fredk. C.
2250 Pte Walton, Robert
2199 C.Q.M.S. Walton, S. R.
60781 Pte Wanhope, George V.
6599 Pte Warburton, H. W.
6572 Pte Ward, Albert H.
4933 Pte Ward, Joseph
4513 Sgt Ward, Percy A.
2047
1627 Pte Ward, Roy
    K.I.A. France, 25/4/18
2048 Pte Ward, Sidney W.
2470 Cpl Wardle, Clarence A.
— Lieut Wardrop, A. H.
2679 Pte Ware, Albert Wm.
3508 Dvr Warke, Thomas
 562 Pte Warlond, Theodore
4339 Pte Warmald, James L.
    (stated to be Wormald,
    J. L. W.)
 333 L/Cpl Warne, Thomas
— Lieut Warne-Smith. I. P.
7081 Pte Warner, Charles H.
    Died, Melbourne, 9/3/18
7579 Pte Warner, Alfred
7082 Pte Warren, George
 272 Pte Warren, George

(stated to be Warren, G. W.)
  K.I.A. Anzac, 25/4/15
271 Pte Warren, Stanley G.
  K.I.A. Gallipoli, 8/5/15
306 Dvr Warren, William H.
2680 Dvr Warwick David
7336 Pte Warwick, Ernest
522 C.S.M. Waterhouse, T. C.
— Lieut Waters, Arthur J.
  (M.I.D.)
650 L/Cpl Waters, Stanley
  K.I.A. Gallipoli, 8/5/15
3289 Pte Waters, W. M. J.
976 Pte Watkins, Thomas J.
2049 Sgt Watkins, William H.
1842 Pte Watson, Alfred
3509 Pte Watson, Alfred
  K.I.A. France, 6/5/17
3290 L/Cpl Watson, A. C.
2225 Cpl Watson, Albert F.
2695 Pte Watson, Clarence A.
1060 Pte Watson, Fredk. W.
  K.I.A. Gallipoli, 25/4/15
1203 Pte Watson, George M.
1200 Pte Watson, Henry
— Lieut Watson, Hubert C.
— Lieut Watson, Harry W.
  (M.M., M.I.D.)
3291 Sgt Watson, James
3292 Cpl Watson, Joseph E.
7359 Pte Watson, James Keith
2469 Cpl Watson, James M.
4934 Pte Watson, S. A.
  D.O.W. France, 20/8/16
2254 Pte Watson, Thomas A.
3500 Pte Watt, Allan
  K.I.A. France, 19/7/16
4332 Pte Watt, Bernard John
1201 Pte Watt, Robert
977 L/Sgt Watterston, B. W.
  K.I.A. Gallipoli, 8/5/15
1043 Pte Watterston, H. C. B.
1306 Pte Watts, Leslie James
1440
5968 Pte Watts, William
1727 Pte Watty, John
  (Stated to be Khya, W.)
2838 Pte Waud, Arthur Henry
2468 Pte Wayland, Claude F.
  K.I.A. 14/12/15
55724 Gnr Wealand, Andrew G.
2716 L/Cpl Wearne, F. R. G.
6594 MT/Dvr Wearne, F. W.
303 Cpl Weatherhead, H.
1850 Sgt Weatherhead, R.
2836 Pte Weaver, Joseph H.
2471 Pte Webb, David James
60787 Pte Webb, Franklin R.
1839 Pte Webb, James
  K.I.A. Belgium, 4/10/17
509 Cpl Webb, Harry
  (D.C.M.)
  D.O.W. Anzac, 9/8/15
7333 Pte Webster, George

1121 Pte Webster, Horace
1205 (M.M.)
— Mjr Weddell, Robert H.
1637 Pte Weeding, Harold
703 Pte Weir, David
  K.I.A. Belgium, 4/10/17
6374 Pte Weir, Frederick W.
— Lieut Weir, Michael
  (M.I.D.)
  D.O.W. France, 18/8/18
6844 Pte Weir, Stephen W.
1636 Pte Weir, William
5777 Pte Welch, Alexander B.
583 Sgt Welden, Rex
2223 Pte Wellington, Daniel
  K.I.A. France, 18/8/16
1025 Pte Wells, Albert Anson
1450 Pte Wells, Cecil F. J.
  D.O.W. Gallipoli, 7/7/15
979 Dvr Wesley, Jack
— Lieut West, John Melville
682 L/Cpl West, Percy
2700 Pte West, Reginald H.
1207 Pte Westaway, Fredk.
  D.O.D. England, 9/9/15
3332 Pte Westaway, H. C.
3511 Dvr Westerbeck, William
4331 Pte Wetherall, Leslie C.
1445 Pte Whaite, Andrew T.
  (Correct name White, A. T.)
— Lieut Whalley, Rupert P.
3293 Pte Whatmough, R. H.
  K.I.A. France, 17/8/16
2697 Sgt Whelan, Frank R.
1841 Pte Whilde, Thomas
694 Pte Whinfield, James V.
616 Pte Whitaker, F. A.
7580 Pte Whitbourne, C. W.
315 L/Cpl Whitbourn, G. F.
2710 Dvr White, Alfred James
55703 Pte White, Albert Victor
159 L/Sgt White, Benjamin
7581 Sgt White, Charles S.
3294 Pte White, Edward W.
631 Pte White, Frederick
2050 Pte White, Frederick
5235 Pte White, Frederick E.
3512 Pte White, George H.
2051 Pte White, James
7080 Pte White, John Stanley
  D.O.W. England, 26/8/18
4341 Pte White, Robert C.
  K.I.A. France, 23/7/16
5775 Pte White, Robert Steele
  K.I.A. Belgium, 20/9/17
7088 Pte White, Thomas Geo.
1929 Pte White, Thomas P.
4021 L/Cpl White, William
  (M.M.)
553 Sgt White, William Geo.
5236 Pte White, William Jas.
980 Pte Whitecross, William
  K.I.A. Anzac, 25/4/15
1029 Pte Whitehead, Leslie T.

3501 Pte Whitehead, John F. R. (M.M.)
    K.I.A. France, 23/8/18
3295 Pte Whitehead, Robert J.
    K.I.A. Belgium, 4/10/17
1449 Pte Whitehurst, John
    K.I.A. France, 19/7/16
5465 L/Cpl Whitelaw, C. M.
  57 Pte Whitelaw, John
— Lieut. Whitelaw, John S.
1447 Pte Whitelaw, W. E.
2052 Cpl Whitford, John
3046 Pte Whitford, James S.
3296 Pte Whitmore, George
    K.I.A. France, 25/4/16
5237 Cpl Whittles, F. F. R.
2200 Pte Whitty, George
1021 Pte Wickman, Harold W.
    K.I.A. Belgium, 4/10/17
6859 Dvr Widdup, J. W. T.
3297 Pte Wiffen, Charles B.
7583 Pte Wigg, William P.
1711 Pte Wignall, Robert
    D.O.W. Gallipoli, 29/7/15
  20 L/Cpl Wignell, C. W. (M.M. and Bar)
  19 Trans/Sgt Wignell, E.S.A.
6834 Pte Wilcock, Thomas
    D.O.W. France, 9/3/18
 194 Pte Wilden, Arthur
    K.I.A. Gallipoli, 25/4/15
1199 Pte Wilding, Leslie E.
55702 Pte Wilkins, John S.
2458 Pte Wilkins, Llewellyn H.
1026 Pte Wilkinson, R. H.
1862 Pte Willcocks, Albert H.
    (Alias Willcocks, Bert)
1703 L/Cpl Williams, Arthur
2904 Pte Williams, Alfred
6603 L/Cpl Williams, Arthur
7584 Pte Williams, Albert
1202 Pte Williams, Albert H.
    K.I.A. Gallipoli, 25/4/15
2053 Pte Williams. Arthur H.
    (Correct name Lowe, A. A)
7108 Pte Williams, Arthur J.
2457 Cpl Williams, Charles C.
— Lieut Williams, C. S.
4945 Pte Williams, David John
1629 Cpl Williams, Edgar F.
710 Pte Williams, Edward G.
2701 Pte Williams, Ernest G.
1443 Pte Williams, Edmund T.
    K.I.A. Gallipoli, 8-9/8/15
5240 Pte Williams, Francis
828 Pte Williams, George
457 Pte Williams, G. C. M.
161 L/Cpl Williams, Geo. J.
— Lieut Williams, H. E.
    K.I.A. France, 21/9/18
3156 Pte Williams, Henry J.
7339 Cpl Williams. H. M.
6838 Pte Williams, James
4340 Pte Williams, Norman C.

3298 Pte Williams, Paul
1199 Pte Williams, Robert H.
981 Dvr Williams, Ray Wm.
6366 L/Cpl Williams, T. J. J.
404 Pte Williams, Thomas P.
2054 Pte Williams, William
2702 Pte Williams, Wilfred
3299 L/Cpl Williamson. A. G.
4968 Pte Williamson, George
4939 Pte Williamson, Robert R.
    K.I.A. France, 26/7/16
55713 Pte Williamson, Thomas
6837 Pte Willis, Albert E.
60783 ER/Sgt Willis. Alfred R.
7089 Pte Willis, Francis J.
6596 Pte Willis, Harold A.
2225 Pte Willis, John
    K.I.A. France, 19/7/16
160 Cpl Willmore, Phillip C.
401 Pte Willmott, Charles J.
    K.I.A. Anzac, 25/4/15
2905 Sgt Wills, Frank S.
983 Pte Wills, George
6597 Pte Wills, Joseph
436 Pte Wills, William H.
    K.I.A. Anzac, 25/4/15
1451 Pte Wills, William Thos.
274 Pte Wilson, Alexander
3154 Pte Wilson, Alexander H
    K.I.A. France, 23-27/6/18
7585 Pte Wilson, Alfred Henry
7091 Pte Wilson, Allan Stanley
173 Pte Wilson, Charles
2258 Pte Wilson, Charles
2906 Pte Wilson, Edward G.
5242 Pte Wilson, Edward J. (M.M.)
2460 Pte Wilson, Frank O.
2907 Pte Wilson, Herbert C.
2841 Sgt Wilson, Harrie R.
    K.I.A. France, 18/8/16
1628 Pte Wilson, John
    (stated to be Reaburn, J. A.)
563 Pte Wilson, John Edward
— Lieut Wilson, James M. (M.I.D.)
    K.I.A. Belgium, 20/9/17
3301 Pte Wilson, Norman J.
713 Pte Wilson, Peter Daniel
7079 L/Cpl Wilson, Richard L.
162 Pte Wilson, Richard N.
    K.I.A. Anzac, 25/4/15
2465 Pte Wilson, Stanley M.
    D.O.W. Belgium, 26/9/17
6369 Pte Wilson, Timon C.
    K.I.A. France, 23/4/17
2908 Pte Wilson, William E.
4941 Pte Wiltshire, Walter
5470 Pte Windle, P. V., S.B.V.
2686 Pte Windley, Harry
    K.I.A. France, 19/7/16
6836 Pte Windows, Ernest
2055 Pte Wing, Ralph
    K.I.A Anzac, 7-9/8/15

2198 Pte Wilton, James
60784 Pte Winning, John Alex.
1206 Pte Winslet, Bertram
    K.I.A. Anzac, 25/4/15
3302 Pte Winter, Herbert W.
    K.I.A. France, 26/3/17
1837 Pte Winter, Joseph S.
2269 Pte Winter, Richard
    K.I.A. Gallipoli, 8/5/15
2691 Pte Wintle, Richard F.
— Lieut Wisewould, A. E. (M.C.)
4435 Pte Wishart, David
    K.I.A. France, 22-25/7/16
1024 Pte Witcombe, John A.
165 ER/WO(1) Withers, A. J.
560 Pte Witton, Sydney W.
978 Pte Wodetzki, Victor E.
    K.I.A. Gallipoli, 8/5/15
1472 Pte Wolseley, Arthur
    D.O.W. Gallipoli, 9/5/15
55704 Pte Womersley, A. S.
6376 Pte Womersley, L. V. R.
    K.I.A. France, 23/8/18
2685 Pte Wood, George C.
759 Dvr Wood, Gordon L.
511 Pte Wood, George W.
    K.I.A. Anzac, 25/4/15
6368 Pte Wood, Harry E. W.
3303 Pte Wood, Herbert V.
2683 Pte Wood, Henry W.
760 Dvr Wood, Keith L.
2684 L/Cpl Wood, Leslie H.
289 Pte Wood, Stanley H.
7334 Pte Wood, William
4334 L/Cpl Wood, William R.
302 Pte Woodberry, F. G.
2667 Pte Woodfine, Walter C.
1062 T/2/Cpl Woodhead, A.
2910 A/Cpl Woodhead, John E.
6843 Pte Woodland, W. H.
2252 Pte Woods, Charles G.
    K.I.A. Gallipoli, 8-9/8/15
— Lieut Woods, Errol F.
5773 Pte Woods, Frederick
464 Pte Woods, Horace J.
1864 Pte Woods, Hugh McM.
3574 L/Cpl Woods, John E.
4333 L/Cpl Woods, Thomas
2202 Cpl Woods, Walter W.
    K.I.A. France, 19/7/16
982 Pte Woolnough, A. J.
2845 Pte Wormald, George H.
— Lieut Wraight, H. T. (D.C.M., M.M.)
163 Cpl Wraith, Mark
(Correct name Odgers, A.)
    K.I.A. Gallipoli, 8/5/15
1214 Pte Wren, Clarence A.
6601 Pte Wrench, E. J. R.
    K.I.A. Belgium, 4/10/17
825 Pte Wright, Charles
    K.I.A. Gallipoli, 25/4/15
55707 Pte Wright, Charles H.

1444 Pte Wright, Harry
3513 Pte Wright, Charles R.
    K.I.A. France, 18/8/16
1062 Cpl Wright, Frederick (M.I.D.)
    K.I.A. Gallipoli, 8-9/8/15
2909 Pte Wright, Hugh A.
5780 Pte Wright, H. E. J.
    K.I.A. Belgium, 4/10/17
— Capt Wright, Hewlet J.
5814 Pte Wright, John C.
2057 L/Cpl Wright, Leslie R.
3503 Pte Wright, Maitland
2467 Cpl Wright, Thomas J.
    K.I.A. France, 12/12/16
639 Sgt Wright-Smith, Straun
— Capt Wrigley, Hugh (M.C.)
1174 Pte Wuchatsch, Fredk. J.
1843 Pte Wyatt, Edwin
7588 L/Cpl Wycherley, W. I.
1072 Pte Wylie, Alfred J.
871 Cpl Wylie, Robert Geo.

Y-Z

166 Pte Yager, John George
1681 Pte Yanner, George
4018 Pte Yeld, Douglas
2698 Pte Yendle, George
    K.I.A. France
60791 Pte York, George E.
2912 Pte Young, Arthur H.
276 Cpl Young, Albert Victor
    D.O.W. Alexandria, 22/7/15
414 Sgt Young, Alfred T.
    K.I.A. France, 20/8/16
— Capt Young, Eric M. (M.C.)
672 Pte Young, Frank
3519 Pte Young, Frank
3520 Cpl Young, Francis W.
6606 L/Sgt Young, George E.
    D.O.D. England, 29/10/18
1631 Pte Young, Harry
    K.I.A. Gallipoli, 8-9/8/15
— Capt Young, Harold H.
3517 Pte Young, James G.
2911 Pte Young, James W.
1632 Pte Young, Leslie
1844 Pte Young, Robert
6382 Pte Young, R. E. J.
55714 Pte Young, Robert J.
7589 Pte Young, Thomas W.
    D.O.W. France, 20/8/18
456 Pte Young, Wilfred J.
    K.I.A. Belgium, 4/10/17
805 Pte Yuill, George R.
    K.I.A. Anzac, 25/4/15
55725 Pte Yule, Jack H.
7342 Pte Yung, George A.
    K.I.A. Belgium, 20/9/17
3973 Pte Zerbst, King Fredk.
    K.I.A. Belgium, 4/10/17
984 Dvr Zinzzerella, John

www.ingramcontent.com/pod-product-compliance
Lightning Source LLC
Chambersburg PA
CBHW031955080426
42735CB00007B/396